TREATIES AND

FEDERAL CONSTITUTIONS

BY JAMES McLEOD HENDRY
Professor of Law, Dalhousie University

FOREWORD BY WILLIAM W. BISHOP, JR.
Professor of Law, University of Michigan

Public Affairs Press, Washington, D. C.

TO MY FATHER AND MOTHER

FOREWORD

In this book Prof. Hendry has treated in scholarly and imaginative fashion the problems of federal states in the field of international agreements. It is particularly fortunate that a Canadian lawyer, trained both in Canada and in the United States, should have devoted his efforts to this subject, since both countries have faced similar problems resulting from the division of governmental powers between their national and local governments. Perhaps each may learn something from the experience of the other, and of other federal states throughout the world.

In international legal affairs perhaps the most prominent development of the twentieth century has been the amazing number, complexity and variety of international agreements. Upon the foundation of international customary law there has been built a great suprastructure of bilateral and multilateral agreements, which represent purposeful development of the law and which in practice largely replace custom by more clearly defined rules chosen by the parties to meet their needs. The growth of international law, and its adaption to changing needs, has become largely a matter of treaties. Most of the cases before the World Court since its creation 35 years ago and most of the international law problems which arise today involve international agreements. The subject-matter, importance, and nature of these agreements vary enormously. Whenever nations seek to end a struggle or settle a dispute, to create an international organization, to express a commercial bargain between them, to lay down uniform rules for their peoples to follow, to delimit their territorial authority, to formalize administrative cooperation, or to accomplish almost any task, great or small, which involves two or more nations—then it is to the treaty that they must turn. This instrument must, in the international legal sphere, fill the functions performed on the domestic scene by contracts, conveyances, corporate charters, legislation or constitutions. Hence the growing number of treaties and the ever-increasing importance of legal problems involving the making, entry into force, application, interpretation, enforcement, modification, and termination of international agreements.

These problems involve questions of both international law and of the national laws of the countries involved. They assume added complexity when the country is a federation, or federal state, in which governmental power is divided between a central government and the governments of the component states, provinces, cantons, or other divisions which have their own law-making and law-enforcing authority and machinery. The increasing importance of these federal states in the world of today becomes evident when some are listed: the United States of America, Argentina, Australia, Austria, Brazil, Federal Republic of Germany, India, Libya, Mexico, Switzerland, Venezuela. Other countries like Ethiopia, Indonesia, Union of South Africa, and U.S.S.R. might perhaps be added to the category. In the West Indies and in Africa there are areas now within the British Commonwealth which may soon achieve separate international personality as new federal states.

Each federal state has its own legal problems in matters relating to international agreements, but they have enough in common to warrant study of the treaty problems which arise out of the nature of federations as such. Prof. Hendry has singled out the United States of America, Canada, Australia, and Switzerland for his special study, as the best examples of federal states which have had extensive experience with respect to treaties. He shows how each of these four countries has dealt with the problems involved, and suggests ways in which the successes or failures of one country's methods may be of value in other lands governed according to federal principles. In so doing he clarifies our thinking by distinguishing between capacity to enter into agreements, and capacity to carry them out. He discusses the constitutional law problems of each country, and investigates how far an "unconstitutional" treaty may nevertheless have international effect. He touches upon questions which have become vital political issues in the United States and in Canada, giving us both background and his own ideas as to what seems needed for a more effective treaty power. Upon completion of the volume, the reader of this book should indeed have a good understanding of the treaty problems of federal states.

WILLIAM W. BISHOP, JR.

TABLE OF CONTENTS

PART I

1 : The Problem   1

2 : Historical and Constitutional Considerations
on the Treaty Processes of Federal States   17

PART II

3 : The Treaty-Making Powers of Federal
Executives   39

4 : Governmental Participation in the Treaty-
Making Powers of Federal Executives   66

PART III

5 : Treaty Performance and Fundamental Laws   86

6 : Treaty Performance and the Legislative Powers
of the Component States   107

PART IV

7 : Constitutional Limitations and International
Law   137

8 : Constitutional Limitations and Fundamental
Laws   163

Index   184

CHAPTER 1

THE PROBLEM

Since the international community knows as yet no supreme law-making body or law enforcement agency comparable to that of the modern state, the treaty remains the principal method by which states maintain relations among themselves. It is by this method that rules of international law are formulated and chaos avoided.

The states of the international community have utilized the treaty device in a variety of situations. Political treaties may define boundaries, create alliances, and end wars. Commercial treaties relate to consular privileges, navigation, fisheries and other commercial arrangements. Especially significant is the fact that in recent years treaties have been indispensable in the implementation of such general agreements as the Charter of the United Nations. Treaties have similarly been used to secure adherence to constitutions of such agencies as the International Labor Organization and the World Health Organization. Particularly important at the present time is the "law-making" treaty. Through the League of Nations, and now the United Nations, the states of the international community have sought to implement the realization that the peace of the world depends not only on military disarmament and political accord but also on the economic and social conditions of the peoples. This idea has forerun a change in the nature of treaties.

The international convention or multilateral treaty is today being increasingly employed to regulate many subjects which not so long ago were considered of purely national concern. This phenomenon has many characteristics of international legislation. As Professor Manley O. Hudson says: "the analogy to national legislation is not perfect and cannot be pressed too far; but it may be resorted to for borrowing the general term legislation, and the term is a convenient one for designating the introduction of law governing the relations between states, though there exists in the world of states no single body which is in every respect comparable to any national legislature."[1] However the term "international legislation" is gaining common use and

1

connotes every phase of economic, social and cultural activity embodied in international conventions. One has only to peruse Professor Hudson's comprehensive work[2] to obtain a perspective of the multitude and variety of agreements, conventions, protocols, declarations, acts and regulations, and other multilateral instruments indicative of the volume of "international legislation" now in force between the various countries of the world. Existing "law-making" treaties deal, among other things, with hours of work, sanitation, slavery and white slavery, munitions, monetary arrangements, obscene publications, postal, telegraph and telephone communications, copyrights, trade marks and patents, piracy, maritime law and navigation, submarine cables, customs and tariffs, the drug traffic.

The nature of the "law-making" type of treaty deserves special mention. Unlike political and constitutional types of treaties which, for the most part, are applicable to states as units, "international legislation" is increasingly affecting the sphere of individual rights and duties. Indeed, modern international conventions are invading every phase of our everyday life. States, directly responsible in international law for the observance of these conventions by their subjects, are finding that carrying out their international commitments may place strains on their constitutional structures. We propose to deal with one very fundamental strain: the manner in which the treaty processes in the constitutions of selected states conform to this new trend of internationalism.

The increase in the amount of "international legislation" began largely with the creation of the League of Nations in 1919. Not only was the League created "to promote international cooperation" in the political arena, but it was also empowered to bring about "fair and humane conditions of labor for men, women, and children," and to regulate other matters such as drugs, communications and commerce. After the Second World War, it was realized more than ever that these were indeed questions of general international concern. In addition, many other types of subject matters were considered ripe for international control.

In the United Nations, the General Assembly is empowered to make recommendations on all subjects relating to the promotion of "international cooperation in the political field and encouraging the progressive development of international law and its codification; b. promoting international cooperation in the economic, social, cultural, educational, and health fields and assisting in the realization of human rights and fundamental freedoms for all without discrimination as to race, sex, language or religion."[3] Although recommendations of the General Assembly have a moral force only, and are not legally binding on the member states, they provide a fundamental guide for the conduct of nations, and forerun their embodiment into legally binding conventions. Similar to "international legislation" are the decisions of the Security Council of the United Nations. This Council is directly responsible for the peace of the world; it has considerable powers for the enforcement of its decrees through military action and economic sanctions against aggressor states.

Probably the most important source of future "international legislation" will be the various international agencies established in recent years to achieve peace indirectly by solving economic, social and cultural problems which have been the cause of so much unrest and discontent. Already great strides have been taken by these agencies in health, labor,[4] education, and other fields. It is well recognized that war is to be abolished not only by its outlawry and the peaceful settlement of international disputes but by raising the standards of living in backward countries and trust territories which need assistance in the attainment of economic and social security.

This brief outline of the scope of "international legislation" and its major sources is meant to accentuate the importance of the national treaty process in the furtherance and acceptance of international principles and activities. The effectiveness of the latter depend chiefly on the cooperation afforded to the United Nations and the specialized agencies.

"International legislation" is not true legislation in the municipal sense since the states still refuse to give up their sovereign right of ratification. Its success or failure depends on the ability and desire of the states to accept and carry out international commitments. Those states which signed the United Nations Charter were not willing to set up a more centralized government than that of the defunct and discredited League of Nations. The concept of an international agency endowed with legislative power, an agency having the character of a true government, was not found acceptable at San Francisco. The system of government evolved depends for its efficiency upon the complete cooperation of the member states, except in actions taken by the Security Council against a declared aggressor. Thus, with no power to deal directly with individuals, to proclaim social laws, levy taxes or raise armed forces, its success or failure is dependent on the ability and the inclination of the member states "to fulfil the obligations assumed." In short, the United Nations, its affiliated agencies, and "international legislation" are all based on the principle that states have a duty to fulfil their international obligations in good faith. True, this principle has acquired, in the passage of time, the status of a rule of international customary law[5] and for the most part is scrupulously observed. But if the rule is transgressed, international law must rely on nebulous, usually indirect and rather ineffective sanctions such as self-help, parliamentary censure, general odium and distrust. Such sanctions, possibly sufficient when states can discharge their obligations by executive action alone, are hardly adequate to cope with the changed nature of the "law-making" treaty. The majority of such treaties involve considerations that necessitate inquiry into the constitutional or fundamental laws of the member states. More is necessary than the employment of international legal sanctions to enforce this new type of treaty. The ability "to fulfil in good faith" depends to a great extent on the treaty procedures of the member states, on the mechanism they have at their disposal to enter into international agreements and to carry out the obligations therein incurred. If a state does not have a constitutional treaty process capable of entering into and carrying out these obligations, it cannot "fulfil in good faith." Not only is this delinquency a breach of international law, but it threatens the very stability and structure of the international community. It is axiomatic that the peace of the world depends on international collaboration, but such collaboration depends on the states' ability to conclude and perform international obligations.

The great amount of "international legislation" in force and proposed has led Francis O. Wilcox to write: "Under such circumstances it is not surprising that the states should acquire treaty indigestion. The pace has been so rapid that the process of ratification has naturally been retarded. National governmental machinery must now be adjusted so as to conform to

the requirements of the new internationalism."[6]   This statement needs no elaboration and serves to raise the fundamental
questions with which our present study is concerned.   The first
is how should "national governmental machinery . . . be adjusted so as to conform to the requirements of the new internationalism" compatibly with the pervading spirit of modern
constitutionalism?   The second is how far should international
law be cognizant of the limitations which the individual states
place on their treaty processes, in a possible solution to the
problem?

   To date, international law has deemed the making and performance of treaty obligations a national problem, the sole
concern of the states, and subject to no international interference.   It is a cardinal principle of international law that a
state may organize itself as it chooses, perhaps subject to the
qualification that it may not organize itself in such a way that
it cannot fulfil its duties as a member of the international community.[7]   In the language of William E. Hall, "a state may
place itself under any form of government that it wishes, and
may frame its social institutions upon any model.   To foreign
states the political or social doctrines which may be exemplified
in it, or may spread from it, are legally immaterial.   A state
has the right to live its life in its own way, so long as it keeps
itself rigidly to itself, and refrains from interfering with the
equal rights of other states to live their own life in the manner
which commends itself to them, either by its own action, or by
lending the shelter of its independence to persons organizing
armed attack upon the political or social order elsewhere established."[8]   This principle involves no international legal consideration of the constitutional laws of the states.   But the principle is meeting criticism.   Professor Edwin D. Dickinson, for one,
urges that international recognition be given to national capabilities or capacities to enter into international agreements.   He
maintains that "the subject of internal limitations has never
received adequate consideration.   More often than otherwise
it has been dismissed with the dictum that the law of nations
has no concern with the constitution of the state.   This dictum,
it is submitted, requires revaluation.   It has been universally
approved in the sense that each people must be free to determine
its own form of government without external interference; but
it cannot certainly be taken to mean that the law of nations

is blind to important capacities and incapacities arising out of the organic constitutions of its subjects."[9] With respect to this statement, it is submitted that the question is whether the law of nations can assist the states in greater international collaboration. If the formulation of international legal rules places the states in a better position to enter and perform international obligations, such rules should be made, and to this extent international law should be cognizant of "capacities and incapacities arising out of the organic constitutions." But before an answer to the question is attempted,[10] it is necessary to determine these "capacities or incapacities," their national operation, and their international effect. Henceforth we shall refer to them as constitutional limitations or constitutional restrictions.

Definition and Classification of Constitutional Limitations

The broad definition of a constitutional limitation on the treaty process is any limitation or restriction contained in the fundamental law of a state which prevents a state from entering into a treaty, or, having entered into one, from performing the obligations incurred thereunder. This definition can be readily broken down into two general classifications: namely, the one referable to the entering into the treaty and the other referable to the performance of its obligations once it has been validly concluded according to the constitutional law of the state. The former are those limitations which pertain to the capacity of a state's executives to enter into international agreements; the latter affect the ability of the state to perform commitments incurred under them. This classification is by no means arbitrary; it is quite logical for several reasons. In the first place, it is inherent in many of the treaty processes in vogue today. In the British countries there is a decided distinction between the formation of the treaty obligation, which is the responsibility of the Crown, and its performance, which lies within the power of Parliament.[11] Secondly, the very nature of most modern constitutions makes such a classification necessary. Although not so obviously as the British system, most of the European states require a similar separation of function to validate certain types of treaties.[12] A state's adherence in some degree to the doctrine of the separation of governmental powers will inevitably separate the treaty process into the act of the execu-

tive in entering into treaties, and the participation, more or
less, of the legislature in performing the treaty obligations.
Thirdly, many authorities recognize this classification in the
determination of the international validity of treaties invalidated
by the states' constitutional limitations.   Some authorities contend that constitutional limitations affecting the capacity of a
state to enter into international agreements must be observed before a treaty will be recognized as valid in international law.   On
the other hand, most authorities are in accord that constitutional
limitations pertaining to the states' performing power are of no
consequence in this determination.[13]   Finally, the nature of the
constitutional structures of federal states makes this classification important, and most necessary, for analysing the treaty
processes of federal states.   This is the major purpose of the
present study.   In federal states, the control over foreign relations is given to the central authority; but it is the essence of
federalism that there remains in the component states a certain
sphere of legislative action.   If the performance of treaty obligations invades this legislative sphere residing in the component
states, it is manifest that there is a sharp distinction between
the conclusion of a treaty and the performance of its obligations.

Constitutional Limitations on the Capacity
of a State to Enter Into International Obligations

Constitutional limitations affecting the capacity of a state
to enter into international agreements are those pertaining to
the negotiation and ratification of treaties.   They prescribe the
type of treaty to be undertaken, and the form and procedure
necessary to render the treaty nationally valid.   Such limitations can be conveniently divided into three separate categories.
The first pertains to situations where the head of a state may
enter into international engagements without any constitutional
restriction whatever.   Of course, most modern constitutions
stipulate some measure of participation in this process by the
legislative organ.   In our age there is no counterpart to the
autocratic authority of the Russian Emperor to enter into international agreements on his own initiative and at his own inclination.[14]   The last clear example of the autocratic treaty-making
authority disappeared with the defeat of Japan in 1945.[15]   It
is true that in the British system a treaty is a voluntary act of
the executive, requiring no formal procedure either by law or

convention to render it nationally valid. But every treaty is subject to such stringent regulatory measures relating to enforcement, that it is hardly realistic to place the British countries in this category. However, as their procedure is anomalous, it may conveniently be included here.

The second category comprises those states whose constitutions restrict the autonomy of the treaty-making authority in connection with such matters as the declaration of war, the cession of territory, the appropriation of money, the private rights and duties of citizens, and certain types of commercial arrangements. Some form of legislative approval is generally necessary. This is the continental European method. In Sweden, for example, Article 12 of the Constitution permits the King to enter into agreements after the Council of State has been heard on the subject; but in matters affecting financial commitments legislative approval is a prerequisite to ratification. Moreover, in matters of great importance the King must seek the opinion of the Committee of Foreign Affairs.[16] Somewhat less autonomy in foreign affairs is granted to the King under the Danish Constitution. Article 18 of the Constitution of 1915 declares that the King cannot, without the consent of the Rigstag, declare war, conclude peace, contract or cancel alliances and commercial treaties, nor cede any part of the territory nor contract any obligation which may change the existing condition of the public law. This leaves little that the King can do alone.[17] Varying degrees of legislative participation in the treaty process are stipulated in the Constitutions of France[18] and Belgium;[19] these countries require that their legislative houses shall approve all treaties concerning the cession of territory, financial obligations, and the modification of legal rights.

The third and final category includes those states which permit the head of the State to conduct all foreign negotiations and to sign treaties, provided that the advice and consent of one or both of the legislative bodies is obtained. This procedure has been characterized as the American system and most Latin American states have adopted it from the United States model. Article 68 of Argentina's Constitution typically declares that it is for the Congress to approve or reject treaties concluded with foreign powers.[20] In the United States, a two-thirds vote of the Senate only is necessary to give complete validity to a treaty.

These subclassifications of the different types of constitutional limitations affecting the capacity of the state to enter into international agreements, indicate that, though different, they pertain to the actual form or procedure of negotiation and ratification which must be observed before such agreements become nationally effective. These limitations may be so restrictive as to preclude a state from entering into a particular type of treaty completely. The Mexican Constitution, for example, prohibits the making of treaties that provide for the extradition of political offenders and agreements which in any way modify the constitutional guarantees accorded to Mexicans.[21] This stringent type of limitation is rare, and it is difficult to imply that it is denied by international law, although possibly the qualification exists that it must be reasonable and directed to contributing to the well-being of the state.[22] More commonly, such limitations restrict the right of the treaty-making authority to enter into certain international agreements without the advice and consent of the legislative body concerned, but do not categorically deny the right of the state to enter into these treaties.[23] The problem in this type of limitation is the advisability and effect of placing too many restraints on the treaty-making authority to conclude valid international agreements. It is conceivable that too much legislative participation in the treaty process will lead to more unfavorable results than too little. This problem will be considered in Chapter 4.

Constitutional Limitations Affecting the Performance of Treaty Obligations

When considering the other type of constitutional limitation, it is to be assumed that the treaty has been validly concluded according to the states' constitutional requirements affecting "capacity."

The problem is now one of performance, and the treaty may be nationally ineffective for three reasons. The first is due to the division of governmental powers within the state. Every modern state has to a lesser or greater extent adopted Montesquieu's theory that, to obviate autocratic government, the three main organs of government, the executive, the legislature and the judiciary, must be kept separate and free from recipro-

cal interference. This means that the capacity to enter into
treaty obligations may be vested in one organ, whereas the ability
to perform the obligations incurred, is vested in another. For
example, the Constitution of the United States vests the treaty-
making authority in the President but the control of the federal
revenues is within the exclusive power of Congress. Thus,
treaties which embody financial obligations necessitate congressional legislative action for implementation. Again, in Great
Britain, though the executive has the capacity to enter into any
type of agreement with another state, it has not the power to
enforce the provisions of agreements that come before the courts
for adjudication or impose a financial burden on British subjects. This can be done only if fulfilling legislation is forthcoming from Parliament. For example, a treaty that provides
for the extradition of political and social offenders requires legislation to be of internal effect, since it affects common law rights
of subjects. Without necessary legislation, the obligations in
the treaty are not nationally effective.[24]

The second reason why a treaty can be nationally ineffective
is that its subject matter may contravene a provision in the written constitution of the state, and the treaty's application as national law may be declared unconstitutional and void by the
judiciary. In the United States, a tentative draft covenant
arising out of the Declaration of Human Rights and Fundamental Freedoms[25] has been held by some to pose a threat
to the basic rights of Americans, and to the constitutional relationship between the several states and the federal government.[26] The fears engendered by this tentative draft covenant
has led recently to the most serious attempt in history to curtail the President's treaty-making power. The attempt, embodied in Senate Joint Resolution 1, brought before the eighty-
third Congress in January, 1953, and commonly known as the
Bricker Amendment, was defeated in the Senate by one vote
in February, 1954.

The third and final reason that a treaty may be nationally
ineffective is peculiar to states with federal constitutions. It
is the essence of the federal form of government that legislative powers are distributed between a central government
and the governments of component states, each sovereign within
a defined sphere of legistlative action. So, though the central
authority may have the power to enter into treaties, it may rest

with the component states to enact necessary implementing legislation to make the treaty effective. In other words, the necessary legislative measures may be *ultra vires* for the government that entered into the treaty. If the central government has not the legislative authority and the attitude of the component states is either questionable or hostile to a proposed measure or subject of international negotiation, obviously it is not feasible for the former to undertake the obligation. This means a severe curtailment of the nature of agreements which the central authority can enter. It has not the latitude of a unitary state to partake of the benefits of international intercourse. If the constitutional situation is so serious that the state is hamstrung in its conduct of international relations, the form of government is hardly in the best interests of the people, of the component states, or of the international community in general.

Thus, constitutional limitations in unitary states relative to the performance of treaty obligations are of two types. But an additional type is observed in federal states. As in unitary states, the performing power of federal states is limited by the division of governmental functions and judicial interpretations of their constitutions. Unlike in unitary states, the distinctive federal problem is that the central authority often does not have the legislative power to perform the obligations upon which it has entered, that power being vested in the component states.

THE OBJECT AND SCOPE OF THIS STUDY

This study has two objectives. The first is to make an exhaustive analysis of constitutional limitations of four federal states, compare their effect, and determine their real and supposed validity in restricting the participation of these states in international affairs. The second is to ascertain what scope there is for international law to assist the states in better international collaboration by the development, change or institution of international legal rules for international agreements.

Four states — Canada, Australia, the United States and Switzerland — have been chosen for detailed study for several reasons, principally because they are the only ones that conform to the accepted definition of a federal state.

The federal principle, as Professor Kenneth C. Wheare points out, is the principle of a division of powers between the general

and regional governments, each independent within a sphere.[27]
To make this principle clearer and to support the choice of the
four selected federations, a few observations on other states
with federal constitutional organizations are in order.

Doubtlessly the Latin American states possess some of the
attributes of federal states but on close examination it becomes
obvious that they do not fit into the principle defined above.
The Argentine Constitution permits the central authority to
interfere with the internal affairs of the component states almost
at will, and economic and political stagnation, the lack of population and resources, give the federal government ample excuse
for such interference.   Provincial governors and legislatures
unfriendly to the federal regime soon find themselves in an ineffective position.   "Federal intervention is one of the abuses
of the Argentine political practice which makes impossible that
equilibrium between the federal and provincial governments
which was anticipated by the members of the Constituent Congress eighty-five years ago."[28]   Recent political unrest in Brazil
leaves the situation rather obscure; but it is unlikely that present conditions approximate our definition of a federal state.
Professor Wheare[29] contends that the article in the Constitution of 1891, which provides that the Constitution can be
amended if approved by a two-thirds vote in both chambers in
two successive years, is in itself sufficient to destroy the reality of
federalism.   Venezuela, which has endured one of the most
oppressive dictatorships in Latin American history, has moved
from political tyranny to relative freedom since 1936.   But in
practice (and this observation may be applied to all Latin
American federations), the federal aspect in Wheare's definition has been ignored.   Finally, Mexico's Constitution of 1917,
modelled on the American example, pays only lip service to
federal principles.   "Although there is emphatic and almost
unanimous opposition to formal centralism in Mexico, para-
doxically, the Mexican federal government has from the beginning been strongly centralistic in fact.   The will of the center
has been consistently imposed upon the *sovereign* states by constitutional and extra-legal methods."[30]

It would seem at first sight that the Union of South Africa
presents some of the characteristics of a federal state.   In
reality it is unitary; this was intended by the framers of the
South African Constitution.   In the debates preceding the adop-

tion of this Constitution, the unpopularity of the American model was obvious. In a country so overwhelmingly populated with Negroes, South Africans considered a strong central government necessary to maintain write supremacy. A supreme central legislature was desirable. A judiciary like that of the United States, with wide powers of review over central legislation, was also found repugnant, for it would tend to delimit the omnipotence of the central government. Section 59 of the Constitution simply provides that "Parliament shall have full power to make laws for the peace, order and good government of the Union." Although the provinces have maintained their own administrative functions and their own legislatures, these bodies are actually subordinate. They have wide powers but their ordinances are valid only when they do not conflict with the acts of the central parliament, and are subject to review by the Governor General in Council.[31]

To complete the picture, Northern Ireland and the U.S.S.R. should be briefly mentioned. By virtue of an act of 1932, the Parliament of Northern Ireland has the right to make laws relating to "peace, order and good government." But in matters such as defense, external affairs, and custom duties the Imperial Parliament is the supreme authority. The Imperial Parliament can not only reduce the powers of the regional and central legislatures, but is also has the power of disallowance over all laws passed by Northern Ireland. The U.S.S.R. might be termed a quasi-federal state since its regional governments are subordinate to the general government and not coordinate with it. But article 14 of the Constitution gives to the all-union legislature such comprehensive powers that it leaves little control to the regional governments. Recent events have so obscured the constitutional structure, that any detailed study would not be practicable.

The second reason for the choice of the four federations listed above is that they fall within each of the three subclassifications of constitutional limitations affecting "capacity" previously mentioned.[32] Canada and Australia illustrate the anomalous procedure employed in the British countries; the United States utilizes a high degree of legislative participation in the formation of its international agreements; and the Swiss procedure can be regarded as typical of the European method.[33]

The third reason is the existence of the opposing "monistic" and "dualistic" doctrines in vogue in the American and British treaty processes respectively.[34]   This permits a relative comparison of the two different concepts in the application of treaties in the realm of national law.   The United States and Switzerland are true adherents of the "monistic" view that treaties validly made *ipso facto* become law of the land without further governmental action.   Australia and Canada, on the other hand, illustrate the "dualistic" concept; their treaties and national laws have not the same internal effect.   Before a treaty is effective as the law of the land, it must be embodied in a statute.

The final reason for the choice of these four states is that they illustrate the different types of executive authority extant among modern states.   An attempt will be made in these pages to compare the efficacy, relative to the treaty processes, of the so-called "fixed" executive, as in the United States, with the parliamentary type of executive as in Australia and Canada. Switzerland offers an interesting compromise.

This study is divided into four parts.   Part I (Chapters 1 and 2) present the problem, and some constitutional and international considerations which, it is hoped, will provide a more suitable background for the subsequent material.   Part II is concerned with the authority of the governmental organs of federal states to enter into international agreements.   Chapter 3 examines the treaty-making authorities of the states, their power to bind the states, and how far the component parts are excluded from the process.   Chapter 4 is concerned with governmental control and participation in the treaty process other than the main treaty-making authority.   Part III is a study of the problem of treaty performance.   Chapter 5 deals with the effect of the division of powers, and with the judicial construction of the constitutions which pertain to the states' performing powers.   Chapter 6 is arbitrarily separated to deal exclusively with the federal problem of the effect of the legislative powers of component states. In Part IV, Chapter 7 deals with the question of how far constitutional limitations should be taken into consideration by international law in providing a possible solution to the problem of making treaty processes conform with modern international conditions.   Finally, in Chapter 8, an attempt has been made to submit constitutional remedies that the writer considers will be more conducive to better international participation and collaboration by federal states.

In conclusion, it should be noted that Switzerland, although truly a federal state, does not develop the problems that are evident in the other federations. For example, the judiciary has not the same power that it enjoys in the United States, so that legislative supremacy over the Constitution precludes many of the difficulties relative to the implementation of treaty obligations. Also, its high degree of centralization of the past fifty years tends to place it more in the category of a unitary state than of a federal state. However, its peculiar executive, its principles of direct democracy, its lack of a supreme judiciary and other peculiarities of its governmental organization help to bring out in greater relief problems that will be observed in the other federations.

[1] Hudson, Manley O., *International Legislation*, (1929-1949), introduction to Vol. 1, p. xiii.

[2] *Ibid*. Eight volumes have been published to date.

[3] United Nations Charter, Article 13 :1.

[4] For example, the International Labor Organization, the oldest and most prolific instrument of "international legislation." It has in force over one hundred conventions on questions relating to conditions of work.

[5] Whitton, John B., "Sanctity of Treaties," *International Conciliation*, (1935), p. 395.

[6] Wilcox, Francis O., *The Ratification of International Labor Conventions*, (1935), p. 113.

[7] "International Law of the Future," Principle 5, (1944) 38 *American Journal of International Law* (Supplement), pp. 41, 80.

[8] Hall, William E., *International Law*, (8th edition by Higgins, Alexander P., 1924), p. 50.

[9] Dickinson, Edwin D., *Equality of States in International Law*, (1920), p. 219.

[10] *Infra*, Chapter 7. [11] *Infra*, pp. 87 ff. [12] *Infra*, p. 8. [13] *Infra*, Chapter 7.

[14] Wilcox, Francis O., writing in 1935, says, "from the Russian Constitution of today, one cannot get a clear picture of the treaty making process in the Soviet Republic." *The Ratification of International Labour Conventions*, (1935), p. 96. The same observation applies, *a fortiori*, today.

[15] Article 13 of the old Japanese Constitution placed the treaty-making authority without reservation in the hands of the Emperor, who made all treaties without interference from or concurrence of the Japanese Diet.

[16] Peaslee, Amos J., *Constitutions of Nations*, (1950), Vol. 3, p. 98.

[17] *Ibid*, Vol. 1, p. 646. [18] *Ibid*, Vol. 2, Article 27, p. 12. [19] *Ibid*, Vol. 1, Article 68, pp. 135-36.

[20] *Ibid*, Vol. 1, p. 76. Other states which require the approval of Congress are Bolivia, Chile, Costa Rica, Columbia, Dominica, Guatemala, Paraguay and El Salvador.

[21.] *Ibid*, Vol. 2, Article 15, p. 418.

[22.] Harvard University Research in International Law, Draft Convention on the Law of Treaties, (hereinafter cited as the Harvard Draft Convention), (1935) 29 *American Journal of International Law* (Supplement), Article 3, pp. 705 ff.

[23.] External limitations, such as the illegality or immorality of the subject-matter, which may affect the validity of a treaty, are of no concern in this discussion.

[24.] *Infra*, pp. 87 ff.

[25.] Passed and proclaimed by the General Assembly of the United Nations, December 10, 1948.

[26.] For example, Holman, Frank E., "Treaty Making; A Blank Check for Writing a New Constitution," (1950) 36 *American Bar Association Journal* 707.

[27.] Wheare, Kenneth C., *Federal Government,* (1947), Ch. 1. Sir Robert Carran in the *Report of the Royal Commission on the Australian Constitution,* (1929), defines a federal state as a "form of government in which the sovereignty or political power is divided between the central and local governments so that each of them within its own sphere is independent of the other." Moore, Sir William H., *Constitution of the Commonwealth of Australia,* (2nd ed., 1910), p. 68, maintains that a "federal government exists where, in a political community, the powers of government are distributed between two classes of organization—a central government affecting the whole territory and population of the sovereignty, and a number of local governments affecting different localities and the persons and things therein—which are so far independent of each other that the one cannot destroy the other or limit the power of the other, or encroach upon the sphere of the other as determined by the sovereign in the constitution."

[28.] De Kiewiet, Cornelius W., "Federalism in Latin America," writing in *The Constitution Reconsidered,* (1938), p. 347.

[29.] *Federal Government,* (1947), p. 23.

[30.] Martin, Percy A., "Federalism in Mexico," writing in *The Constitution Reconsidered,* (1938), p. 365.

[31.] De Kiewiet, Cornelius W., "The Frontier and the Constitution in South Africa," writing in *The Constitution Reconsidered,* (1938), p. 329. Jennings, W. Ivor, and Young, Charlotte M., *Constitutional Laws of the British Empire,* (1938), p. 268.

[32.] *Supra,* p. 7.

[33.] Switzerland could be properly placed in the category of American states, since theoretically all treaties obtain the consent of the Federal Assembly. Actually, however, Swiss constitutional law recognizes that certain types of treaties do not require this legislative approval. *Infra,* pp. 45-46.

[34.] See Oppenheim, L., *International Law,* (7th edition by Lauterpacht, H., 1947), Chapter Four, for terminology and summary of the premises of these conflicting doctrines.

CHAPTER 2

HISTORICAL AND CONSTITUTIONAL CONSIDERATIONS ON THE TREATY PROCESSES OF FEDERAL STATES

Since federal constitutions raise many intricate and basic problems of pure constitutional law, certain fundamental constitutional propositions will be examined in this chapter. Better understanding of constitutional problems will help to illuminate subsequent chapters, precluding elaborate explanatory notes. In any case, the clearest possible separation of constitutional issues should bring into sharper focus the strictly international legal problems.

CONSTITUTIONAL ORGANIZATION OF THE FEDERATIONS

The American Articles of Confederation, signed on July 9, 1778, established a military league of thirteen colonies to prosecute the war of independence against the oppressive rule of England. But these Articles soon proved too loose to provide for adequate governmental machinery. They contained no provision for a judiciary; Congress had no power to compel the states to raise money for taxation; treaties entered into by the young republic were not only unenforceable but openly disregarded by the component states; and the individual was not subject to any direct control by the national government. That a strong central government was necessary was evidenced by the mutual commercial interests of the states, the possibility of future wars, the trend toward westward expansion, and the continued presence of England and Spain on the same continent. These were the factors that chiefly influenced the states to seek a more compact union.

A unitary constitution did not seem possible not only because of the general attachment to individual states but, in the main, because of the fear that a strong central government meant the substitution of England's monarchy by another arbitrary government. The result was the Constitution of 1787, which laid down the framework of the present American government. The framers of this document sought to establish a strong national government without derogating too far from the autonomy of the states. They gave to this government legislative authority over foreign and interstate commerce, the right of coining money, and control over bankruptcy. Moreover, they empowered the new government to establish post offices, issue patents, promulgate national policies, and maintain armed forces. Another provision gave the central government the right to "lay and collect taxes . . . to pay the debts and provide for the common defence and general welfare of the United States," but Congress was to have all powers necessary and incidental to effectuating these powers. Important to the individual states is the Tenth Amendment, which provides that "the powers not delegated to the United States by the Constitution, nor prohibited by it to the states, are reserved to the states respectively or to the people."

As in the United States, the formation of a unitary state was not practicable in Canada. Communication between the various provinces was difficult. Language, customs and traditions were greatly at variance, and this meant a pronounced racial antagonism between different provinces. On the other hand, the weakness of the individual colonies, the desire for a better system of communication (particularly in the Maritime Provinces), and the movement for more and better trade made some type of union desirable.[1]

These factors, among others, led to the enactment of the British North America Act of 1867.[2] Sir John A. MacDonald's concept of the federation was that of provincial subordination to a central authority. Canada's first Prime Minister, and leading luminary of the period, visualized a powerful central government, a powerful legislature, and a powerful decentralized scheme of minor legislatures for local purposes.[3] He considered that a union on the principle of the United States would mean the death of the confederation scheme in Canada. In the United States, specific powers were given to Congress, and the residue was reserved to the states by the Tenth Amendment of the Constitution. Sir John A. MacDonald thought that this provision was the cause of the American Civil War, since it permitted too much freedom to the individual states. To avoid this, he advocated and obtained specific and local functions for the provinces, and gave the residue to the central government. To complete the process of central omnipotence, other specific methods of control were given to it. The Governor General was given the power to disallow bills of the provincial legislatures, even those measures within their specific powers.[4] He was also empowered to appoint the Lieutenant Governors of the provinces, but since these act on the advice of the provincial cabinet, this power is of little consequence.[5]   Finally a provision gave the Governor General the power to appoint provincial judges.[6]

The most important provisions that distribute the legislative powers between the provinces and the central Parliament are contained in Sections 91 and 92 of the Act.   Section 91 gives the central Parliament the residual power to "make laws for the peace, order and good government of Canada" and "all matters not coming within the classes of subjects by this Act assigned exclusively to the legislatures of the provinces."   Further, and "for greater certainty, but not so as to restrict the generality of of the foregoing terms," Section 91 continues to enumerate twenty-nine subjects within the Parliament's exclusive jurisdiction. As the scheme of the Section is one of exclusive enumerated powers, the last paragraph permits federal legislation to override any conflicting provincial legislation if it is found to be truly within the federal power   The provincial legislative powers are derived from Section 92, an enumeration of sixteen classes of subject matters, that gives the provinces exclusive jurisdiction over all subjects mentioned therein.   These include the all-important clauses relating to "property and civil rights in the provinces" and "all matters of a purely local or private nature in the province."   The other provision relevant to the consideration of the treaty process in Canada is Section 132, which will be considered in detail later in this chapter.

Although before 1900 Australia did not have the diversity of race so evident in Canada, there were various economic interests and traditions that precluded the possibility of a unitary state. But a federal union of the states was desirable for several reasons.   The encroachment of the political and economic power of Germany and Japan was feared in many circles.   Also the growing population of the Eastern Australasian colonies resulted in tariff barriers which were becoming a major hindrance and needed central regulation.   Finally, the concept of a united and strong Australasia appealed to many Australians.[7]

In creating their federal state the framers of the Australian Constitution[8] had before them the benefit of the American and Canadian experiences.   As a result of an extensive examination of the problem, they concluded that the difficulties encountered in the United States resulted from the paucity of enumerated powers given to the central government, and not from the principle of the distribution of powers, which Canada considered the reason. Consequently, with these limitations removed, the United States' example was preferred to the Canadian. The result in Australia was that the central or commonwealth government was assigned specific powers, intentionally broad and inclusive, and the residuary powers were left to the states.

The general legislative powers of the Commonwealth Parliament are defined in Section 51 of the Act. This Section gives the Parliament power to make laws "for the peace, order and good government of Australia" on thirty-nine different subject matters. The residue is reserved to the states in Section 107. The Commonwealth is given all necessary incidental powers to implement its legislation by *placitum xxxix* of Section 51, and Commonwealth paramountcy, when in conflict with state legislation, is authorized in Section 109. Although there are no express legislative powers to implement treaty obligations, comparable to Canada's Section 132, nor a provision that treaties are to have the force of law, as in the American Constitution, *placitum xxix* of Section 51 gives the Commonwealth Parliament power to legislate on "external affairs."

In Switzerland, by the middle of the sixteenth century, nearly all the cantons were connected with the Confederation.[9] After the defeat of Napoleon, the Congress of Vienna vested the highest power of the Confederation in a Diet composed of ambassadors from each canton. As in the Confederation in America, the fatal weakness was the inability of the Diet to enforce its decrees. Economic conditions, popular representation, the advancement of manufactures, communication, and transportation called for more political unity. After two forceful though abortive revolutions, the gravity of the situation became obvious by 1846. On September 12, 1848, the organic law which at present forms the basis of the fundamental law of the Confederation was adopted by a large majority of the Swiss people. Thereafter, the combined effects of centralization in Europe, the movement of Kulturkampf and the economic liberalism in social matters, and the spread of the doctrines of Engels and Marx, led to a revision of the Constitution in 1874. This document is practically identical with the present Constitution.

Article 71 of this Constitution provides that, subject to the rights of the people and the cantons, the supreme authority of the Confederation is exercised by the Federal Assembly. The Assembly is composed of two sections: the National Council and the Council of States. Article 3 provides that the cantons may exercise all the rights not delegated to the central government. Various Articles enumerate the rights exercisable by the Confederation.[11] Thus the federal Constitution establishes the legislative power of the central legislature, and only within the limits of the Constitution can the Federal Assembly legislate. However, the Swiss Constitution is very flexible and can readily be amended either by the "popular initiative" (Article 121) or by action on the part of the Assembly (Article 120). The Constitution cannot be termed a permanent distribution of legislative powers but only a guide to their current distribution between the Assembly and the cantons.

FUNDAMENTAL CONSTITUTIONAL DISTINCTIONS AND THE TREATY PROCESSES

The distinction between the different types of executives is important to this study. The framers of the American Constitution vested the executive of the government in one man. His relation to his cabinet is that of superior to subordinate and, subject to the approval of the Senate, cabinet members are nominated by him and hold office during his pleasure. The final responsibility for their actions rests with him alone; the cabinet is his executive council and must do his bidding. The American Chief Executive or President is practically irremovable except by the extraordinary method of impeachment. His office cannot be abridged without his consent. Very important, and unlike the Swiss and British systems, is the fact that he is not bound to be in political agreement with Congress. Finally, the Constitution vests in him the right to veto bills of Congress, subject to the limitation that the bill can always be passed over his veto by a majority of two-thirds in both Houses.

The Swiss Constitution provides for an executive of seven men, theoretically subject to the strict control of the Federal Assembly. This executive body is known as the Federal Council and is elected for a term of four years by the Assembly, in joint session, shortly after the election of the National Council. The Assembly annually elects the Chairman and Vice Chairman of this executive body. All its members are of equal status. Like the President of the United States, the Federal Councillors are not members of the Assembly but, unlike the President, they are always represented on the floor of each House whenever any important subject is under discussion. The powers of the Federal Council are very extensive. Although legally the servant of the Assembly, it exerts in practice almost the same power as the British cabinet, for it is the dominating force in the introduction and passage of public legislation. This great influence is due mainly to the fact that it is composed of the leaders of the Assembly and thus of the people.

Briefly, the chief characteristic of the executive of the British federations is that it is based on the theory of responsible government which, in essence, means that the cabinet or executive is responsible to the legislature, which in turn is responsible to the people. The King is represented by the Governor General, but the active head of the cabinet and the policy-making executive is the Prime Minister, the leader of the party in power. He appoints his cabinet and other executive posts with the same authority as the American President. The Prime Minister and the members of his cabinet each must have a seat in the Parliament, and by this means a direct control is exercised over the executive by Parliament. This implies a fundamental agreement and sympathy between the actual head of the government, the House and the people.

The constitutional position of the American executive in foreign affairs seems untrammelled at first glance. It has often given rise to the fear of lack of checks. On the other hand, the parliamentary type of executive may, in foreign affairs, be moved by the transient mood of the people and politics, though firm, prompt and purposeful action may be called for. With the Swiss Federal Council having in fact much more authority than theory would give it, the position of the executive would appear to be a compromise. Other considerations, however, such as the popular referendum,[12] are important in any appraisal of its true position.

Four other constitutional distinctions must be taken into account in analyzing the treaty processes of these federations. The first is the residue of powers. The American, Swiss and Australian Constitutions give certain enumerated powers to the central government and reserve the residue to the states. In Canada, the residue of legislative powers is in the central authority, and the provinces are given definite powers. The result is a different interpretative process by the courts, which is particularly important in determining the power of performance of treaty obligations. In Australia and the United States, courts need only to point to some affirmative grant of power to the central government in the Constitution; but in Canada the further question must be asked whether this power has been limited by any express grant to the provinces.[13] One consequence of this distinction in the residuary powers is that the Australian courts have referred to the freer interpretation of the American courts.[14] In result, in the course of constitutional interpretation, the express powers granted to the federal government in Canada by Sections 91 and 132[15] have been delimited by the powers contained in Section 92. The courts in Australia have not the burden of "classifying disputed legislation under two already given heads of power." Obviously it is a much easier task to "expand" than to "balance" legislative powers. Here is a prime reason why Canada now finds itself in a disadvantageous international position with respect to its treaty process. The freer method of interpretation employed in the American courts is illustrated in *DeGeofroy v. Riggs*.[16] Had it been followed in Canada, it would have done much to solve the Canadian dilemma; but because of the wide differences in the constitutional structures, such a decision is considered inapplicable there.[17]

The second constitutional distinction to be observed in these federations is that the executive power of the British federations Canada and Australia, is vested in and exercisable by the Crown, which is one and indivisible throughout the Empire.[18] The Crown in these federations is in theory the King, represented by the Governor General, but in practice it is the cabinet. Though the consequences of this doctrine are confused and obscure, at least two principles of judicial construction emerge from it. In the first place, it has influenced the courts to interpret the Australian and Canadian Constitutions as "statutes" rather than as "living things."[19] This has resulted in a stricter interpretation of the federations' central performing power. Secondly, under this doctrine both Canada and Australia have inherited the common law and the many constitutional documents that so richly embody it. This common law determines the fundamental rights of the subjects, for the Constitutions of these states contain nothing to compare with the "Bill of Rights" in the first ten amendments of the American Constitution. It also fills in gaps of executive power.[20]   The Canadian and Australian constitutional documents show a most disconcerting omission of any reference to executive power.   This power must be ascertained from prerogative instruments granted to colonial governors, the Governors General, from statutes conferring it, and, of great importance, from the remnants of the ancient royal prerogative that are still exercisable by the Crown.   Executive power in the domain of foreign affairs rests, for the most part, on this source. It is likewise on the basis of this doctrine of the inclusion of the common law in the constitutional law of Canada and Australia, that the courts there control the executive power.   Since it is exercisable according to law, the courts can determine and pass upon the validity of its exercise.   In foreign affairs, this control of the executive action is considered under the doctrine of the "act of state," and courts may be called upon to determine whether an act of the executive comes within this doctrine or not.[21] A similar consequence—and a question of a perplexing nature— is the extent to which the royal prerogative has been delegated to Canada and Australia.   The theoretical control over foreign affairs has been in strict law, and possibly still is, in the Imperial Parliament at Westminster, although constitutional practice or convention now places the effective control in the federation.   This concept will be discussed in the next chapter.

In all federations except the United States, the executive is responsible to the legislature.   This is the third constitutional distinction to be considered.   Executive acts, such as treaty-making, are under the direct control of the legislature.   In theory and practice, this concept has done much to preclude judicial control over higher executive action.[22]   It emphasises legislative rather than judicial control, but the judicial control over treaty performance, involving questions of constitutional interpretation, is not affected.[23]   It must be noted that this distinction has rendered the theory of separation of powers very indistinct in the British federations.   The executive, composed of members of Parliament and holding office only because of parliamentary support for its policies, exercises a close union personally over legislative and executive matters to a much greater extent than is possible in the United States.   Indeed, it is unlikely under the British system that an executive will enter with a foreign state into an agreement that will not have the support of Parliament.   On the other hand, such a limitation can very well restrict the executive from entering into a treaty which may prove advantageous in the long run, although lacking popular support at the time.   Such a course would be open to an American executive.[24]

The final constitutional distinction to be brought out in this central government are not the delegates of the component parts theory has support in the Swiss and American Constitutions, particularly the latter.   The doctrine that the central government can operate only within the powers which the states and the people have delegated to it has had considerable effect on the course of constitutional interpretation in the United States; but it may now be considered at least dormant in the field of foreign affairs.[25]   In this field, apparently, the sovereignty of the states and of the people has bowed to an omnipotent central government.   Under the systems of government of Canada and Australia, this principle has no legal function.   The Constitutions of these states are in the form of Imperial enactments, and the central governments are not the delegates of the component parts.

Within those legislative spheres specifically allotted to them by the Constitutions, they are as sovereign and plenary as the Imperial Parliament itself.[26]   This principle might be thought to give the central governments a wider authority than in the United States, but the course of constitutional interpretation of the powers of the central and local governments has not borne this out.   The courts have successfully kept the central governments of the British federations within strict spheres of operation so that their concept of sovereignty, compared to that of the Imperial Parliament, has a much narrower meaning.

ORIGIN OF THE TREATY PROVISIONS IN THE FUNDAMENTAL
LAWS OF THE FEDERAL STATES
In the United States and Switzerland

The framers of the American Constitution realized that the control of foreign affairs must be in the central government, so the states were specifically prohibited from entering into foreign alliances and treaties.   Under the Articles of Confederation, though the right of entering into treaties was vested solely and exclusively in Congress, its legislative powers were few and ill-defined, and each state retained "its sovereignty, freedom, and independence," and "every power, jurisdiction and right" not expressly delegated to Congress.   Thus the states and only the states had the power to regulate commerce.) In the commercial treaties concluded, most-favored nation treatment was accorded to the subjects of France, the Netherlands, Sweden and Prussia.[27]   But by the Articles, Congress had no means of enforcing their provisions and had to rely on legislation by the states to carry out the obligations incurred under the treaties.   Consequently many treaties were openly flouted, and American negotiators abroad found difficulty in concluding desirable agreements.   However, though Article 9 did not expressly mention that treaties so contracted by the United States should have the force and effect of law, contemporary political and judicial interpretation paved the way for the later provision giving treaties such status.[28]   It was early realized and strongly urged that the United States must eventually answer for the conduct of the Union and that the power of the individual states to "involve the confederacy in difficulties and war" must be removed.[29]   The situation was rectified at the Convention in Philadelphia in 1787.   (The Constitution drawn up by the representatives of the States gave to the executive the right to enter into treaties on the advice and consent of two-thirds of the Senators present.   The more important provision was that of Article 6, Section 2, which reads: "This Constitution, and the laws of the United States which shall be made in pursuance thereof; and all treaties made, or which shall be made, under the authority of the United States, shall be the supreme law of the land; and the judges in every state shall be bound thereby, anything in the Constitution or laws of any state notwithstanding."   A clearer exposition of the superiority of the treaty-making authority of the central government could not have been made.[30]   No state law was to stand in the way.) In the words of Alexander Hamilton: "The treaties of the United States, under the present Constitution, are liable to the infractions of thirteen different legislatures, and as many different courts of final jurisdiction, acting under the authority of those legislatures.   The faith, the reputation, the peace of the whole union, are thus continually at the mercy of the prejudices, the passions, and the interests of every member of which these are composed.   Is it possible that foreign nations can either respect or confide in such a government?   Is it possible that the people of America will longer consent to trust their honour, their happiness, their safety on so precarious a foundation?"[31])

The Constitution of Switzerland does not give the Federal Assembly any express right to implement treaties; but, under Article 8, the power or capacity to conclude international agreements belongs exclusively to the Confederation, and only within strict limits and exceptionally have the individual cantons the right to conclude their own agreements with foreign states. The capacity to enter into any type of agreement has, by constitutional practice, been recognized as inherent in the federal government even on matters which lie within the domain of cantonal legislative competence.[32]   The procedure in matters which actually do relate to cantonal legislation will be discussed in a subsequent chapter.[33]

The Act of Mediation of 1803 and the Act of 1815 both placed the treaty-making power within the control of the Diet and restricted the right of the cantons to enter into agreements with foreign states.[34]   Although these provisions were wide enough to prevent them from entering into foreign alliances, the cantons actually retained considerable freedom in the matter, particularly with respect to the capitulations, resulting from the service of Swiss troops under the flags of alien states. This practice was not considered conducive to a strong central state. Besides abuse of the cantonal treaty-making power, rivalries between Catholics and Protestants in the frontier cantons, particularly in the Sonderbund, brought the Swiss to the realization that a strong central authority with the power to control not only political but also commercial arrangements with foreign states was desirable. Although this change from the Constitution of 1848 met some opposition from the frontier cantons, the majority were firmly resolved to bring to an end the abuses that had manifested themselves after the Act of 1815. The wording of Articles 7, 8 and 9, the treaty-making clauses, is essentially the same today as when they were drawn up in 1848. But in Article 9, which reserves the right to the cantons to conclude exceptional alliances, the opening word "toutefois" has been replaced by the word "exceptionellement." This is an indication of the centralization process now in progress in Switzerland.

In Canada and Australia

The origin and development of the treaty provisions in the Constitutions of the British federations must be considered in the light of the great constitutional changes undergone by these states in the international community during the past half-century.

Section 132 of the British North America Act reads as follows: "The Parliament of Canada shall have all the powers necessary and proper for performing the obligations of Canada or of any province thereof, as part of the British Empire, towards foreign countries, arising under treaties between the Empire and such foreign countries." The scope of this clause will be fully appreciated after a brief survey of the treaty-making history of the Dominions of the British Commonwealth which, for the most part, is manifest in the Canadian experience. A most important consideration is that at the time of Confederation in 1867, Canada had little autonomy in foreign affairs, such matters being within the exclusive control of Westminster.[35] Prior to 1867, in political treaties concerning local interests of the British North American colonies, the colonial representative had no official status in the negotiation of treaties. He acted only in an advisory capacity. In 1865, a dispatch from the Foreign Office at Westminster to the Colonial Office accurately defined the colonial position. It read in part: "His Lordship (the Earl of Clarendon) concludes that as regards foreign countries, the agents who may be sent from the British North American Colonies will not assume any independent character, or attempt to negotiate or conclude arrangements with the governments of foreign countries but will only . . . be authorized to confer with the British Minister in each foreign country, and to afford him with information with respect to the British North American Provinces."[36]

At the time of Confederation, Section 132 had nothing to do with Canada's capacity to enter into international agreements. There was only one state, namely the British Empire, and only one Crown for treaty-making. For this purpose the Crown was one and indivisible in the strictest sense. But this did not mean that the Imperial authorities could enter into international agreements which would be applicable *ipso facto* as the law of the land in Canada. The constitutional practice was already well established at this time, that legislation was required for the implementation of treaties that altered existing law or imposed a charge on British subjects.[37] The conclusion, then, is inevitable: the Section was intended to give the central authority the legislative power to fulfill the obligations of treaties which had been made by the Imperial authorities. This power was to be exclusive. The Section specifically declares that the central government "shall have all the powers necessary and proper for performing the obligations of Canada *or of any province thereof.*" Thus, the Section extends to those treaties made by His Majesty the King on behalf of Canada in the usual form prior to the close of the First World War. This conclusion is adequately supported by reference to a case arising in British Columbia, decided in 1908.[38] A treaty was concluded between His Majesty the King and the Emperor of Japan in January 31, 1906, signed by the English plenipotentiary with Full Powers, issued in the usual way, and ratified by His Majesty in the same year. This treaty extended to Canada two agreements relating to commerce and navigation. The federal Parliament passed subsidiary legislation giving effect to the treaty in Canada. There arose the question of the validity of provincial legislation that circumscribed the admission of aliens to the province in direct contradiction to the terms of the treaty and of the Federal statute. The Supreme Court of British Columbia had little difficulty in denying effect to the provincial statute, upholding the validity of the federal legislation under Section 132 of the B.N.A. Act.

But soon after Confederation, the status of Canada and of the other British Dominions began to undergo a radical change in the international community, which was duly reflected in the evolution of the treaty process. Immediately after the union, in 1871, Sir John A. MacDonald took a very active part in the negotiation and signing of the Washington Treaty with the United States. This precedent was followed in 1874 when the Honorable George Brown acted in a similar capacity. Further developments marked the course of evolution when, in 1888, and 1893, commercial treaties with France and the United States were negotiated by the Canadian Minister alone. These treaties, however, were followed in 1898 by a dispatch from Lord Ripon, then Colonial Secretary of State, indicating the procedure to be followed in the future regarding the negotiation of treaties affecting Canada.[39] It laid down the rule that important treaties were not to be signed by the Canadian representative, but by the representative of the British Government, regardless of their respective roles in the actual negotiation. The next step of consequence was taken at the Imperial Conference of 1911.[40]

At this Conference, the Canadian Prime Minister obtained the privilege for the Dominion to withdraw from the operation of a treaty affecting it, without impairing the treaty's effectiveness for the rest of the Empire.   The foreign powers concerned were to be informed of this arrangement before the treaty was concluded.   It was likewise at this Conference that the Dominions were conceded the right to be consulted on all important matters in international relations.   This was to be accomplished by establishing a permanent Dominion representative in London, who should be regularly summoned to the Committee on Imperial Defence, and kept informed on all Imperial matters before action was instituted.   These events led to the enunciation, at the Imperial Conference of 1917, of the important principle that the Dominions are autonomous nations in an Imperial Commonwealth.   This principle was carried to its logical conclusion at the signing of the Treaty of Versailles in 1919.   Prior to the signing of this document, at a conference of Prime Ministers, Sir Robert Borden, then Canadian Prime Minister, was granted the request that the Dominions and India appear as contracting parties and signatories.   This was the procedure followed at the signing, although the Dominions signed as members of the British Empire and not as individual states.   The British Empire alone was named in the treaty as one of the principal allied and associated powers.[41]   Thus the signatures of the Dominions were so grouped as to make it obvious to foreign states that they were mere constituents of the British Empire.[42]   This procedure was employed throughout the period 1919-1923.

With this background in mind, the then current legal position of Section 132 of the B.N.A. Act may now be observed by considering one case.[43]   Canada, along with twenty-six other states, was a party to the Convention Relating to the Regulation of Aerial Navigation.   Canada sent her own plenipotentiary, who signed in the style above-mentioned; that is, Canada was separately mentioned as a member of the British Empire.   The Convention was ratified by the King on behalf of the British Empire as a unit.   The Privy Council held that Section 132 operated to give the Dominion exclusive authority to implement such conventions when entered into in this manner.   So this type of treaty comes within the Section's ambit, as well as those types of treaties made by the Imperial Government before this procedure was adopted.

The focal point of Canadian, and thus Dominion treaty-making practice, was the Halibut Fisheries Treaty of 1923 between Canada and the United States.[44]   Fully apprised, it was the Imperial Government, that secured the issuance by the King of the formal Full Powers authorizing the Canadian Minister of Marine and Fisheries to sign the treaty.   This was the first time in history a Canadian (and Dominion) appointee of the Canadian Government alone negotiated and signed a treaty with another power on behalf of Canada.   The British Ambassador in Washington, departing from the practice heretofore followed, played no part in the proceedings.   However, from an international standpoint, the Canadian Minister was a representative of His Britannic Majesty as such, not of the Canadian government as such, and the Senate of the United States, in its ratification of the treaty, acknowledged it as a treaty concluded on behalf of the British Empire and not of Canada.   At the Imperial Conference of 1926,[45] the procedure of the Halibut Fisheries Treaty was confirmed.   Pursuant to resolutions recommended at a previous Imperial Conference in 1923,[46] it was resolved that the existing practice in connection with the ratification of treaties should be maintained.   The entire subject of signing and ratifying treaties was discussed and principles and procedure formulated to govern future occasions.   In general, the Conference affirmed the right of the Dominion Government to negotiate and to enter into treaties affecting its own interests, but not without consideration of the other parts of the Empire, and ratification was to be effected at the instance of the Dominion concerned.   Further, the Conference not only recognized the right of the Dominions to commence active negotiations and incur individual obligations with foreign powers, but also gave the Dominions the right of legation and of establishing direct diplomatic relations with foreign powers; the right to create and recognize consular services; the privilege of not being bound by any obligation without the consent of the Dominion concerned; separate representation at international conferences; the right to appoint their own plenipotentiaries; the right of separate ratification of treaties.

With respect to Section 132, the 1926 Report changed one important aspect of the procedure.   It recommended that all treaties should be henceforth "made in the name of the King as the symbol of special relationship between the different parts of the

Empire," and renounced the style of signing under the title of the British Empire. The Report also recognized the existence of types of agreements less formal than treaties, that is, those made between governments or departments thereof, as distinct from heads of state. In result, the King is henceforth to be named as the High Contracting Party except in those special circumstances when this less formal type of agreement is used.[47]

The effect of Section 132 on both these types of agreements is illustrated in *The Radio Communications Case.*[48] Seventy-four governments were parties to the International Radio Telegraph Convention, Canada signing in her alphabetical position and in accordance with the new procedure as laid down in the Report of the Imperial Conference of 1926. The Canadian plenipotentiaries were appointed by the Canadian Government and the ratification was accomplished by a written instrument signed by the Secretary of State for External Affairs. When regulations made under it were attacked as being *ultra vires,* that is, exceeding the Dominion legislative authority contained in Section 91, it was countered that Section 132 gave the government the necessary power to implement such conventions which had been concluded by the new method. The Privy Council held that this Convention was "not a treaty between the Empire as such and foreign countries, for Great Britain does not sign as representing the Colonies and the Dominions."[49] As the Dominion conformed to the new procedure, which obviated the method of signing under the title of the British Empire, the Convention is not an Empire treaty within the wording of Section 132, and that Section may not be validly cited by the central government in such connection. Consequently both the formal and informal types of agreements less formal than treaties, that is, those made the new procedure are not "Empire" treaties, and fall outside the scope of Section 132.

We may now make a few general observations on the content of Section 132. With reference to its wording at the time when the Section was framed, it will be noted that a treaty made on behalf of the British Empire was neither in existence nor contemplated. Canada had no autonomy whatsoever in external relations. The Section was manifestly directed at giving the central government all power to discharge treaty obligations made by the Imperial Government for the benefit of Canada. The provinces were not to participate in the process. No treaty was entered into by a Dominion under the style of the British Empire until the Treaty of Versailles in 1919 and, at this point, the judiciary defined the term "Empire treaty" and permitted Section 132, by a literal reading, to give the central government power of implementation. As Professor Vincent C. MacDonald points out, the wording of the Section was not a work of art, but was intended to give the central government power to perform all obligations which were incurred by a treaty, just as before Confederation it would have been made good by the action of the Imperial Parliament.[50] Historical reason and logic gives no firm foundation for the restrictive interpretation placed on this clause by the Privy Council. Indeed the Section has now been relegated to cover a situation which no longer exists.

The history of the treaty process in Australia is similar to that of Canada. The Commonwealth, being part of the Empire, had no authority to enter into treaties with foreign powers except so far as authority was expressly delegated to it by the Imperial Government. The Bill of 1891, proposing the forthcoming Constitution of 1900, contained a provision empowering the central government to legislate with respect to "external affairs and treaties." After the American model, Clause 7 of the Bill read: "The Constitution established by this Act, and all laws made by the Parliament of the Commonwealth in pursuance of the powers conferred by the Constitution, and all treaties made by the Commonwealth, shall, according to their tenor, be binding on the courts, judges and people of every state, and of every part of the Commonwealth anything in the laws of any state to the contrary notwithstanding." From the context, it can be seen that the framers were attempting to give to the commonwealth executive an unprecedented and possibly unrestricted power, in which the role of Parliament was obscure. However, in the final draft, the phrases "and treaties" and "all treaties made by the Commonwealth" were omitted from the *placitum* and from Clause 7, respectively, without much debate.[51] Sir John Quick and Sir Robert Garran remark that the words were omitted because they might have been construed as involving a claim on the part of the Commonwealth to a power to make treaties.[52] Had these clauses remained, it would have been interesting to observe how constitutional practice would have reconciled an uncontrolled executive in treaty making, with the doctrine of the Supremacy of Parliament.

The views of the authoritative constitutional writers at the time the Australian Constitution Act was passed are of practical concern. Mr. Augustus H. F. LeFroy considered that the Clause 7 indicated the intention on the part of the Imperial Parliament to divest itself of legislative control over the implementation of treaties concerning Australia. He reasoned that, as in the interpretation of the Canadian Constitution, the federal Parliament had power to legislate exclusively on matters within Section 91, subject only to the restriction not to encroach on provincial matters within Section 92, and, as there was no corresponding restriction in the Australian Constitution, the legislative power over external affairs was unrestricted. This theory would be supported by the omission of a similar section to Section 132.[53] Sir William H. Moore, writing in 1910, was of the opinion that the "power to give effect to international arrangements must, it would seem, be limited to matters which *in se* concern external relations; a matter purely domestic, and therefore within the exclusive power of the states, cannot be within the range of federal power merely because some arrangement has been made for uniform national action."[54] Thus Sir William H. Moore would not at that time give the federal power even the efficacy of Section 132 in the Canadian Constitution which, as has been shown, permitted the central government to take implementing action on certain types of treaties. Professor A. Berriedale Keith would further restrict it, by not permitting it to be extended outside the ambit of the other powers of Parliament.[55] Sir John Quick and Sir Robert Garran,[56] writing in 1901, did not think that the *placitum* indicated any intention on the part of the Imperial Parliament to divest itself absolutely of all authority over the external affairs of Australia, and to commit such matters exclusively to the Parliament of the Commonwealth. These writers considered that this grant of power must be construed with the other *placita* and that it has its limitations: "It must be restricted to matters in which political influence may be exercised, or negotiation and intercourse conducted, between the Government of the Commonwealth and Governments of countries outside the limits of the Commonwealth. This power may therefore be fairly interpreted as applicable to (1) the external representation of the Commonwealth by accredited agents where required; (2) the conduct of the business and promotion of the interests of the Commonwealth in outside countries, and (3) the extradition of fugitive offenders from outside countries."

At the time, Mr. LeFroy was the only one to give the *placitum* the power and effect that it was eventually to receive. He recognized that the future interpretation of this *placitum* did not have to depend on the fate of Section 132 of the B. N. A. Act. Sir John Quick and Sir Robert Garran, influenced by the Imperial tie, wrote under conditions that obtained before Imperial constitutional law underwent such a radical change in the period immediately succeeding the First World War. Sir William H. Moore and Professor A. Berriedale Keith were apparently concerned that a broad interpretation of "external affairs" would infringe and possibly obliterate the powers reserved to the states. They advanced the same arguments that have received much support from the advocates of "state rights" in the United States. They express the imaginative fear that the central government will use this power in quest of autocratic domination.

[1.] See the resolutions and correspondence leading up to Confederation, in Kennedy, William P. M., *Statutes, Treaties and Documents of the Canadian Constitution,* (1930), pp. 535 ff.

[2.] 30-31 *Statutes of Victoria,* Ch. 3, (hereinafter referred to as the B.N.A. Act).

[3.] Kennedy, William P. M., *The Constitution of Canada,* (2nd ed., 1938), pp. 289, 305, 307, 404, 489.

[4.] Section 90 of the B.N.A. Act. [5.] Section 59 of the B.N.A. Act. [6.] Section 96 of the B.N.A. Act.

[7.] Jennings, W. Ivor and Young, Charlotte M., *Constitutional Laws of the British Empire* (1938), p. 211; Moore, Sir William H., *Constitution of the Commonwealth of Australia,* (1910), pp. 26 ff; Sir John Quick and Sir Robert Garran, *Annotated Constitution of Australia,* (1901), Part IV.

[8.] Commonwealth of Australia Constitution Act, 1900, 63-64 *Statutes of Victoria,* Ch. 12, (hereinafter referred to as the Australian Constitution Act).

[9.] Rappard, William E., *La Constitution de la Suisse, 1884-1948,* (1948), *passim.*

[10.] *Ibid,* p. 280. [11.] *Infra,* pp. 127-128. [12.] *Infra,* pp. 79-80.

[13.] "Section 91 of the B.N.A. Act vests the exclusive power in the Dominion Parliament to make laws for 'the regulation of trade and commerce.' But section 92 of the same Constitution vests exclusively in the Legislatures of the Provinces exclusive power to make laws in relation to 'property and civil rights in the Province.' It was, therefore, not possible to ascertain and define the extent of the Dominion power over trade and commerce without maintaining the exclusive provincial power over local civil rights. Central and local claims to power had to be balanced. Neither power was greater or less than the other . . . In such cases, the double enumeration of exclusive powers of Dominion and Province respectively in sections 91 and 92 made the problem one of classifying disputed legislation under two already given heads of power." *Huddart Parker Limited v. The Common-*

wealth, (1931) 44 Commonwealth Law Reports (Australia) 492, pp. 526-27, (*per* Justice Evatt).

[14.] For example, see the references to the American decisions in *The King v. Burgess: ex parte Henry,* (1936) Commonwealth Law Reports (Australia) 608, pp. 638-39, (*per* Chief Justice Latham), and p. 680, (*per* Justices Evatt and Mc-Tiernan).

[15.] *Infra,* p. 28.   [16.] (1890) 133 United States 266. *Supra,* p. 56.

[17.] Australian courts have been cautioned against the persuasiveness of American authority. See *Amalgamated Society of Engineers v. Adelaide Steamship Company Limited* (hereinafter cited as *The Engineer's Case*), (1920) 28 Commonwealth Law Reports (Australia) 129, p. 146. Their "usefulness," however, is illustrated in *The King v. Burgess*: *ex parte Henry,* (1936) 55 Commonwealth Law Reports (Australia) 608; *Infra,* pp. 56, 121.

[18.] *The Engineer's Case, ibid; Theodore v. Duncan,* (1919) Appeal Cases (England) 696, p. 706.

[19.] *The Engineer's Case, ibid.*   [20.] *Infra,* pp. 46 ff. 99-100.   [21.] *Infra,* pp. 68 ff.

[22.] *The Engineer's Case,* (1920) 28 Commonwealth Law Reports (Australia) 129, pp. 146-48; *Orpen v. Attorney-General for Ontario,* (1925) 56 Ontario Law Reports (Canada) 327, p. 337.

[23.] *Infra,* pp. 99 ff., Ch. 6.   [24.] *Infra,* pp. 88 ff, 168 ff.   [25.] *Infra,* pp. 95 ff.

[26.] *Infra,* p. 99. *Hodge v. The Queen,* (1883) 9 Appeal Cases (England) 117, p. 132; *Attorney-General for Canada v. Cain,* (1906) Appeal Cases (England) 542, p. 547.

[27.] Crandall, Samuel B., *Treaties, Their Making and Enforcement,* (2nd ed., 1916), pp. 32 ff.

[28.] Crandall, Samuel B., *ibid,* pp. 41-2. Mr. Crandall quotes Chief Justice Ellesworth as summing up the prevailing opinion in his decision in *Hamilton v. Erle,* (1796) 1 Hughes (United States Supreme Court) 249. "The treaty now under consideration was made on the part of the United States by a Congress composed of deputies from each state, to whom were delegated by the Articles of Confederation, expressly 'the sole and exclusive right and power of entering into treaties and alliances'; and being ratified and made by them, it became a national act and law of every state."

[29.] Detailed accounts of the difficulties in this period may be found in Butler, Charles H., *Treaty Making Power of the United States,* (1902), Vol. 1, Ch. 6. Crandall, Samuel B., *ibid,* Chs. 2 and 3. Corwin, Edwin S., *National Supremacy,* (1913), Ch. 3. Dangerfield, Royden J., *In Defense of the Senate,* (1933), pp. 11ff.

[30.] The framers had little difficulty with the concept involved in making treaties the law of the land. It was generally accepted that customary international law was an integral part of the law of the land; *a fortiori,* conventional international law. See Scott, James B., "The Legal Nature of International Law," (1907) 1 *American Journal of International Law* 831, and Sprout, Harold H., "Theories as to the Applicability of International Law in the Federal Courts of the United States," (1932) 26 *American Journal of International Law* 280.

[31.] *The Federalist,* No. 22, (edited by Max Beloff, 1948), p. 109.

[32.] Burckhardt, Walther, *Le Droit Fédéral Suisse,* (1935), Vol. 5, pp. 1, 414.

[33.] *Infra,* pp. 127-128.

[34.] Rappard, William F., *Le Constitution de la Suisse, 1848-1948,* (1948), pp. 191, 207 ff.

[35.] As early as 1846, Canada had obtained a degree of control in tariff matters. Ollivier, Maurice, *Problems of Canadian Sovereignty,* (1945), pp. 84-5, reports that in other matters the colonies often hurdled Imperial objections by agreements which did not take the form of treaties but were ratified by subsequent legislation. Such a procedure was employed as early as 1822 and as late as 1873 but at the later date the Orders-in-Council, necessary to bring the legislation into effect, were shelved because Imperial authorities were of the opinion that the legislation ran counter to outstanding British treaties, and so were in contravention to the Colonial Laws Validity Act of 1865, which rendered such legislation void.

[36.] Quoted in MacDonald, Vincent C., "Canada's Power to Perform Treaty Obligations," (1933) 11 *Canadian Bar Review* 581, 664, pp 583-84.

[37.] For the origin of this practice, see *infra*, pp. 87 ff. See also Clement, William H. P., *The Law of the Canadian Constitution,* (3rd ed., 1916), pp. 134 ff.

[38.] *In Re Nakane and Okazake,* (1908) 13 British Columbia Reports (Canada) 370.

[39.] "A foreign Power can only be approached through H.M. Representative, and any agreement entered into with it, affecting any part of Her Majesty's dominions, is an agreement between Her Majesty and the sovereign of a foreign State . . . . . To give the colonies the power of negotiating treaties for themselves without reference to H.M. Government would be to give them an international status as separate and sovereign states . . ." Stewart, Robert B., *Treaty Relations of the British Commonwealth of Nations,* (1939), Appendix II.

[40.] Kennedy, William P. M., *Constitution of Canada,* (2nd ed., 1938), p. 352; Stewart, *ibid,* Appendix IV.

[41.] There was no separate mention of the Dominions and India among the minor powers. Another qualification to the signatures of the Dominions and India at this time was that they were not made under the authority of their respective governments, but under the Full Powers issued by the King on the advice of the Imperial Government.

[42.] See Stewart, Robert B., *Treaty Relations of the British Commonwealth of Nations,* (1939), pp. 146 ff, for details of this procedure and other treaties signed in this way.

[43.] *Reference re Regulation and Control of Aeronautics in Canada,* 1930 Supreme Court Reports (Canada) 663; (1932) Appeal Cases (England) 54. (hereinafter cited as the *Aeronautics Case*)

[44.] For detailed considerations of this treaty, see Read, Horace E., "Canada as a Treaty Maker," (1927) 5 *Canadian Bar Review* 229, 301; Stewart, Robert B., *Treaty Relations of the British Commonwealth of Nations,* (1939), pp. 71 ff.

[45.] Imperial Conference, 1923, Summary of Proceedings; text may be found in Kennedy, William P. M., *Statutes, Treaties and Documents of the Canadian Constitution,* (1930), pp. 702 ff.

[46.] Imperial Conference, 1923, Summary of Proceedings; text may be found in Kennedy, William P. M., *ibid,* pp. 701-2.

[47.] The heads of states formula for treaty making is generally employed in arrangements of the highest dignity and importance. Agreements between governments are those usually of a technical or administrative nature. The national and international effect is exactly the same but the classification is important since it determines the nature of the Full Powers to be issued and Instruments of Ratification. Formal documents issued at Westminster are probably required when the formal procedure is employed; but see *infra*, p. 52 ff. Intergovernmental agreements require only written authority from the Secretary of State for External Affairs. See Read, "International Agreements," (1948) 26 *Canadian Bar Review*. 520.

[48]. *In re Regulation and Control of Radio Communication in Canada*, 1931 Supreme Court Reports (Canada) 541; 1932 Appeal Cases (England) 304. (hereinafter referred to as *The Radio Communications Case*).

[49]. 1932 Appeal Cases (England) 304, p. 311.

[50]. MacDonald, Vincent C., "Canada's Power to Perform Treaty Obligations," (1933) 11 *Canadian Bar Review* 581, 664.

[51]. A brief and uninformative discussion on this point may be found in the *Official Records of the Debates of the Australian Federal Convention: 2nd Session*, Sydney, 1897, pp. 238-40; and Melbourne, Vol. 1, p. 30.

[52]. *Annotated Constitution of Australia*, (1901), p. 770.

[53]. "Commonwealth of Australia Bill," (1899) 15 *Law Quarterly Review* 281, p. 290.

[54]. *Constitution of the Commonwealth of Australia*, (2nd ed., 1910), p. 461.

[55]. *Responsible Government in the Dominions*, (2nd ed., 1928), Vol. 2, pp. 620-21.

[56]. *Annotated Constitution of Australia*, (1901), pp. 631-32.

CHAPTER 3

THE TREATY-MAKING POWERS OF
FEDERAL EXECUTIVES

It is to the advantage of federations, as it is for unitary states, to have a strong agency to conduct foreign relations. It often follows that if control over foreign relations by the central agency is weak, the federation's policy will be weak; if strong and guided by a competent executive, its policy will be strong. In other words, the control of foreign affairs in the central government is often determinative of the state's policy. The effectiveness of international cooperation necessarily depends upon strong national agencies. It is not practical for foreign states to cooperate with the various separate entities that compose a federation. Even if this were feasible, it would soon prove unworkable because of jealousy and competition, as exemplified by the American experience prior to 1787.[1] Hence international law requires for admission to the world community that a state have an organ capable of speaking authoritatively in foreign affairs.[2]

Source and Extent of Authority in the United States and Switzerland

The two clearest examples of federations which derive their executive authority from written instruments are the United States and Switzerland. In the United States, Article 2, Section 2 of the Constitution vests the executive treaty-making authority in the President, with the proviso that he obtain the advice of two-thirds of the Senate. In Switzerland, Article 102:8 of the Constitution confers on the Federal Council the power and responsibility for conducting external affairs; however, Article 3 gives the Confederation alone the right to declare war, to conclude peace, and enter into alliances with foreign states.

The Constitution of the United States not only confers the treaty-making power on the President but it also grants him other powers distinctly relevant to foreign affairs. He has the power to appoint and receive ambassadors and other plenipotentiaries. Further, though this has been disputed, he may appoint special plenipotentiaries to determine the current of world political opinion. As Head of State, he has the inherent authority to make official visits to other Heads of States. He has by the Constitution the authority over the armed forces, and although it is for Congress to declare war, it is manifest that by this authority it would not be impossible for him to precipitate a war. Finally, there is, probably inherent in his capacity as Chief Executive, the President's acquired right to enter into executive agreements, a less formal type of international agreement than the treaty, and not requiring the two-thirds vote of the Senate.

Of all the federations under study, it is the United States that has the most specific measures for excluding the component states from the treaty process. The Constitution declares in no uncertain terms that the treaty-making power is vested in the central government. In the first Section of Article 1, it is provided that "no state shall enter into any treaty or alliance or confederation," and in the third Section of the same Article is found the provision that "no state shall without the consent of Congress . . . enter into any agreement or compact with another state or with a foreign power." Thus the Constitution envisages two types of agreements which the framers, familiar with the practice of nations and of international law, must be deemed to have had in mind. With respect to the formal treaty, the situation is adequately summed up in the words of an eminent American statesman, ". . . the people of the United States, by the Constitution of 1787, vested the whole treaty-making power in the national government . . . The treaty-making power is not distributed; it is vested all in the national government; no part of it is vested in or reserved to the states. In international affairs there are no states; there is but one nation, acting in direct relation to and representation of every citizen in every state. Every treaty made under the authority of the United States is made by the national government, as the direct and sole representative of every citizen in the United States . . . "[3]

Is there any scope left to the individual state in foreign affairs? The above-quoted constitutional provisions indicate at least that the states cannot enter into an agreement with a foreign state without the consent of Congress; but this means inferentially that some types of agreements may be concluded. The determination of this question necessarily involves an interpretation of the expression "an agreement or compact." A clear distinction is obviously intended, but what this distinction is has

not been authoritatively determined.[4]   Doubtlessly treaties connote agreements or arrangements with other states, that involve
political considerations affecting the whole nation.   The component states have no voice in this process.   On the other hand,
by elimination, there is argument that other types of treaties,
such as commercial agreements, are permissible with the consent
of Congress.   Actual practice has shown that compacts have
been utilized from a very early time between the states themselves, even without the consent of Congress, but they did not involve political entanglements apt to embarrass the central government.[5]   Political treaties with foreign countries and between
the states themselves were prohibited; yet some scope remains to
individual states to enter into "agreements or compacts" of a
non-political nature.   One writer, on an examination of the
problem, concludes that "only political compacts or agreements
which affected their sovereignty as between themselves or between them and the federal government were sought to be regulated or controlled."[6]   Another writer is of the opinion "that
these 'agreements and compacts' must be distinguished from
treaties, probably referring to 'trifling and temporary arrangements between states and, foreign powers without substantial
political and economic effect."[7]   But even in these inconsequential
arrangements between the states the central government apparently has maintained a strict control, and in practice the scope
for such agreements with foreign powers remains ill-defined and
vague.[8]   Finally, it is clear from the Constitutional Convention
of 1787 that the executive was to be supreme in this field.   Although we find divergent opinions expressed concerning the residence of the treaty-making power, there was definite unanimity
among the framers that the central government was the exclusive
and sole authority in foreign affairs.[9]   In the United States there
is no doubt that the component states are effectively excluded
from the treaty process, and foreign states need not look beyond
the central organ.

   In the Swiss treaty-making procedure, an adequate explanation
is afforded in the relevant articles in the Swiss Constitution.
Article 8 confers on the Confederation the sole right to declare
war, to make peace, and to conclude alliances with foreign powers, particularly treaties relating to tariffs and commerce.   According to Article 9, by exception, the cantons retain the right
to conclude agreements with foreign states regarding the admin-

istration of public property, and border and police regulations;
but the Constitution specifically provides that such arrangements
should contain nothing contrary to the Confederation of the
rights of the other cantons. Even over these types of agreements that lie within the authority of the cantons, the Federal
Council maintains a definite measure of control in virtue of the
provision in Article 10, to the effect that official relations between the cantons and foreign governments or their representatives shall be conducted through the Federal Council. However, by the same Article, the cantons are permitted to correspond, and thus negotiate, with inferior officials and officers of
foreign states in regard to the subjects enumerated in Article 9.
Hence the cantons may conclude certain minor treaties, under
the surveillance of the Federal Council. This is similar to the
situation in the United States. The Federal Council, maintaining direct control over all such agreements, is authorized to prevent their execution if they contain anything contrary to the
Constitution, of if they infringe the rights of other cantons.
Although the covenanting cantons are authorized to invoke the
aid of the federal government in carrying out such obligations,
and though, in case of dispute over the application of the rules,
appeal may be made to the Supreme Court, the Federal Council's
determination is generally final.[10]

The complete supremacy of the American executive in treaty
making is authoritatively outlined in the opinion of the court in
United States v. Curtiss-Wright Corporation: "The President
is the constitutional representative of the United States with
regard to foreign nations. He manages our concerns with foreign nations and must necessarily be most competent to determine
when, how and upon what subjects negotiation may be urged
with the greatest prospects of success. For his conduct he is responsible to the Constitution."[11] The control of American foreign relations is an executive act of the widest import. In the field
of negotiation, the President is empowered to enter into any international arrangements he sees fit, and he is the sole judge
of the expediency of instituting and conducting them. By his
inherent power under the Constitution he is not bound by any
action of the Senate before or after a treaty is negotiated. He
is not bound by resolutions of the Senate or of the House of
Representatives, though Congress has considerable power of
implementation and delegation in the field. Also, the President

is under no obligation to put into effect an agreement that has received the "advice and consent" of the Senate. There is no legal or political barrier to discarding the senatorial acceptance if in his opinion it is in the best interest of the state. There is no obligation to ratify, and by this means the President has some measure of control over amendments that may be proposed in the Senate. The President, however, is precluded by the Constitution from ratifying treaties which do not receive the "advice and consent" of the Senate.

The President's authority to terminate treaties is questionable. Congress has the undoubted right to supersede treaties by enacting conflicting legislation, and a resolution to the effect of directing the President to terminate an international agreement would be a most "effective and unquestionable method" of termination. However, the treaty procedure itself could be effectively employed, and termination accomplished by the President, by and with the advice and consent of the Senate. Also, the method of altering and abrogating international agreements by simple executive agreement would in all likelihood be constitutionally upheld. It may be fairly said that the right of termination is also within the control of the President, at least coequally with the power of Congress in this regard.[12]

The situation in Switzerland is not as clear as that in the United States. The Federal Council has not, in theory at any rate, such a free hand as the American President. Theoretically, the Council must do the bidding of the Federal Assembly, and any resolution passed with respect to foreign affairs must be meticulously performed by the council. Yet in practice the Council's position as a leader in initiating policy legislation approaches the predominant status of the British cabinet,[13] and it may be properly considered the actual instigator and negotiator in foreign relations. With respect to ratification the procedure is clearer. The treaty must be submitted to the two chambers for their approval, and this approval is requisite for the treaty's internal application. Once approved, it is for the Federal Council to ratify and communicate its acceptance or rejection to the foreign state concerned.[14]

In addition to his constitutional authority to enter into treaties, by and with the advice of two-thirds of the Senators present, the American President, under various constitutional powers, has the right to enter into a particular type of international agree-

ment generally known as the executive agreement. This is a
less formal type of agreement than the treaty, but its effect in
international law is analogous to that of the more formal procedure.[15]   Its effect in national law will be discussed at a later
point.[16]

Executive agreements are of two kinds. The first are those
issued under a congressional authorization, that is, made under
some authority within the constitutional right of Congress and
within the required bounds of valid delegation.[17]   It is sufficient
here to note that this type of executive agreement should offer
no constitutional objection. Although this procedure is not in
strict conformity with the terms of the Constitution, the objections to it seem to stem from this fact rather than from logical
constitutional practice, usage and good government. Professors
Myers S. McDougal and Asher Lans, in an exhaustive examina-
tive examination of this subject,[18] conclude that "the result is that
our constitutional law today makes available two parallel and
completely interchangeable procedures, wholly applicable to the
same subject matters and of identical domestic and international
legal consequences, for the consummation of intergovernmental
agreements."

The second type of executive agreement is more controversial.
It includes those agreements entered into with foreign states
under the President's own initiative and without Senatorial advice or consent. The constitutional authority for the making
of such agreements is to be found, first and probably foremost,
in the President's constitutional capacity of Commander-in-Chief
of the Army and Navy. For example, the arrangement effected
with Great Britain in 1941 concerning the trade of overage
American destroyers for certain concessions on British territory
was upheld under this power, and supported by the President's
paramount power in foreign affairs inherent in his capacity as
Chief Executive. Also, under this authority, the President may
validly effect armistice arrangements, such as the 1898 pre-
liminary peace protocol with Spain, and the settlement of international claims arising out of hostilities after the First World
War. Under his constitutional right to "receive Ambassadors
and Other Public Ministers," another source of authority is
available to the President to make such agreements. Thus the
famous Litvinoff assignment of Russian assets in the United
States to the United States and the consequent recognition of

Russia in 1933 were accomplished by this means. In determining the validity of the assignment, the court supported the procedure by emphasizing the presidential capacity as "sole organ" of the government in the conduct of foreign affairs.[19] All types of international agreements have been made under this procedure, and the general view that presidential executive agreements were legally interchangeable with the treaty led to the specific prohibition of the former in the recently defeated Bricker Amendment.

The use of the executive agreement has been severely criticised. It incurs opposition in the Senate and supports the argument that a stricter constitutional observance by the executive in foreign affairs is necessary. However, the use of these agreements may well be the result of an incomplete and faulty treaty process, which, as laid down in the United States Constitution, does not permit the necessary facility in modern international relations. At the present time, though many decry its use, the efficacy and value of the executive agreement, in the present constitutional system of the United States, cannot be denied.

The American use of the executive agreement is to a small extent paralleled in Switzerland. Although the Federal Council is the servant of the legislature, and responsible to it for all its actions, Swiss constitutional law fully recognizes the right of the Federal Council to enter and conclude international agreements in certain instances without the approval of the Federal Assembly.[20] The first instance is when the Assembly has given the Council special or prior authorization to enter into a treaty. This, of course, is analogous to delegation in the United States. The theory is that the legislature still retains control over the process, but the details are relinquished to the Council for consummation. The second instance is "when the matter in issue is concerned with the exchange of declarations touching accessory questions." Presumably of lesser importance to the main subject under consideration, protocols, annexes and appendices, similar to the above authority, may be worked out in detail by the Federal Council alone. The third situation when the Federal Council does not require Assembly approval is in cases of emergency or "provisional ordering of international relations and especially with the view to commercial adjustments." Speed and secrecy are often essential in the conduct of foreign affairs, and the Swiss Constitution, presumably, was making provision for such cases.[21]

The above, of course, are also the prime reasons for the use of executive agreements in the United States. Current conditions justify the continued use of such expedients as an integral part of the present treaty-making process.

Fourthly, the Swiss Assembly allows the Council full authority to arrange for the execution of agreements that have already been approved. As approval of an agreement also empowers the Council to apply it, this provision would enable the Council to make subsidiary rules with the other state with regard to the application of the agreement. Finally, the Assembly's approval is not necessary when Switzerland acquires rights only, and incurs no obligations under an international agreement.

In conclusion, it may be stated that the Swiss and American treaty-making power is effectively vested in the central executive of each federation. The component parts are excluded from participation in international affairs except in a narrow, and from an international standpoint, inconsequential sphere. Each of these federal states presents a solid united front to foreign states in this respect.

SOURCE AND EXTENT OF AUTHORITY
IN CANADA AND AUSTRALIA

The Constitutions of Canada and Australia vest the executive power of the federations in the Queen (or King), exercisable by the Governor General, the Queen's representative, on the advice of the Privy Council, that is, the cabinet.[22] But, whereas the broad limits of executive power are contained in the written constitutions of the United States and Switzerland, it is otherwise in Canada and Australia. The constitutions of Canada and Australia merely state that the executive power is conferred in the Governor General, who represents the Sovereign. The Canadian document does mention that all powers, authorities and functions exercised by the pre-Confederation provinces or colonies shall pass to the Governor General with respect to matters concerning Canada.[23] But this expression in no way indicates what these powers are. They must be found in the instructions and commissions of the old colonial governors, the Letters Patent and Instructions of the present office of Governor General, the statutory authority conferred on the executive by Parliament and, most important for the study of the power in foreign affairs, the prerogatives of the King. It is evident that, from such sources, these prerogative powers are obscure, ill-defined and subject to continual judicial interpretation.

The statutory authority, the more readily ascertainable source of executive power, is not important for the purpose of defining the authority of the executive in foreign affairs. Both Parliaments, being omnipotent under the English doctrine of supremacy of Parliament, and restrained only by the Constitutions, can expand or delimit the statutory executive power as they see fit. Also as a consequence of this omnipotence, they can restrict the King's prerogative by statute, if the authority to do so can be found in the express words of the Constitutions, or by necessary intendment therefrom.[24] Neither Canada nor Australia has yet attempted to confer this authority expressly on the central executive. Indeed there is doubt whether they have the constitutional power to do so.[25]

With no assistance from the statutory authority conferred on the federal executives, the determination of the nature and extent of the treaty-making power in these two federations is dependent entirely on the prerogative of the Crown. Before this determination is made, the prerogative must be defined and explained; and no clearer explanation of the prerogative power of the Crown can be found than that contained in William F. O'Connor's Report to the Senate of Canada on the B. N. A. Act in 1939.[26] It reads: "Anciently the prerogative of the Crown embraced, alike, the executive, legislative and judicial powers of government and in legal theory, evidenced by familiar forms and expressions, it yet does . . . In fact, however, the Crown . . . has lost its former legislative and judicial powers. They have been assumed by Parliament. It is only in the executive sphere that any large tract of prerogative remains to it . . . When we speak of a prerogative of the Crown we mean a right that remains in the Sovereign as one of that bundle of discretionary common law rights which were, at and by the common law, exercisable by the Sovereign in person, and we use that term whether the Prerogative in question is or is not now exercisable by the Sovereign in person, or through him by his representative, and though that Prerogative may now be exercisable in his name by his constitutional advisers, and so only; and when we speak of an executive power we mean a right exercisable in the name of the Crown by the Sovereign's constitutional advisers, whether the right be one of prerogative origin or be one that arises from, or is aided by, statute . . ." Thus, in the absence of any statute bearing on the question, Parliament having never legislated to take away this right from the Crown, it is necessary to define the extent of the prerogative of the Crown in foreign affairs and to consider how far it is exercisable in the Dominions.

To answer the first question: it is the Crown that represents the community in external or foreign relations. It is the Crown to whom foreign states look when consummating international agreements. The cabinet advises the Crown and actually negotiates and concludes such agreements; there is no responsibility to Parliament for the actual negotiations. In negotiating, signing and ratifying treaties, the Crown is supreme and untrammelled by constitutional restrictions. Sir William R. Anson says: "No person or body save the King by his ministers or his accredited representatives, can deal with a foreign state so as to acquire rights or incur liabilities on behalf of the community at large."[27] The prerogative in respect to foreign affairs has been left untouched and complete in the hands of the executive.

The second question, that concerning the delegation of the prerogative to Canada and Australia, is of wider import. It is more nebulous and demands much more explanation. Ostensibly, the prerogative with respect to foreign affairs is not delegated to the federations. Nowhere in the documents tracing the course of constitutional evolution of these two states can express provisions be found permitting their executives to enter into treaties with foreign countries, exclusively as sovereign states. The treaty-making power is still vested in the Crown; and this means the Imperial Crown. Thus it is not the Canadian Crown that ratifies the more important type of treaty.[28] Intergovernmental agreements, the less formal type of agreements, are concluded on behalf of Canada alone; but this procedure has not been interpreted as a devolution of the royal prerogative of the Imperial Crown in treaty making, though it is strong evidence of present Canadian autonomy. Although the actual negotiation, signing, and formal ratification of a treaty are effected at the instance and on the advice of the Canadian government, the procedure for the formal treaty is still in the Imperial form.

Since this procedure still exists, it is obvious that there are two types of prerogative powers in the British federations. First, there are those which are exercised by the Governor General;

that is, the Crown in the state concerned, on the advice of its cabinet. The rules relative to the acquisition of these prerogative powers will be discussed in the following pages. Second, there are those prerogative powers exercised by the Queen (King) or Crown in England, the Imperial Crown, on the advice of the government concerned. Ostensibly, the treaty-making power of the British federations is of the latter type, since it has not been delegated—at least not to Canada—as will be presently explained. It might be maintained that, as Canada has the actual power to enter into treaties, the form and theoretical control by the Imperial authorities are of no concern. It is not disputed that Canada and Australia conduct their own destinies, and that the Imperial procedure is only an instrument of form and not a substantive control. But it is submitted that the legal as well as the actual control of the treaty-making power should reside in these federations. In Australia, the central executive is sufficiently endowed with executive power to enter into treaties; but this cannot be said for Canada. For two reasons at least, it is important to find legal authority for the exercise of this power by the Canadian central executive. First, the fact that such legal authority has not been found in Canada creates uncertainty as to where, in fact, the power does reside. The fact sustains the provincial contention that the provinces should have a voice in this part of the treaty process.[29] Second, if the authority were found to reside within the exclusive central control, it would be a long stride in the direction of determining with greater precision the legislative control over the implementation of treaty obligations. The questions to be considered now are the exact location and the extent of the legal power to conclude international agreements, in the British federations.

There are three different views advanced respecting the right of Canada and Australia to exercise the prerogative powers originally vested in the Queen (King) in person. The first is that all prerogatives necessarily incidental to the conduct of an independent state now reside in these states. This would naturally include the delegation of the prerogative power of treaty-making. The second and the more prevalent opinion is that the only prerogatives the federations can legally exercise are those which have been expressly delegated by statute, Letters Patent and Instructions of the Governors, and convention. The third view considers there is an undoubted devolution of the prerogatives, namely, of those executive powers that are incidental to the exercise of expressly conferred legislative power. These views will be examined in turn.

One prominent authority, Professor A. Berriedale Keith, indicates in his *Constitutional Laws of the British Dominions*[30] that he favors the wide view. He says that "formerly the extent of the delegation of the prerogative in the case of the Dominions had to be judged on the basis of their subordinate position; now that equality of status has been asserted,[31] it may be argued that prima facie every royal prerogative has by necessary intendment passed to the Governor General." The force of this assertion is considerably abated by his next sentence in which he declares: "but . . . this is not accepted law as regards the vital external prerogatives . . . "[32] This view, of course, demands a detailed study of the Dominions' rise to the status of a full-fledged state in the international community. This, aside from the observations made later in this chapter, lies beyond the scope of the present work. Mr. William F. O'Connor, in an exhaustive study of the B. N. A. Act, urges this view in a qualified way,[33] basing his authority on the rise of Canada to the status of an international entity, and on the doctrine of "immunity of Crown instrumentalities." He considers that this doctrine, borrowed from the United States by Australia, but never adopted in Canada, should be applied to give powers of a truly "governmental" character to federal executive. He expands this argument and concludes that the Governor General of Canada may "rightfully exercise in Canada, on the advice of his Canadian Ministers, all such prerogatives of the Crown as are necessary for the conduct of the executive government of Canada." He would not include the exercise by the Governor General of those prerogatives which, since the Statute of Westminster in 1931,[34] are exercised by the Imperial Government; but, of course, would comprise the prerogatives respecting foreign affairs.

There is little legal support for this wide view of the delegation of the prerogatives to the British federations. In *Bononza Creek Gold Mining Company v. the King*,[35] it was advanced in the argument of counsel. The Privy Council[36] evasively replied: "But their Lordships abstain from discussing at length the question so raised. They will only say that when, if ever, it comes to be argued, points of difficulty will have to be considered. There is no provision in the British North America Act corresponding even to Section 61 of the Australian Commonwealth Act, which, subject to the declarations of the discretionary right of delegation by the Sovereign in Chapter 1, Section 2, provides that the executive power, though declared to be in the Sovereign, is yet to be exercisable by the Governor General.   Moreover, in the Canadian Act (i.e., the B. N. A. Act) there are various significant sections, such as Section 9, which declares the executive government and authority over Canada to continue and be vested in the Sovereign; Section 14, which declares the power of the Sovereign to authorize the Governor General to appoint deputies; Section 15, which, differing from Section 68 of the Commonwealth Act, says that the command in chief of the naval and military forces in Canada is to be deemed to continue and be vested in the Sovereign; and Section 16, which says that, until the Sovereign otherwise directs, the seat of the Government of Canada shall be Ottawa.   These and other provisions of the British North America Act appear to preserve prerogative rights of the Crown which would pass if the scheme were that contended for, and to negative the theory that the Governor General is made a viceroy in the full sense, and they point to the different conclusion that for the measure of his powers the words of his commission and of the statute itself must be looked to."   In view of these observations, there is little judicial support for the maintenance of this view of prerogative devolution in Canada.[37]

Notwithstanding Canada's rise to independent status in the community of nations, it does not necessarily follow that all the prerogative powers of government, exercisable by the Crown in England, are transferred to the Crown in Canada.   Judging by the inference in the above-quoted decision by the Privy Council, support may be found for an argument that the prerogative has devolved upon the central executive of Australia by this means.[38]

However, the required devolution of prerogative powers in Australia is more realistically found in the second view on the delegation of prerogative powers, which will now be examined. This view is that the federal executives can exercise only those prerogative powers expressly given to them by delegation.[39]   The question now is whether it can be reasonably inferred from statutes, Governors' General instructions, commissions, and Letters Patent creating the office, and from other sources, that the prerogative with respect to foreign affairs has indeed been delegated.   There is no express provision for the devolution of the prerogative powers. If such devolution is to be found, it has to be inferred. The Imperial prerogative and the procedure necessary for formal treaties are still available for both federations. But particular factors relating to the office of the Governor General in Canada, and the recent establishment of a Great Seal for Canada may be valid sources for the necessary inference.

The appointment of the Governor General and the delegation of power to him occur through the prerogative instruments —i.e., Letters Patent that empower the office—which are of a permanent nature and do not vary with each Governor. Each Governor is appointed by a commission which constitutes his power to act on behalf of the King and to fill the office. Finally, instructions are issued to each Governor, which set out his individual powers. The Letters Patent of the Australian Commonwealth were constituted in 1900. They "authorize the Governor General to do and execute all things that shall 'belong to his said command, and to the trust We have reposed in him, according to the several powers and authorities granted or appointed him, by virtue of the Commonwealth of Australia Constitution Act 1900'." Mr. Donald Kerr concludes: "With the exception of Cl. VIII of the Instructions and Cls. III and IV of the Letters Patent (appointment and dismissal of officers) above-mentioned, the Crown has not delegated any of its prerogatives."[40] Presumably the Australian prerogative instruments contain nothing to support an inference of the devolution of the prerogative. In Canada, however, the situation is different.

Prior to 1890 the Governor General was appointed by the Sovereign alone, without advice or assistance from the Dominions. After this date the practice was for the Dominion to be consulted prior to an appointment. At the Imperial Conference of 1926[41] it was declared, as "an essential consequence of equality of status existing among the members of the British Commonwealth of Nations, that the Governor General of a Dominion is the representative of the Crown, holding in all essential respects the same position in the relation to the administration of public affairs in the Dominion as is held by His Majesty the King in Great Britain, and that he is not the representative or agent of His Majesty's Government in Great Britain or of any Department of that Government." As a consequence of this new status, and with the aid of certain other rules laid down in the Imperial Conference of 1930, new Letters Patent were created for the office of Governor General in Canada. These may have a considerable bearing on the question of the devolution of the prerogative. Article 2 of the new Letters declares: "And We hereby authorize and empower Our Governor General, with the advice of Our Privy Council for Canada or of any members thereof or individually, as the case requires, to exercise all powers and authorities lawfully belonging to Us in respect of Canada . . . " Article 3 adds: "And We do hereby authorize and empower Our Governor General to keep and use Our Great Seal of Canada for sealing all things whatsoever that may be passed under Our Great Seal of Canada."[42]

As Professor William P. M. Kennedy points out in a note on the subject, the exact extent of the legal nature of the innovations remains to be determined in the future. However, from their broad terms, read in conjunction with the 1939 provision for a Great Seal for Canada, there would seem to be a strong argument to the effect that the prerogative has now devolved in respect to Canada. At least, the central authority in Canada has the legal authority to conclude international agreements, and any provincial interference in this procedure is effectively denied.

In both states, Full Powers and Instruments of Ratification are usually passed under the Great Seal of the Realm, the Imperial seal issued under the authority of a warrant under the Sign Manual and Signet, a procedure set into motion on the advice of the federal executive but accomplished by the powers of the Imperial Government. This is the only method by which the more formal type of treaty may be concluded by Australia. However, to facilitate Canadian acts of state performed by His Majesty the King when he visited Canada in 1939, a Seal Act[43] was passed which provided for a Great Seal for Canada. Therefore in Canada either procedure may be employed for concluding formal agreements, and conceivably, intervention of the Imperial Government avoided. At this time, though the Imperial procedure is still available, the existence of the new mode, together with the operation of the new Letters Patent, affords sufficient basis for a judicial determination that the prerogative has now devolved to the central government. Legal authority and procedure exist for such construction; but as yet there has been no authoritative ruling, hence the matter still needs clarification. Although there is no complaint with respect to the use of the Imperial procedure,[44] the national treaty process is undeniably confused and irritating.   Canada has the procedure and should use it, thereby removing doubts about where this executive power lies.[45]

The validity of this conclusion was given much weight by the judgment of Chief Justice Duff of the Canadian Supreme Court in *The Labor Conventions Case.*[46]   Directed specifically to the question whether the Canadian executive had the power to enter into international agreements, he rejected the argument of the provinces involved that the power resides nowhere in the B. N. A. Act or in any other constitutional document, and he declared that the Governor General now has the power.   He arrived at this conclusion from the position of the Governor General and the alteration of his status, as contained in the Imperial Conference Report of 1926.[47]   He also referred to the declarations of both Imperial Conferences of 1923 and 1926, particularly the assertion that "agreements between Great Britain and a foreign country or a Dominion and a foreign country, shall take the form of treaties between heads of states (except in the case of agreements between governments), the responsible government being in each case the Government of Great Britain or the Government concerned upon whose advice plenipotentiaries are appointed and full powers granted."   He then categorically denied the contention of the provinces that these declarations of the Imperial Conferences have no legal basis and have not yet reached the status of a convention of the Constitution. In his opinion, "there could hardly be more authoritative evidence as to constitutional usage than the declarations of such a Conference" and that they must be "recognized by the Courts as having the force of law."   The Chief Justice considered these reasons sufficient for the devolution of the necessary prerogative power to the central government.

When the case came before the Privy Council,[48] their Lordships were not concerned with this problem and, although recognizing Canada's new status in the international community, they passed no specific judgment on the question of the devolution of the prerogative powers.   But the inferences from the decision support Chief Justice Duff's opinion.   Concerning the rule in the British countries that the treaty process involves two acts, the act of the executive in entering into the treaty and the act of the legislature in performing its provisions, the Privy Council recognized that performance may have to be undertaken by different legislatures, "and the executive have the task of obtaining the legislative assent not of the one Parliament to whom they may be responsible, but possibly of several Parliaments to whom they stand in no direct relation."[49] Their Lordships obviously had the central executive in mind as the lawful treaty-making authority. They then considered the new international status of Canada, declaring that "it follows from what has been said that no further legislative competence is obtained by the Dominion from its accession to international status, and the consequent increase in the scope of its executive functions."[50] This increase in executive functions is, of course, referable to the central authority's treaty-making power. Finally, in the same paragraph, their Lordships inferentially recognized the executive authority in the central executive by affirming that "the Dominion cannot, merely by making promises to foreign countries, clothe itself with legislative authority inconsistent with the constitution which gave it birth." Unfortunately there was no express pronouncement on the important point of how the prerogative devolved. The problem still remains unsolved.

The rise of Australia to the status of an independent state was indeed the basis of decision in *The King v. Burgess; ex parte Henry*[51] in which the High Court of Australia held that the executive power in foreign affairs was vested in the Commonwealth Government and denied to the states. But the Court did not sustain that power under the broad view of the devolution of the prerogative to the Dominions.

The decision turned on the executive and legislative ability of the Commonwealth Government to enter into and legislate on the provisions of the Convention Relating to Aerial Navigation. With regard to the executive power of the Commonwealth,[52] Chief Justice Latham referred to the treaty-making power or prerogative of the Crown, and to the change in the international and constitutional position of Australia, concluding that the executive had power validly to sign and ratify the treaty. The decision is qualified by the fact that the Convention had been made after the signing of the Treaty of Versailles when the procedure gave the Commonwealth the right of a separate signature but under the title of the British Empire.[53] The Chief Justice, without intending to expand the central executive power unduly, extended it to this type of treaty at least.[54] Justice Starke directed his opinion solely to the question of Commonwealth legislative competence; but the phrasing of the opinion makes it obvious that he assumed the executive power to be in the central organ.[55]

The single judgment of Justices Evatt and McTiernan leaves no doubt of the constitutional position of the executive of the Commonwealth. Approaching the problem of legislative ability to implement the provisions of the Convention under the power to legislate on "external affairs," they find the executive authority to be broad and adequate. First, they answer Sir William H. Moore's argument,[56] by holding that his method of construing the Constitution was wrong. They assert that "accordingly it is wrong to prejudice the examination of the content of the subject of 'external affairs' by assuming or asserting in advance that there are certain matters such as conditions or terms of employment which are necessarily excluded from Commonwealth legislation in exercise of the power."[57] They then referred to the judgement of Justice Field in *DeGeofroy v. Riggs,*[58] expressing the unlimited treaty-making power in the United States subject to the qualification that the treaty must be "properly the subject of negotiation with a foreign country." They rightfully conclude: "But it is a consequence of the closer connection between the nations of the world (which has been partly brought about by the modern revolutions in communications) and of the recognition by the nations of a common interest in many matters affecting the social welfare of their peoples and of the necessity of co-operation among them in dealing with such matters, that it is no longer possible to assert that there is any subject matter which must necessarily be excluded from the lists of possible subjects of negotiation, international dispute or international agreement."[59] The executive power was certainly wide enough for the executive government of the Commonwealth to enter into such a convention with a foreign state. But it must be stressed that all these judgments were restricted to the consideration of the actual treaty before the Court, that is, a convention relating to aerial navigation. The decision cannot be advanced as wholly covering the treaty-making power. However, the real position of the Commonwealth is indicated by the reference to the American decision in which the power is restricted only to subjects properly within the sphere of international negotiation and by the unimpeachable observation that all subjects may now be properly brought within the ambit of international negotiation.

Consequently, though Australia still employs the Imperial procedure for formal treaties, the central government has the legal control over the "capacity" part of the treaty process, and the component states are effectively silenced as entities from the international point of view.   The High Court, in effect, found the requisite devolution of the prerogatives in the rise of Australia to the status of a member state in the international community, in Imperial constitutional documents, and in a determined purview of the needs of the time.

The third and last view of the delegation of prerogative powers from the Imperial Crown to Canada and Australia is that, in addition to those prerogatives expressly given, there are those prerogatives which are coextensive with federal and provincial legislative power, and which are sufficiently broad to enable the executive government to be carried on effectively.   Thus, Sections 91 and 92 of the B.N.A. Act, which distribute the legislative powers between the Canadian central government and the provinces, carry with them coextensive executive powers.[60]

In Australia, the High Court did not resort to this method of ascertaining the Commonwealth's executive power.[61]   But the doctrine that legislative power determines the extent of executive power is very much in vogue, at least with respect to those subjects over which the Commonwealth has exclusive control.[62] Furthermore, the differences in the constitutional structure of the Canadian and Australian federations have given rise to different interpretations concerning the authority of the Australian states in foreign affairs.[63]   It has been contended that, as in the United States, all that the Australian Constitution Act did was to create an agency to serve as the states' representative in certain defined areas.   The opposing view is that the creation of the central body was tantamount to a new entity, and changed the fundamental status of the states in their relation to a central government and to the outside world.[64]   These concepts have had a particular significance in foreign affairs.   However, the latter view has been upheld by the Imperial Government and the question may now be considered as conclusively settled by the decision in *The King v. Burgess; ex parte Henry.*[65]   The Commonwealth Government is the exclusive agency in international affairs.

In Canada, the central government had the necessary executive power to enter into international agreements when Canada

signed as a member of the British Empire.[66]   But this procedure
is now obsolete.   At the present time, either the more formal
type of treaty-making method (the "Heads of States" form) or
inter-governmental agreements are used—the former by the
Queen (King) acting on the advice of the Canadian ministers,
the latter by the Canadian ministers acting through the instru-
mentality of the Secretary of State for External Affairs.   The
authority to legislate to implement these types of treaties is not
contained in Section 132[67] nor is the legislative authority to
perform the obligations incurred under these agreements necessarily within the power of the central government.[68]   *The Labor Conventions Case*[69] held categorically that the Canadian
Parliament did not possess the legislative competence to implement conventions, the subject matters of which were within provincial legislative jurisdiction.   In result, with respect to the
acquisition of executive power by coextension with legislative
power, in the possible absence of the legislative power, the executive power is absent also.

A rather remote problem remains: if the provinces have the
right to legislate on subject matters or international agreements
within their legislative competence, does not the theory of the
executive power following legislative power give them the right
to enter into, or at least assist in, the negotiation of such agreements?   Chief Justice Duff in *The Labor Conventions Case*[70]
answers the question in these words: "In regards all such international arrangements, it is a necessary consequence of the respective positions of the Dominion executive and the provincial
executives that this authority resides in the Parliament of Canada.   The Lieutenant-Governors represent the Crown for certain purposes.[71]   But, in no respect does the Lieutenant-Governor of a province represent the Crown in respect of relations with
foreign governments.   The Canadian executive, again, constitutionally acts under responsibility to the Parliament of Canada and it is that Parliament alone which can constitutionally
control its conduct of external affairs."[72]   In other words, the
provincial executive authority is derived from the delegated power of the Governor General, and this authority extends to all
matters necessarily implied in the grant of legislative powers
contained in Section 92, and no further.   Section 92 nowhere
gives it any authority to enter into agreements with foreign
states.   Fortunately the provincial argument has not been taken

seriously, and it is patently futile for other reasons. It is contrary to the spirit in which the Constitution was framed,[73] indeed to its very provisions, as Section 132 of the B.N.A. Act is specifically directed against provincial participation in the treaty process.[74] It leaves little doubt that legislative power at least was to be exercised by the central government alone, although subsequent judicial interpretation has nullified this apparent intention. It is clear, too, that the contention advocated by the provinces is contrary to the very spirit of internationalism, and detrimental to Canada's status as an international entity. Further, as already noted,[75] the provincial contention has not been upheld by judicial interpretation. Definite constitutional restraints can also be brought to bear against the argument. These are contained in the federal power of control over the provinces, such as the appointment and removal of Lieutenant-Governors, the appointment of judges and, probably most important of all, the power of disallowance of provincial acts.[76]

'The whole situation, however, remains obscure. Though actually the central government does exercise the treaty-making authority, legally the provinces have not been effectively excluded from participation, which results in the present vagueness and unsatisfactory position of the treaty process in Canada.

The problem of ratification will now be dealt with briefly. In the British federations this aspect of the treaty process is an exclusive executive function. The negotiation, signing, and ratification of a treaty are all included within the prerogative of the Crown, exercised by the Cabinet. There is no constitutional law or convention which requires concurrence by Parliament before any of these acts are effected,[77] although in most instances the cabinet will obtain the approval of Parliament either in the form of a statute or of a resolution, before accomplishing the final act of ratification.[78]

The provinces advance the argument that, since ratification is an executive act, that, since the legislative authority to perform treaty obligations involving subject matters within provincial control is within the power of the provinces, that, since the legal executive power is not in central government, the provinces have the power of ratification of such treaties. To answer this argument it is again necessary to refer to *The Labor Conventions Case*.[79]

The Privy Council was not concerned with the executive function and so did not pass on the ability of either the central government or the provinces to ratify the conventions. But in the Supreme Court of Canada various opinions were given. Chief Justice Duff[80] reasoned that, as the Privy Council had upheld the validity of Canada's obligations under the International Radio Telegraph Convention in *The Radio Communications Case,*[81] it indirectly upheld the right of ratification in the Canadian executive. The learned Chief Justice declared that "ratification was the effective act which gave binding force to the convention. It was, as respects Canada, the act of the Government of Canada alone, and the decision mentioned appears, therefore, to negative decisively the contention that, in point of strict law, the Government of Canada is incompetent to enter into an international engagement."[82] He found that Section 132 provides the necessary authority for the Canadian executive to enter, to ratify, and also to legislate to effectuate the provisions of the conventions.

The three dissenting judges were directed to the specific problem of interpreting paragraphs 5 and 7 of Article 405 of the Treaty of Versailles, which provide that such conventions as are considered in *The Labor Conventions Case* should be brought "before the authority or authorities within whose competence the matter lies, for the enactment of legislation or other action." This, of course, narrowed the issue, making it dependent on the determination of legislative competence rather than upon the question whether the Canadian Government has the power to ratify, irrespective of its legislative competence. Justices Rinfret and Cannon were of the opinion that the Canadian Government did not have the legislative authority to implement, either under Sections 91 or 132, and so, in accordance with Article 405, the proper authorities, not to ratify but to concur before ratification, were the provinces. This had been disregarded, and so the Canadian ratifications were ineffective.[83] Justice Crockett was also of the opinion that the central government could not rely on Section 132 for the necessary legislative power. He said: "While I agree with the learned Chief Justice that the Government of Canada must now be held to be the proper medium for the formal conclusion of international conventions, whether they affect Canada as a whole or any of the provinces separately, I do not think that this fact can be relied on as altering in any way the provisions of the B.N.A. Act as regards the distribution of legislative power as between the Dominion Parliament and the provincial legislatures or as necessarily giving to any matter, which may be made the subject of legislation in Canada, any other meaning or aspect than that which it bears in our original constitution."[84] The three judges did not, in conclusion, deny the ability of the Canadian Government to ratify treaties. On interpretation, it was the peculiar provisions of the Treaty of Versailles, requiring the Canadian Government to bring certain subject matters before the competent authorities for approval, that provided the reason for the denial of the effectiveness of these particular ratifications.

CONCLUSION

It is obvious that the American and Swiss arrangements of executive powers in foreign affairs are more clearcut and defined than those of British federations. Of course, the actual limits of executive power is, in the United States, left to the courts, and is still in the process of evolution. In Switzerland, with the doctrine and actual practice of legislative supremacy, it is the Federal Assembly itself which determines the limits of its own competence. But the path of construction in both federations is clear. The judiciary in the United States is more and more denying itself interference in the field of foreign affairs. This will be considered in some detail in the next chapter. The Swiss constitutional practice leaves little doubt that the central authority is supreme in this field.[85] It is true that in both states the component parts still have some voice in effecting arrangements with other countries. In the United States, this is restricted to a very indefinite and, no doubt, small compass. In Switzerland, there is possibly a larger scope of cantonal operation in foreign affairs, but resultant agreements must be of local significance only. The Federal Council would not permit any interference with a subject of national importance.

In Australia, the capacity of the federal government to enter and ratify international agreements is apparently assured, not withstanding the cautious phraseology of the judgments and the qualifications mentioned therein. The High Court has now found the necessary executive power in the central executive, and the states are effectively subordinated to the central government in external matters.

In Canada, the executive power in the central government in foreign affairs is indefinite. As a matter of actual practice and from inferences of Privy Council remarks, the authority, as a fact, conforms to international requirements, and is in the cental government. But, strictly speaking, this result has not been judicially established and this has unfortunate consequences. It may be contended that Canada lacks a firm and active authority in international affairs. And foreign policy is bound to be weak and vacillating if the central executive has doubts as to its authority to contract binding international agreements.[86]

[1.] *Supra,* pp. 25-26; *Infra,* p. 88.

[2.] Hackworth, Green H., *Digest of International Law,* (1940-44), Vol. 1, pp. 47 ff.

[3.] Root, Elihu, "The Real Questions under the Japanese Treaty and San Francisco Board Resolution," (1907) 1 *American Journal of International Law* 273, pp. 278-79.

[4.] McDougal, Myers S., and Lans, Asher, "Treaties and Congressional-Executive or Presidential Agreements; Interchangeable Instruments of National Policy." (Hereinafter cited "Treaties and Executive Agreements") (1945) 54 *Yale Law Journal* 181, 534, pp. 226 ff; Frankfurter, Felix, and Landis, James M., "The Compact Clause of the Constitution-A Study in Interstate Adjustments," (1925) 34 *Yale Law Journal* 685; Crandall, Samuel B., *Treaties: Their Making and Enforcement,* (2nd ed., 1916), Ch. 10

[5.] Frankfurter, Felix, and Landis, James M., *ibid.*

[6.] Bruce, Andrew A., "The Compacts or Agreements of the States with One Another and With Foreign Powers," (1918) 2 *Minnesota Law Review* 500.

[7.] Wright, Quincy, "The Constitutionality of Treaties," (1919) 13 *American Journal of International Law* 242, p. 251, note 22.

[8.] For example, refer to the two unsuccessful attempts of states to enter into "trifling" agreements with foreign states, reported in Hackworth, Green H., *Digest of International Law,* (1940-44), Vol. 5, p. 25.

[9.] Farrand, Max, *The Records of the Federal Convention,* (3 Vols., 1911), *passim.* Possibly the most illuminating legal opinion on point is that given by Justice Taney in *Holmes v. Jennison,* (1840) 14 Peters (United States Supreme Court) 540.

[10.] Vincent, John M., *State and Federal Government in Switzerland,* (1913), p. 202

[11.] (1936) 299 United States 304, p. 319, (*per* Justice Sutherland). But see *Youngstown Sheet & Tube Co. v. Sawyer,* (1952) 343 United States 579, p. 635, where Justice Jackson refers to this decision in footnote 2. He says that "much of the Court's opinion is dictum." See also *United States v. Belmont,* (1937) 301 United States 324, p. 330: "Negotiations, acceptance of the assignment and agreements and understandings in respect thereof were within the competence of the President may not be doubted. Governmental power over internal affairs is distributed between the national government and the several states. Governmental power over external affairs is not distributed, but is vested exclusively in the national government. And in respect to what was done here, the Executive had authority to speak as the sole organ of that government."

12. Hackworth, Green H., *Digest of International Law,* (1940-44), Vol. 5, p. 319.

13. Rappard, William E., *The Government of Switzerland,* (1936), pp. 82 ff.

14. Arnold, Ralph, *Treaty Making Procedure,* (1933), p. 65.

15. See the Harvard Draft Convention, Article 1, and the authorities quoted therein, (1935) 29 *American Journal of International Law* (Supplement), p. 681.

16. *Infra,* pp. 92-93.   17. *Infra,* p. 76.

18. McDougal, Myers S. and Lans, Asher, "Treaties and Executive Agreements," (1945) 54 *Yale Law Journal* 181, 534, p. 187.

19. *United States v. Belmont,* (1937) 301 United States 324; *United States v. Pink,* (1942) 315 United States 203. The inherent powers of the President in internal affairs have undoubtedly been restricted by the decision of the Supreme Court in *Youngstown Sheet & Tube Co. v. Sawyer,* (1952) 343 United States 579. The powers of the President in external affairs would appear to be unaffected.

20. These observations are made on the basis of the reply of the Swiss Government to a questionnaire in 1933. They are contained in Arnold, Ralph, *Treaty Making Procedure,* (1933), p. 64.   21. *Infra,* pp. 165 ff.

22. Australian Constitution Act, Sections 61-70; B. N. A. Act, Sections 9-16.

23. B.N.A. Act, Section 12.

24. *Nadan v. The King,* (1926) Appeal Cases (England) 482, p. 492; *British Coal Corporation v. The King,* (1935) Appeal Cases (England) 500, p. 520.

25. *Infra,* p. 64, note 45.

26. O'Connor, William F., "Report to the Honourable Speaker of the Senate on the British North America Act, 1867," (hereinafter cited as "Report to the Senate"), (1939), pp. 145-46.

27. Anson, Sir William R., *Law and Custom of the Constitution,* (4th ed., 1935), Vol. 2, part 2, p. 131.

28. *Supra,* p. 32.   29. *Infra,* pp. 58 ff.   30. (1933), p. 137.

31. Imperial Conference, Summary of Proceedings, 1926. This Conference laid down the well-known proposition that all Dominions of the Commonwealth are autonomous nations, in no way subordinate to one another.

32. *Constitutional Law of the British Dominions,* (1933), p. 137. Presumably the reason is that these states (no longer considered or termed Dominions) still use the formal procedure as laid down by the Imperial Conference of 1926, *supra,* pp. 31-32.

33. "Report to the Senate," (1939), pp. 145 ff.

34. 22 *Statutes of George V*, Ch. 4. Presumably Mr. O'Connor thinks that Section 7, paragraph 3, would preclude Canada from asserting this power. This Section restricts federal legislation to powers within its competence by the B. N. A. Act.

35. (1916) 1 Appeal Cases (England) 566.   36. *Ibid,* p. 586, (*per* Lord Haldane).

37. But see *infra,* pp. 52 ff.

38. *Infra,* pp. 55 ff. Opinion appears to be to the contrary. See Keer, Donald, *Law of the Australian Constitution,* (1925), p. 224, and the authorities quoted therein.

39. Minty, Leonard L., *Constitutional Laws of the British Empire,* (1928), p. 113. Kerr, Donald, *ibid,* concludes that "it is clear, therefore, that the Governor-General of the Commonwealth is not a general agent of the Crown, with general power to exercise the royal prerogative; but is a special agent, armed only with power to carry out the Constitution and the laws of the Commonwealth, and such prerogative powers and functions as the Crown may lawfully assign to him."

[40.] Kerr, Donald, *ibid*, p. 225.

[41.] Summary of Proceedings, Part IV, Section (b).

[42.] *Letters Patent Constituting the Office of Governor General of Canada, Effective Oct. 1, 1947.* See text in Kennedy, William P. M., "The Office of the Governor-General of Canada," (1947-48) 7 *University of Toronto Law Journal* 474.

[43.] (Canada), 3 *Statutes of George VI*, Ch. 22.   [44.] Infra, p. 164.

[45.] The legal difficulty of parliamentary action to bar the Imperial prerogative is to be recognized. Canada, by the operation of the Statute of Westminster, 1931, can only legislate with respect to powers within her competence as laid down in the B. N. A. Act. Thus, Canada could not legally pass a statute denying the existence of this prerogative. But there is no legal obstacle to a request to the Imperial Parliament to legislate to this effect. This process, perhaps, has the danger of unnecessarily stirring up political and legal issues better left alone.

[46.] *References The Weekly Rest in Industrial Undertakings Act, The Minimum Wages Act and The Limitation of Hours Act,* (hereinafter referred to as *The Labor Conventions Case*), (1936) Supreme Court Reports (Canada) 461, pp. 474 ff.

[47.] *Supra,* p. 52.

[48.] *The Labor Conventions Case,* (1937) Appeal Cases (England) 326.

[49.] *Ibid,* p. 348.   [50.] *Ibid,* p. 352.

[51.] *The King v. Burgess; ex parte Henry,* (1936) 55 Commonwealth Law Reports (Australia) 618.

[52.] The Commonwealth's legislative power is examined in Chapter 6, *infra,* pp. 120 ff.   [53.] *Supra,* p. 30.

[54.] *The King v. Burgess; ex parte Henry,* (1936) 55 Commonwealth Law Reports (Australia) 618, p. 635.

[55.] *ibid,* pp. 655 ff. Justice Dixon also assumes it, pp. 669-70.

[56.] *Supra,* pp. 34-35.   [57.] Also, see *supra,* p. 23.

[58.] (1890) United States 258, p. 267.

[59.] *The King v. Burgess; ex parte Henry,* (1936) 55 Commonwealth Law Reports (Australia) 618, pp. 680-81.

[60.] LeFroy, Augustus H. F., *Canada's Federal System,* (1913), pp. 23-24; *Liquidators of the Maritime Bank of Canada v. Receiver-General of N. B.,* (1892) Appeal Cases (England) 437; *Bonanza Creek Gold Mining Company v. King,* (1916) 1 Appea Cases (England) 566, p. 580.   [61.] *Supra,* p. 55.

[62.] By Section 108 of the Constitution respecting concurrent powers, the executive power would remain in the state until the Commonwealth exercises valid legislation which will automatically bring with it the necessary executive power.

[63.] For example, the states in Australia enjoy the right of direct appointment of their governors by the Imperial Crown, and their laws are subject only to the obsolete veto control of the Imperial Government. Compare with the situation in Canada, *supra,* pp. 18-19.

[64.] Keith, A. Berriedale, *Responsible Government in the Dominions,* (1928), Vol. 2, pp. 607 ff.

[65.] (1936) 55 Commonwealth Law Reports (Australia) 618. The interpretation placed on the states' position is illustrated by the *Vondel* incident in 1902 and set out in detail by Keith, *ibid*, p. 612. In this instance, the Netherlands Government made representations to the Imperial Government regarding the failure of the State of South Australia to arrest the crew of the Dutch ship *Vondel,* in accordance with the terms of an existing Anglo-Dutch treaty. South Australia maintained that its governor was the proper channel of communication rather than the central government, but this contention was not accepted. The Imperial Government took the position that foreign nations were entitled to look to the Commonwealth and not to South Australia for the redress of wrongs.

[66.] *Supra*, p. 30.   [67.] *Supra*, p. 32.   [68.] *Infra*, p. 122 ff.

[69.] (1937) Appeal Cases (England) 326, *infra*, pp. 254-56.

[70.] (1936) Supreme Court Reports (Canada) 461.

[71.] It was long ago made clear that the Lieutenant-Governor in the province is the representative of the King for provincial purposes, and that he possesses under the Constitution all the power necessary for local purposes, so far as that belongs to the Crown for such local purposes. *Liquidator of the Maritime Bank of Canada v. Receiver-General of New Brunswick,* (1892) Appeal Cases (England) 437.

[72.] (1936) Supreme Court Reports (Canada) 461, p. 488.

[73.] *Supra*, pp. 18-19.   [74.] *Supra*, pp. 28 ff.   [75.] *Supra*, pp. 54-55.

[76.] For a recent discussion of this still existing power of the Canadian Government, (Section 90, B. N. A. Act), see *Reference re Power of Disallowance and Power of Reservation,* (1938) Supreme Court Reports (Canada) 77.

[77.] Except possibly a treaty involving cession of British territory. With respect to such a treaty there is argument that modern precedents have created a constitutional convention that prior parliamentary concurrence must be obtained.

[78.] *Infra*, p. 90.   [79.] (1937) Appeal Cases (England) 326.

[80.] (1936) Supreme Court Reports (Canada) 461, p. 477. *Supra*, p. 32; *infra*, pp. 125-126.   [81.] (1932) Appeal Cases (England) 304.

[82.] (1936) Supreme Court Reports (Canada) 461, p. 478.

[83.] *Ibid*, pp. 502 ff.   [84.] *Ibid,* p. 535.   [85.] *Infra*, pp. 78-79.

[86.] For example, the Canadian position on the establishment of an International Commission of Human Rights and Fundamental Freedoms. In conformance with Article 68 of the United Nations Charter, Canada proposed the establishment of a special committee to study the problem and report on the best method of ensuring the complete fulfilment of her obligations. The hesitant and unsatisfactory attitude of the Government is evidenced in the Canadian *Debates of the House of Commons,* May 19, 1947, Vol. IV, pp. 319 ff.

CHAPTER 4

GOVERNMENTAL PARTICIPATION IN THE TREATY-MAKING POWERS OF THE FEDERAL EXECUTIVES

A sharp distinction has been made between the capacity of states to enter into international agreements and their ability to perform treaty obligations. These are distinct and separate parts of the treaty process. But the distinction is not so evident in the states with written constitutions, the United States and Switzerland, as in the British federations. The reason is that in the former states it is either provided in the constitution, or in accordance with constitutional practice that treaties constitutionally concluded become *ipso facto* the law of the land. Once treaties are validly concluded, they automatically have the same operation as a statute. Thus, the "capacity" and "performance" parts of the process are to an extent indistinguishable because the legislative act is often not necessary.[1]

This chapter is devoted to determining how far other governmental organs control and participate in the negotiating, signing and ratifying of treaties. Though the treaty-making power of the executives of the four federations is wide, it certainly is not uncontrolled. This control over and participation in the treaty-making power of the executives will be examined in both its theoretical and practical aspects. The desirability of such control and participation will also be commented on but many conclusions relative thereto will await final consideration in the last chapter.

THE JUDICIARY

In all the federations except Switzerland, the judiciaries exercise considerable control over the powers of the governments to perform treaty obligations. This is the subject of discussion of Part III. The judiciaries in these federations are the interpreters of the constitutions, and define the executive and legislative limits of constitutional competence.[2] But in so doing the courts act only when disputes come before them for determination, that is, actual sets of facts in dispute between two or more parties, which they then decide by interpretation of previous decisions, relevant statutes, and possibly, the constitutions themselves.   Both in the United States and in Australia, the courts may not be called upon to decide questions which have not arisen in litigation between parties.   Article III, Section 2 of the American Constitution confers on the American judiciary jurisdiction only over "cases" and "controversies."   This means that the judiciary will not of itself declare statutes unconstitutional in most cases, nor permit itself to be called upon for advisory opinions.[3]   This is not so in Canada.   In that state, the courts have more voice in legislative and executive affairs because of their power, or possibly their duty, to give advisory opinions when requested to do so by the Government.[4] So, even prior to an actual dispute, the courts may be called upon to render an opinion on the constitutionality of any executive or legislative act.   The Canadian experience has proved that this procedure is mainly utilized to determine the constitutional effect of statutes within the powers of either Sections 91 or 92.   But it could also be employed to determine the "capacity" of the treaty-making authority to enter into any type of treaty.   Such a request has not yet been made.

Obviously the main judicial duty in the treaty process regards the performance of treaty obligations, that is, to ascertain whether the treaty-making authority has acted constitutionally when it allegedly infringed some right of a subject.   This means that in federations other than Canada, judicial interference in the treaty process cannot arise until after a *fait accompli*.   Consequently the judiciaries of these federations have no direct participation in the "capacity" part of the process.   However, their potential power of indirect control by passing judgment on the *faits accomplis* is very real indeed.

In three of the four federations under consideration, the judiciaries have reached a remarkable position in the governments by their undoubted right to interpret the constitutions.   Not only do they interpret the written constitutions in the United States, Canada and Australia, but in the British federations they are also the exponents of the common law, the age-old method of controlling the executive.   Nowhere in the United States Constitution may be found the power of the judiciary to declare unconstitutional legislative acts of Congress or executive acts of the President.   The courts have assumed this power.   Although opinions about its existence may be found in early chronicles of the Constitution even before the advent of Chief Justice Marshall to the Supreme Court, it was this jurist who laid down the doctrine unequivocally in the now celebrated decision of *Marbury v. Madison.*[5]   He maintained that, as the Constitution is the supreme law, as all governmental organs must act within this supreme authority, the judiciary was the appropriate and natural department of government to determine the constitutionality of disputed legislative and executive acts. In Canada and Australia, the power was found inherent in the immemorial prerogative of the judiciary to interpret statutes.   The B. N. A. Act and the Australian Constitution Act are both Acts of the Imperial Parliament and interpretation is necessary to define the legislative and executive authority of the central governments, of the provinces, and of the states.[6]

In the British federations, the interpretative powers of the courts of statutory law are important in considering the question of the performance of treaty obligations; but they are of little assistance in ascertaining the control of the judiciary over the executive, and especially, the power of the executive in foreign affairs.   This, of course, is due to the fact that the executive power with respect to foreign affairs is not contained in a statute, but derived from the ancient prerogative powers of the English Kings.   Also, the courts' use of the prerogative writs, such as *mandamus* and *certiorari,* to control acts of the executive is restricted.   They are generally utilized to control the use of the statutory powers of the executive and not the prerogative powers. Here the courts must consider whether the executive is acting in conformance with some statutory authority conferred by Parliament.   If it is not so acting, the particular act in question is *ultra vires* and void. But the control of the judiciary over foreign affairs would necessarily be at cabinet level, and the applicability of such writs, to permit judicial review of the actions of cabinet members, is highly doubtful.[7]   Further, the cabinet is responsible to Parliament.[8]   In result, since the executive power in foreign affairs is exercisable under the prerogative, still ill-defined but considerably restricted, the remaining authority has the sanction of Parliament.   This, together with the doctrine of the responsibility to Parliament, has led the courts to abstain from interfering with the actions of the executive in foreign affairs.

But the prerogative must at all times be exercised according to law; its exercise by the cabinet is not uncontrolled.   This proposition brings up consideration of the doctrine of "act of state."

Acts performed under the prerogative power with respect to foreign affairs are called "acts of state." Generally, such acts are outside the orbit of municipal judicial regulation, and must be governed entirely by rules of diplomacy and international law. But it is the function of the courts to determine whether such acts performed by the executive are indeed "acts of state," and in this wise the courts do maintain a measure of control over the executive in this field.

The term "act of state" in English law, came, during the 17th and 18th centuries, to connote primarily the defense available to public servants against allegations of criminality or tortious acts committed by them in the course of their duty, against foreigners. The defense availed only against foreigners because it is the common law alone that determines all rights of British subjects. It is a cardinal principle of the common law that no British subject can be denied access to the courts by executive action alone.[9] But the term was extended to indicate "an act of the executive as a matter of policy performed in the course of its relations with another state, including its relations with the subjects of that state, unless they are temporarily within the allegiance of the Crown."[10]

The term is employed here in the sense that the Crown, in exercising this aspect of its prerogative, is not accountable to the courts. In the strong words of David L. Keir and Frederick H. Lawson:[11] "At municipal law and in the eyes of municipal Courts the Crown is absolute in relation to foreign affairs. Therefore it may act towards foreign states and their subjects outside the realm in a perfectly arbitrary fashion; towards them the Crown has no duties but only powers."[12] Thus the transactions between British countries and foreign states are governed by other laws than those applied in British municipal courts.

The making of treaties is within this doctrine. As was explained in *Rustomjee v. The King*:[13] "The making of peace and the making of war, as they are undoubted, so they are, perhaps, the highest, acts of the prerogative of the Crown. The terms on which peace is made are in the absolute discretion of the Sovereign . . . The Queen might or not, as she thought fit, have made peace at all . . . She acted throughout the making of the treaty and in relation to each other and every of its stipulations in her sovereign character, and by her own inherent authority; and, as in making the treaty . . . she is beyond the control of municipal law, and her acts are not to be examined in her own Courts."[14]

But as the exercise of the prerogative must be according to law, it is within the jurisdiction of the courts to determine whether the alleged act is indeed an act of state or not.   To refer to Lord Justice Fletcher Moulton's judgment in *Salaman v. Secretary of State for India:*[15] " . . . if an act is relied upon as being an act of State, and as thus affording an answer to claims made by a subject, the Courts must decide whether it is in truth an act of State, and what was its nature and extent . . . But in such an inquiry the Court must confine itself to ascertaining what the act of State in fact was, and not what in its opinion it ought to have been . . . In like manner municipal Courts may have to consider the results of acts of State, i. e., their effects on the rights of individuals, and even of the Government itself."   Thus the Crown may not alter the existing law of the land by the exercise of the prerogative or impose a charge on the subjects.[16]   Such attempts would not be valid acts of state, and the courts would declare them void.   However, once the courts do consider the act to be an act of state, municipal law is no longer applicable.[17]

The use and extent of the doctrine of "act of state" in the two British federations is indefinite.   Doubtlessly within the scope of their delegated powers from the Imperial Government, Dominion and colonial governors can act towards foreigners and foreign states with the immunity of "acts of state" in English law.[18]

But prior to the determination whether the act was one of state or not, the validity of the particular act would be considered.   This would depend on the question of devolution of the prerogative power to the federation, the interpretation of the various instruments of the Governor's office, such as the Letters Patent and other relevant documents instructing him in the performance of the duties of his office.[19]   Yet, once the prerogative power is found to reside in the federations,[20] there still remains the question whether or not the act of the executive is one of state.   If it is an act of state, in accord with English decisions, there still remains another judicial control on the "capacity" of the Canadian and Australian executives.   This control is derived from the fact that the executives of these states cannot do by the treaty process what is forbidden to them by the constitutions. The use of the treaty processes must be kept within the strict confines of constitutional provisions.

In the Australian decision of *The King v. Burgess; ex parte Henry*,[21] all the judges made reference to the limitations of the Constitution on the capacity of the executive to enter into international agreements.[22] They all indicated that no breach of the Constitution would be permitted, and treaties made in contravention of it would fall.

In Canada the situation is not so clear. It was argued in *The Labor Conventions Case* before the Supreme Court that Section 132 is limited only to those matters which are properly the subject of international arrangement.[23] Chief Justice Duff in his judgment merely said that "no authority seems to indicate that such matters are excluded from the scope of the prerogative in relation to treaties."[24] It is difficult to interpret this statement. Possibly, considering the Canadian situation analogous to the uncontrolled British executive, the Chief Justice was not concerned with the effect of the Constitution. He may have meant that the effect of Section 132 was to give the executive omnipotent power over the Constitution, but this is unlikely. Probably the best interpretation is that he considered the executive power broad enough to cover the valid entrance of Canada into this particular type of convention, and that this convention was a proper subject of international negotiation. There is no reason to think that the Canadian judiciary will permit the executive to enter into an international agreement derogatory to the provisions of the B. N. A. Act.

In the discussion of the control of the American judiciary over the capacity of the executive to enter into international agreements, it is again to be recalled that the different methods of implementation of treaties make the "capacity" and "performance" parts of the treaty process not as distinguishable in the American system as in the British.[25] With treaties, by the American Constitution, operating as law of the land, without fulfilling legislation, it is manifest that the judiciary is concerned with both parts of the process in any judicial determination. Let us look now at the American judicial standpoint to the "capacity" part of the treaty process.

By Article 6 of the Constitution, it is laid down that "all treaties made . . . shall be the supreme law of the land . . . (and) that the judges shall be bound thereby, anything in the Constitution or the laws of any state to the contrary notwithstanding." From the provision, judicial respect for duly made treaties has been apparent in the United States, and the general attitude of the judiciary has been one of self-abnegation in this part of the process of treaty making.[26]   To explain the process, Professor John Bassett Moore notes that the courts have considered treaties in two lights, the political and legal, and the former has most consistently availed.[27]   On the other hand, if a treaty involves questions relative to the determination of private rights, the courts will declare it their duty to pass on its constitutionality.[28]   Other than this it is difficult to find indications of the possibility of judicial interference; indeed, the path of construction would appear to the contrary.   For example, in *Ware v. Hylton*,[29] the Court held that it would require "a very clear case indeed" before it would hold a treaty void.   A similar modern expression may be found in *United States v. Reid:*[30] "It is doubtful if courts have the power to declare the plain terms of the treaty void and unenforceable thus compelling the nation to violate its pledged word, and thus furnishing a *casus belli* to the other contracting party."   Even in interpreting treaties similar indications of judicial self-abnegation are evident.   As Professor Charles C. Hyde says[31] the Department of State is confident that the Supreme Court will interpret a treaty correctly, that is, in accordance with its own views.   If there is any doubt, the judiciary will not hesitate to look to the Department for guidance, thereby considering it a political question.[32]   Also indicative of the judicial attitude in foreign affairs are the numerous examples given by Professor Moore illustrating subjects that constitute political questions.[33]   Although these illustrations point to a definite hesitancy on the part of the judiciary in the United States to interfere with the executive treaty-making power, it is not to be concluded that the judicial control over the "capacity" part of the process is removed.   Possibly the most exact expression of the judicial attitude in the making of treaties is expressed in *DeGeofroy v. Riggs*,[34] where it was held that the power extended to all proper subjects of international negotiation.   What might constitute proper subjects of international negotiation is, of course, a difficult and changing problem of interpretation.

The scope of judicial control in these three federations over the executives' capacity to enter into international agreements is still considerable.   Although control and participation are indirect in the sense that the judiciary does not actually participate in this part of the process but passes on the validity of a *fait ac-*

compli, its indirect control is very real. The Australian position leaves little doubt that an unconstitutional treaty will be declared void, but it is encouraging to note that two of the judgments[35] recognized the difficulty of defining what are proper subjects of negotiation, and that most subjects now can be brought into a category properly within the scope of international regulation. Thus, if the treaty itself does not infringe an express constitutional provision, the judiciary will find no fault with its constitutionality. The indefiniteness of the Canadian position needs no further comment. Assuming that the Canadian executive has the legal authority to enter into all types of international agreements,[36] Canada's judicial authority is as great as that of Australia to keep the executive within constitutional confines and prevent it from infringing on the fundamental law by the treaty process. In the United States there is much strength in the argument that the statement in *DeGeofroy v. Riggs,*[37] referring to the judicial control of defining proper subjects of international negotiation, is the present state of the law.

Assuming that this is the correct legal view of judicial control, the further question arises of the most desirable position of the judiciary in the "capacity" part of the treaty process. Obviously, executives of the three federations are their nations' spokesmen in international affairs. It is to these individuals or groups that foreign states look to express the opinions and perform the necessary acts of international intercourse for their respective states. Foreign affairs, particularly in this period of tension with the Eastern nations, present a most delicate and complex subject; and certainly the courts find themselves inadequately trained and informed, hence disinclined to deal with such questions. It is the executive of a state that presents the nation's policy, and for the sake of conformity, consistency, and the display of a united front to other states, it is essential that uniformity of foreign and internal policy be apparent. These are the major reasons why the judiciary tends to permit great powers to the modern executive in the external field. It is desirable that the judiciary be cognizant of a definite position in the treaty process. Yet, with conditions changing so rapidly, and the need for omnipotent executive in the foreign field becoming stronger, it is well to maintain this control purposely vague and ill-defined. Certainly it is and should be the exclusive domain of the executive to enter and conclude agreements with other states. But this does not imply an

untrammelled "capacity" of the executive,[38] nor does it exclude
judicial review in relation to the other part of the process, that
is, the performance of treaty obligations.[39]

THE HOUSE OF REPRESENTATIVES AND PARLIAMENT

For our present purpose, the position in the treaty processes of
the Parliaments of Canada and Australia and the House of Representatives in the United States can receive identical treatment.
The Senate in the United States and the Federal Assembly of
Switzerland will demand separate consideration. These organs
of government will be viewed in both their legal and actual participation in the "capacity" part of the treaty processes.

Legally, the capacity of the executives of the states of Canada
and Australia is unrestrained except by the limits of the prerogatives, the doctrine of "acts of state" and their Constitutions.[40]
In neither state is there any rule of law or convention which requires the executive to seek prior approval from any organ of
government before initiating negotiations, signing, and ratifying
treaties. These procedures are all embraced in the power of the
prerogative of the Crown and are within the executive's sole discretion. Thus the Parliaments are effectively excluded from this
part of the process, although their performing powers are very
great indeed. Likewise in the United States, the Constitution
has made no provision for any interference in "capacity" by the
House of Representatives. When no legislative aid is required,
the House is completely divorced from the treaty process. However, when legislation is required to give effect to a treaty's terms,
for instance for the appropriation of money, the legal position
of the House has not been authoritatively settled, although constitutional practice seems to preclude any interference. The question came up at an early date in the history of the Republic in
Jay's Treaty, in 1796, which required appropriations to effectuate
certain of its provisions.[41] The claim of members of the House
was that, as they must act to effectuate the treaty, by right and
good government the House should have some voice in the making of the treaty.[42] The House claimed no direct agency in
making the treaty, but it claimed that, as legislation was necessary, it should have the constitutional right to pass on its effectiveness. This would, in effect, give to the House the same position as the Senate with such types of treaties, since the President
would have to seek the approval of the House prior to the con-

clusion of any treaty which required legislative action. The ability to give effect to a treaty is identical to passing on its validity. The last serious attempt of the House to gain for itself this power occurred in the Alaska Purchase Treaty with Russia[43] in 1868; but there is nothing in the circumstances surrounding the conclusion of that treaty to suggest that the House made good its claim. The fact that the House has never refused an appropriation under a treaty made by the United States possibly indicates the lack of conviction behind the argument.[44]

The actual effect of the Parliaments and the House of Representatives on the capacity of executive to enter into international obligations is of different moment. Though it cannot be defined with any degree of precision, it must be considered of substantial impact. By the doctrine of responsibility of the cabinet to the Parliament, the former must at all times know the disposition of the latter, and have its firm support for any move, not only in domestic but also in foreign affairs. Thus the cabinet will conform its policies to the tenor and temper of the Parliament. On the other hand, the ascendant position of the cabinet, its position as the initiator of public legislation and the prime formulator of public policy, places it in an ideal position to lead Parliament. Further, the cabinets in the British federations maintain a close correspondence with the legislature which, of course, is a great advantage in foreign affairs since it permits general homogeneity of action. Contrarily, the American President will often be at odds with either one or both Congressional Houses in the formulation of foreign policy and in regard to the treaties that follow in its course.[45] This might mean that if the differences in policy are too great, the House of Representatives might refuse to implement legislation, although it has not yet done so. Here is an indirect control over the capacity of the executive to enter into international agreements.

Another power of the House, not evident in the Parliaments of the British federations, is the ability of Congress to shape policies within its constitutional powers, to provide for the implementation of such policies, and so to influence the executive to enter into international agreements according to a prescribed plan. For example, the Congressional authorization of the Trade Agreements Act of 1934 laid down limits within which the negotiations of the trade agreements must be carried on. In this way Congress participates indirectly in the actual negotiations.[46]

This power, although resident in the Parliaments of the British states, is seldom used by these bodies, and the initiation of such policies is generally left to the cabinet.

The main issue which has centered about this participation of the American Congress in the treaty-making procedure has not been so much the constitutionality of the procedure as the constitutionality of the delegation of Congressional power to the President. But even this difficulty seems now abated, as witness in *United States v. Curtiss-Wright Export Corporation.*[47] In this case, Congress authorized the President by resolution to prevent the transmission of arms and other war materials to the belligerents in the Chaco War if he, at his discretion, considered that such action would "contribute to the re-establishment of peace" between the countries engaged in the conflict. The law was challenged as an invalid delegation of the legislative power, but it was sustained by the American Supreme Court. Justice Sutherland found an inherent difference between delegation in internal affairs and delegation in external matters. He said: "The two classes of powers are different, both in respect to their origin and their nature. The broad statement that the Federal government can exercise no powers except those specifically enumerated in the Constitution, and such implied powers as are necessary and proper to carry into effect the enumerated powers, is categorically true only in respect of our internal affairs . . . It results that the investment of the Federal government with the powers of external sovereignty did not depend upon the affirmative grants of the Constitution. The powers to declare and wage war, to conclude peace, to make treaties, to maintain diplomatic relations with other sovereignties, if they had never been mentioned in the Constitution, would have vested in the Federal government as necessary concomitants of national sovereignty." Thus, the President of the United States is well supported to enter into executive agreements under Congressional authorization. Further, although Congress may not participate in the actual negotiation, signing, and ratification of treaties, it may indirectly control them by this power.[49]

The United States Senate

The Constitution of the United States provides, in Article 2, Section 2, that the President is empowered to make treaties "by and with the advice and consent of the Senate, . . . provided that two-thirds of the Senators present concur." The Constitution explicitly provided for participation of the Senate in the "capacity" part of the treaty process, but a definite procedure was not contemplated or laid down by the framers.[59] The result is that constitutional practice has determined that the Senate has no power to initiate or conclude treaties. This is entirely within the control of the executive. However, the Senate may, by resolution, recommend the negotiation of a treaty, but the President is under no legal obligation to take action under such resolutions. A senatorial resolution would be a valid means of informing the President that a treaty in the process of negotiation has not the support of the Senate, and so warn the President against continuing with it. Ratification under such circumstances would hardly be forthcoming, following an expression of strong disapproval of the agreement by this means. Although this procedure has not been utilized, such a power represents a potential restriction on the freedom of the executive in the negotiation of treaties.

The United States Constitution includes the word "advice" in the relevant provision quoted immediately above. Obviously the expression was intended by the framers to mean more than merely a subsequent approval of the treaty by the Senate. The Senate was to act as a coordinate equal in the process. The word "advice" itself implies some definite activity during negotiations, and actual participation in the formal conclusion of the treaty. It was intended that the Senate should act as an executive council, with as much voice in the procedure as the Chief Executive himself. At the outset, President George Washington made one or two attempts to carry out the spirit of the constitutional provision,[51] and other half hearted attempts were made subsequently. But the practice never became general. The Senators probably feared too much presidential influence in their determinations. Another reason for the collapse of the practice is that the President's possible political disharmony with Congress would make such participation almost impossible. Thus, to have an executive council as envisaged by the framers, it would be necessary to obviate partisan feeling, perhaps by having such a council composed of appointees of the President himself. It is manifest that any one of these procedures would soon render the Senate ineffective in its role in foreign affairs. However, the President has often formally conferred with the

Senate before the institution of negotiations, and has appointed senators as negotiators.[52] Also it is not unusual for the President to keep the Senate informed during the course of the negotiations.[53]   But it is a frequent practice to give the Senate no advance notice of the negotiating or signing of any treaty.

The Constitution declares that treaties are not to be effective unless two-thirds of the Senators concur, before the President ratifies a treaty.   This provision gives rise to the undoubted right of the Senate to reject, amend or reserve treaties and, in such cases, the President has to conform to the disposition of that body.   This right of the Senate has resulted in the rejection of one hundred and four treaties, and at least another fifty-seven treaties have been so modified that they had to be shelved as not being in conformance with the spirit of the negotiations.[54]   By this means the Senate has effectively prevented many international agreements, negotiated by the President, from being consummated.[55]

Although the original concept of senatorial participation as an executive council has not been fulfilled, the Senate has been an effective "break" on the complete autonomy of the Presidential treaty-making power.   No doubt its utility in this regard is great.   It can "iron out kinks" in treaties, and observe and determine whether their future effects are to the advantage or disadvantage of the commweal.   By discussion, it can better enable the President to foresee the future reception of treaties by the people and by the authorities concerned.   Generally, the Senate provides for sober contemplation and lessens the possibility of rash action.   On the other hand there are definite disadvantages; but before explaining them, it is advisable to observe the situation in Switzerland.

THE SWISS FEDERAL ASSEMBLY

Although the actual negotiation of treaties is within the province of the Federal Council, the Swiss treaty-making procedure indicates the widest type of control over the "capacity" part of the process as yet observed.   In brief the procedure is as follows. After negotiation, treaties are submitted to the two Federal Chambers with the advice and observations of the Council. They are then submitted to an *ad hoc* committee of the Chamber to which they were originally referred, which presents a report, either oral or written, preceding a full debate on the measure.

This procedure is duplicated in both Chambers, which in Switzerland have identical powers. After agreement is reached, the result is communicated to the Federal Council for ratification. Although the Federal Councillors, because of their political reflection of the Assembly, their long-term appointment and their undoubted and proved leadership, have a similar status in the government as British cabinet members,[56] the control of the Assembly is very real. Certainly its control in the "capacity" part of the Swiss treaty-making process represents the supreme degree of legislative participation.

This legislative participation is further enhanced by the principle of full democratic participation in determining the state's foreign commitments. By a constitutional amendment in 1921, Article 89 now provides that treaties concluded by Switzerland which purport to bind the state indefinitely or for a period of more than fifteen years must be submitted for the approval of the people in a referendum before they are constitutionally effective, if thirty thousand people or eight cantons demand it. This is the highest form of control over the executives' treaty-making powers in any of the federations.[57] It has, however, certain drawbacks.

The optional legislative referendum operates to correct faulty work of a legislature, and is a decided control over this body. A legislature which has to consider the direct mandate of the people on single issues will give long and sober thought before the promulgation of any statute, rule or treaty because of the possible adverse effect. It certainly has not the freedom of a legislature that, as in the British federations, does not usually have public sanction of specific measures. The former type of legislature will ascertain with great caution that no law likely to cause public dissatisfaction be passed. In the realm of internal affairs this arrangement has much in its favor, and, though its application will be generally found feasible only in small countries, it is the epitome and the highest expression of democracy. But in external affairs the situation is not the same. Knowledge of international affairs today requires a high degree of specialization, information, and general familiarity with international conditions in addition to a broad perspective of the course of future events. These qualities the people as a whole cannot supply. To subject international agreements to the whim of the electorate would inevitably lead to delay and possible nullification, because of the public's general incompetence. Treaties such as alliances and wartime agreements are often concluded in secrecy. They often require speed and dispatch of promulgation. Commercial as well as political agreements may fall in this category, for instance, when they involve favors to one country and not to another. Such agreements must sometimes be negotiated and concluded in an atmosphere of secrecy, so as to avoid unfavorable publicity and uninformed public disfavor. Too much legislative and democratic participation, as evidenced in the extreme form in Switzerland, is not conductive to the best management of foreign affairs. Of course, these remarks hardly apply to "international legislation." The great argument in favor of this view is that "international legislation" is generally of such momentous effect that it should be effectuated only after the most thorough and careful consideration. This is not an impressive argument, for it again raises the question whether the people as a group are the best and most authoritative medium to determine if "international legislation" is to be applied. Great social and economic conventions often have to be tested and tried, to determine whether they are to the general advantage or not. The leaders of the state are in the best position to decide what is advantageous, and if a treaty is immediately submitted to the whims and caprices of an uninformed public, it is doomed to defeat as often as not.

CONCLUSION

The Senate of the United States has not performed its intended function as an executive council to participate equally in the formation of international agreements with the President. Its role has devolved to concurring or not concurring in the action of the President. It passes on a *fait accompli* in the same way as the Federal Assembly in Switzerland. Yet the analogy cannot be pushed too far, since the Assembly probably has more power in instructing the executive to initiate negotiations than the Senate.

Is the Senate, or rather the two-thirds vote of the Senators present,[58] better able to perform this task than the more democratic method of a majority in both Houses of Congress? The answer is that the smaller the body assisting in the formation of international agreements, the more efficiently can it carry out this part of the process. As it is constituted now, with only a two-thirds vote of the Senate required, the situation is not quite the same as in Switzerland and possibly not subject to the same objections. However, to the extent that it does participate in the "capacity" part of the treaty process, the same objections apply. The patent objection of the constitutional requirement of Senatorial approval has led the executive to find other means of entering into international agreements than the formal treaty. The most obvious method, now in use, is the executive agreement, which permits the executive to conclude international engagements without senatorial interference. Switzerland, owing to her peculiar neutral position defined by the Congress of Vienna in 1815, perhaps has no need of all constitutional instruments of international intercourse that a country like the United States uses to effectuate its policies. Internationalism still demands speed, talents, information, integrity and secrecy in the formulation of treaties, and, if the fundamental laws of the state do not provide the requisite procedure, circuitous methods will be found. It is inevitable that in time they will give rise to claim of usurpation of power, omnipotence and unconstitutionality. Nevertheless, great freedom of action should be permitted to the executive to enter into foreign engagements, and legislative participation in this should be kept to a minimum. There are still many restrictions to prevent the executive from entering into impolitic and unwarranted agreements.[59]

[1.] *Supra*, p. 6; *infra*, pp. 87 ff, 169 ff.   [2.] *Infra*, pp. 94 ff.

[3.] For the Australian position, see *In re Judiciary and Navigation Acts*, (1921) 29 Commonwealth Law Reports (Australia) 257.

[4.] *The Labor Conventions Case*, for example, came before the court in the form of an advisory opinion, (1936) Supreme Court Reports (Canada) 461.

[5.] (1803) 1 Cranch (United States Supreme Court) 137.

[6.] This power has been expressly conferred on the Australian High Court by the Judiciary Act, *Commonwealth Acts*, 1903, No. 6, sec. 30.

[7.] See Schubert, Glendon A., Jr., "Judicial Review of Royal Proclamations and Orders-in-Council" (1951) 9 *University of Toronto Law Journal* 69, particularly his conclusion, p. 106.   [8.] *Supra*, p. 24, note 22.

[9.] In *Walker v. Baird*, (1892) Appeal Cases (England) 491, it was sought to justify the conduct of an official on the grounds that it was an "act of state" when he attempted to enforce the provisions of a treaty against His Majesty's subjects without the necessary legislation. It was held that the plea was not sound.

[10.] Wade, Emlyn C. S., "An Act of State in English Law; Its Relations with International law," (1934) 15 *British Year Book International Law* 98, p. 103, points out the varied use and confusion with respect to the application of the doctrine.

See particularly, p. 100, note 2.   The Earl of Halsbury, *Laws of England,* (2nd ed., 1931), Vol. 23, Article 638 ff., includes two kinds of "acts of state": 1. acts which done by private individuals would be criminal or tortious; 2. acts which can be performed only by a supreme government, such as treaties, declarations of war.

[11.] *Cases in Constitutional Law,* (2nd. ed., 1933), p. 295.

[12.] The classic legal expression is by Lord Justice Fletcher-Moulton in *Salaman v. Secretary of State for India,* (1906) 1 King's Bench (England) 613, p. 639: "An act of state is essentially an exercise of sovereign power, and hence cannot be challenged, controlled, or interfered with by municipal Courts. Its sanction is not that of law, but that of sovereign power, and, whatever it be, municipal Courts must accept it, as it is, without question."

[13.] (1876) 2 Queen's Bench Division (England) 69, p. 73 (*per* Lord Coleridge).

[14.] Nor have the courts any method to prevent an infraction of a treaty by the executive if one is contemplated. In *Republic of Italy v. Hambro,* (1950) Chancery (England) 314, the claimants, under an alleged breach of an English treaty with Italy, were regretfully denied relief because the act of the executive was not contrary to any rule of municipal law and truly an "act of state" beyond the cognizance of municipal law.

[15.] (1906) 1 King's Bench (England) 613, p. 639.   [16.] *Infra,* pp. 87 ff.

[17.] As a consequence of the doctrine of "act of state," a number of questions have been determined by the courts as true acts of state, not to be questioned in the municipal courts. The Earl of Halsbury, *Laws of England,* (2nd ed., 1931), Vol. 26, p. 247, lists a number of examples, such as: the political status of a state, whether a state of war exists, whether a particular territory is hostile or foreign, or within the boundaries of a particular state, the extent of British territory, and so on. The courts have precluded themselves from considering these questions. They adopt, or take judicial notice of, the findings of the executive in these cases.

[18.] As the doctrine extends only to acts with foreigners, it would presumably be ineffective when dealing with other countries of the Commonwealth maintaining British allegiance.

[19.] *Sprigg v. Sigcau,* (1897) Appeal Cases (England) 238; *Musgrave v. Pulido,* (1879) 5 Appeal Cases (England) 102. *Supra,* pp. 52 ff.

[20.] *Supra,* pp. 48 ff.

[21.] (1936) 55 Commonwealth Law Reports (Australia) 608.

[22.] *Ibid,* p. 642 (*per* Chief Justice Latham): "There are, however, limitations upon the power of the Commonwealth to make and to give effect to international agreements. The Executive Government of the Commonwealth and the Parliament of the Commonwealth are alike bound by the Constitution and the Constitution cannot be indirectly amended by means of an international agreement made by the Executive Government and subsequently adopted by Parliament." *Ibid,* p. 658 (*per* Justice Starke): "The Commonwealth cannot do what the Constitution forbids." *Ibid,* p. 669 (*per* Justice Dixon): "The limits of the power can only be ascertained authoritatively by a course of decision . . . It is, perhaps, wise to leave less formal arrangements with other countries and other international agreements relating only to matters otherwise only of internal concern until questions arise under them." *Ibid,* p. 687 (*per* Justice Evatt and McTiernan): "The legislative power in sec. 51 is granted 'subject to this Constitution' so that such treaties and conventions could not be used to enable the Parliament to set at nought constitutional guarantees elsewhere contained . . . "

[23.] (1936) Supreme Court Reports (Canada) 461, p. 480. *Supra,* at pp. 54-55; *infra,* pp. 126-127.

[24.] *Ibid,* p. 480. [25.] *Supra,* pp. 6, 66.

[26.] Hyde, Charles C., *International Law; Chiefly as Interpreted and Applied in the United States,* (2nd. ed., 1947), Vol. 2 pp. 1458 ff.

[27.] *Digest of International Law,* (1906), Vol. 5, pp. 241 ff.

[28.] Hyde, Charles C., *International Law: Chiefly as Interpreted and Applied in the United States,* (2nd ed., 1947), Vol. 2, p. 1462. *In re Cooper,* (1892) 143 United States 472, p. 503. It is to be noted that no treaty has been ever declared unconstitutional by an American court.

[29.] (1796) 3 Dallas (United States Supreme Court) 199, p. 237.

[30.] (1934) 73 Federal (2nd) (United States) 153, p. 155. See also *United States v. Thompson,* (1919) 258 Federal (United States) 257, p. 260.

[31.] *International Law: Chiefly as Interpreted and Applied by the United States,* (2nd ed., 1947), Vol. 2, p. 1460.

[32.] Moore, John Bassett, *Digest of International Law,* (1906) Vol. 5, pp. 243 ff. Note, (1948-49) 97 *University of Pennsylvania Law Journal* 79.

[33.] *Ibid:* "The power of the judiciary to decide on the validity of treaties is as to the form of execution, constitutionality and effect and not as to a question of a public nature, for example, as to whether a treaty has been violated or the right to declare war." Again the Supreme Court will not enforce provisions of a treaty which the Department of State chooses to disregard. Other examples, forthcoming from other sources, are to be noted in passing. It has been held that the wide power of the conduct of foreign affairs is not within the purview of the courts; *Oetzen v. Central Leather Co.,* (1917) 246 United States 304. The termination or continuance of a treaty is exclusively a political question; *Terlinden v. Ames,* (1902) 184 United States 270. Finally, although these are only a few of many holdings, it has been held that the determination which is the *de facto* or *de jure* government of a state, and the time when a new state comes into existence, are political questions; *United States v. Pink,* (1942) 315 United States 203.

[34.] (1890) 133 United States 258.

[35.] *The King v. Burgess; ex parte Henry,* (1936) 55 Commonwealth Law Reports (Australia) 608, p. 640 (*per* Chief Justice Latham): "It is very difficult to say that any matter is incapable of affecting international relations so as properly to become the subject matter of an international agreement. It appears to me that no absolute rule can be laid down upon this subject." Also see the extract from the judgment of Justices Evatt and McTiernan, *supra,* p. 56.

[36.] *Supra,* pp. 46 ff. [37.] (1890) 133 United States 258, p. 266. [38.] *Infra,* pp. 168-169.

[39.] The position of Switzerland needs little comment. The doctrine of the supremacy of the legislature has been so firmly entrenched in the minds of the Swiss, that no power has been given to judges to pass on the constitutionality of economic and social legislation, or fill in gaps in constitutional texts. Article 113 of the Constitution provides a limited jurisdiction of the Federal Court over complaints of individuals concerning violation of treaties. But the Federal Court has practically no power to annul either legislative or executive acts of the federal government. Thus, unlike the Supreme Court in the United States and those of the British federations, it is not the guardian and interpreter of the Constitution. Under Article 13, it is bound to apply to all the laws of the Federal Assembly. However, this lack of control by the judiciary is probably offset by the existence of the referendum on all legislation with few exceptions. But there is no question of any control or participation by the Swiss judiciary in the conduct of foreign relations.

[40.] *Supra,* pp. 47 ff, 56, 71.

[41.] An undoubted Congressional power under Article 1, Section 9 of the Constitution.

[42.] The subject is treated in detail in Crandall, Samuel B., *Treaties: Their Making and Enforcement,* (2nd ed., 1916), pp. 178 ff; Moore, John Bassett, *Digest of International Law,* (1906), Vol. 5, pp. ff; Hackworth, Green H., *Digest of International Law,* (1940-44), Vol. 5, pp. 198-99.

[43.] Moore, John Bassett, *ibid,* pp. 226-28.

[44.] For the international legal effect of a refusal by the House of Representatives to pass the necessary legislation, see *infra,* pp. 137 ff.

[45.] But he has various means by which he may assert political leadership, for example, his constitutional right to recommend to Congress such measures as he deems right. Article 2, Section 3.

[46.] There appears no doubt about the constitutionality of this method of concluding international engagements. See Hackworth, Green H., *Digest of International Law,* (1940-44), Vol. 5, pp. 407 ff; McDougal, Myers S., and Lans, Asher, "Treaties and Executive Agreements," (1945) 54 *Yale Law Journal* 181, 534. But for a strong opinion to the contrary see Borchard, Edwin M., "Treaties and Executive Agreements—A Reply," (1945) 54 *Yale Law Journal,* 616. The situation is well stated by Professor James W. Garner in "Acts and Joint Resolutions of Congress as Substitutes for Treaties," (1935) 29 *American Journal of International Law,* 482, p. 488: "The delegation by the Constitution to the President and the Senate of the power to make 'treaties' does not exhaust the power of the United States over international relations. The will of the nation in this domain may be expressed through other acts than 'treaties' and such acts do not necessarily need to be ratified by the President by and with the advice of the Senate in order to be valid and binding, unless they so expressly provide by their own terms."

[47.] (1936) 299 United States 304; *infra.* p. 96.

[48.] *Ibid.* pp. 315-16, 318

[49.] There is, further, apparently no constitutional objection for Congress to "fill in details" after the general authorization has been given. See note, (1938) 51 *Harvard Law Review* 1069, pp. 1073-74.

[50.] Dangerfield, Royden J., *In Defense of the Senate,* (1933), Ch. 2; Fleming, Denna F., *The Treaty Veto of the American Senate,* (1930), Ch. 1, for details of the origins of this Senatorial power.

[51.] Moore, John Basset, *Digest of International Law,* (1906), Vol. 5, pp. 196 ff; Dangerfield, Royden J., *ibid;* Fleming, Denna F., *ibid,* Ch. 2.

[52.] Dangerfield, Royden J., *ibid,* pp. 291-93. For criticisms of the practice, see Fleming, Denna F., *ibid,* p. 27.

[53.] Crandall, Samuel B., *Treaties: Their Making and Enforcement,* (2nd ed., 1916), pp. 67-76.

[54.] McDougal, Myers S. and Lans, Asher, "Treaties and Executive Agreements," (1945) 54 *Yale Law Journal* 181, 534, p. 555, note 102, quoting from a list prepared by the Legislative Reference Service, Library of Congress, March, 1944. Also see Dangerfield, *In Defence of the Senate,* (1933), Ch. 6.

[55.] Dangerfield, Royden J., *ibid*, Ch. 7. Fleming, Denna F., *Treaty Veto of the American Senate*, (1930), at pp. 307 ff, notes many pertinent criticisms of the practice.

[56.] *Supra*, p. 22.

[57.] This subject will be further explored in the final chapter.

[58.] Alexander Hamilton's remarks in *The Federalist*, No. LXXV, (edited by Max Beloff, Oxford, 1948), p. 385, explain that if a two-thirds vote of all Senators had been necessary it would, in effect, have meant practical unanimity. "And the history of every political establishment in which this principle has prevailed, is a history of impotence, perplexity and disorder."

[59.] *Infra*, pp. 168-169.

CHAPTER 5

TREATY PERFORMANCE AND FUNDAMENTAL LAWS

Once the treaty has been constitutionally concluded, the obligation incurred is one that international law requires to be performed in good faith. We have now to consider how the states perform their treaty obligations, the governmental machinery they employ, their efficiency in so doing and, most important, how the rights of the state's component parts and of the people are protected from the indiscriminate use of the treaty-making power of the central executives.

The problem of treaty performance may be conveniently studied under three main headings. The first is the division of governmental powers. This involves the familiar concept that in a good government there should be three categories, the executive, the legislature and the judiciary; each exercising its functions within a defined sphere. This doctrine is evident in varying degrees in all the federations, but particularly in the United States. In Canada and Australia the separation of governmental functions is not so sharply defined, mainly because of the system of responsible government and relative conventions of the constitution. In all federations this aspect of treaty performance is primarily one of constitutional procedure and practice, rather than of judicial interpretation. The second heading concerns the judicial interpretations of the relevant constitutional provisions. This embraces the judicial attitude towards treaties which are being applied as law of the land. The third category raises the peculiar federal question of the extent of the subordination of the central power's ability to perform treaty obligations for the whole.

The Division of Governmental Powers

Constitutionalism is very recent in its application, although it was utilized in various ways by ancient governments. Its very essence is a system of restraints on the organs of government, with absolutism controlled by a method of "checks and balances." The concept of constitutionalism is to devise a means of government whereby national security, progressive social and economic institutions, security of individual rights, and the achievement of the national commonweal may best be accomplished. The state must satisfy the mass of the community whose best interests it safeguards, and the governmental machinery through which the state functions must be so adjusted as to secure these ends. But the best interests of the community is not secured by too great participation with the executive in matters like international agreements. Possibly the contrary is true for the reasons already advanced and for others that remain to be considered.[1] The best interests are to be served by a strong but not uncontrolled executive to enter into international engagements together with a real but indefinite intervention by other governmental organs in treaty performance.

The modern trend in treaty processes is for states to adopt the monistic doctrine that international and national law are essentially the same, by providing that once the treaty is validly concluded, it has the effect and force of a municipal statute. On the other hand, the concomitant tendency to place the treaty-making power (or the "capacity") in the hands of some organ other than the executive is increasing correspondingly.[2] Thus, in the United States, by Article 6, Section 2 of the Constitution, the treaty, once validly concluded, becomes the law of the land. In Switzerland, by constitutional practice, the effect is the same. The procedure is different in the British federations of Canada and Australia. For the purpose of treaty performance, at least, they adopt the dualistic view that international law and national law are essentially different, and that the former does not become the law of the land without municipal legislation.[3] It is ineffective in the courts when it affects private rights or alters the existing law. Thus the executive in the United States, and, to an extent, in Switzerland, has a much greater performing power, theoretically, than the executives in the British federation. Actually however, the control of the cabinet over Parliament and the legislative role renders this distinction unreal. But the executive in the United States has a high degree of legislative participation,[4] which is continually the subject of criticism, and not evident in the British states.

The English situation is due directly to the English Revolution, ending in 1688, which severely restricted the prerogative of the King. Much of this power, formerly inherent in this prerogative, was wrested from him by Parliament, which from that time became the supreme organ in British government. Though

Bate's Case, decided in Charles I's reign, which held that a tax
levied in accordance with the provisions of a treaty was valid, has
never been legally overruled, the imposition of such a tax by such a
method was definitely contrary to the spirit of the Revolution de-
creeing that parliamentary assent was necessary for any such exercise of the prerogative.[5] This principle was soon thereafter
established[6] and, although Sir William Blackstone's statement,
circa 1758, that there were no limitations on the treaty-making
power of the Crown might be true as to "capacity," it is not an
accurate statement with respect to "performance" even at this
time.[7]

In addition to the reasons already given for the monistic tendency of the United States,[8] there are others. Violations of
agreements by individual states were causing jealousy and disharmony among them. Foreign nations were developing a
practice of favoring one component state over another, particularly in the commercial field. It was soon realized that the
dominating theory of the central government's supremacy in the
treaty process was to the best interests of the national well-being.
Not only must foreign states look to the central government for
the valid conclusion of agreements, but that central government
must have control of the treaty performing power. It was then
felt that this was necessary to prevent external forces from invading national rights and disturbing the national tranquility.
This idea pervaded the making of the new Constitution and the
setting up of the central government as supreme in both aspects
of the treaty process.

There are many advantages in the American system; but it
also has its disadvantages. For example, it obviates the great
difficulty of federalism which has so plagued the Canadian federation, namely the conflict of federal and provincial legislative
jurisdiction in the performance of treaty obligations.[9] In the
United States, there is little room for state interference.[10] Treaties validly concluded take precedence over state constitutions
and state laws. Indubitably the effectuation of international
agreements by the central government gives that body much more
facility and freedom to enter into them. There is less likelihood
of internal constitutional problems forming a barrier to international intercourse. On the other hand, legislative participation means that the legislative branch of the government will
have a greater voice in the "capacity" part of the treaty process,

and the objections mentioned in the previous chapter are applicable.[11] The same observation is pertinent to the judiciary. Finally, this procedure often necessitates executive action to by-pass constitutional requirements by employing other devices of international intercourse, apt to give rise to dissatisfaction with governmental conduct in this field.[12]

The great disadvantage of the English system is that, if the executive cannot obtain the necessary parliamentary approval for a treaty, or if the courts declare the treaty unconstitutional,[13] the state is internationally in default.[14] Also, when the legislation is effected, the judiciary is excluded from the treaty process, and the supremacy of the legislature is substituted, since statutes in British states are the paramount laws of the land.[15] An executive free to conclude treaties has many advantages.[16] How, then, can state and popular interests best be protected from this wide power by the division of governmental powers?

The Senate of the United States is composed of ninety-six members, each state sending two, irrespective of its population. This is the result of a "compromise" between the large and small states.[17] The Senators think of themselves as spokesmen for the individual states rather than as lawmakers for the national whole.[18] Because of this, the individual states argue that the Senate represents sectional interests and is the advocate of state's concerns. Contrary arguments are made to the effect that sectional or state interests should not come before the interests of the national whole. This exposure to sectional interests is enhanced by the two-thirds rule in the treaty process, which permits a small group to defeat the will of the majority.[19] Such a situation leads to the demand for the more democratic procedure of a simple majority approval of the treaty process. At present, it puts foreign affairs on a higher level than national problems and makes a treaty's passage by the Senate more difficult than an ordinary enactment.

Since it is the essence of the American governmental system that Congress as a whole is the law-making authority, the popular as opposed to the state interests suffer to the extent this control is given to another group. It can, of course, be argued that the Senate is composed of senior statesmen, tested and tried in the arts of political science, generally abler and wiser men than their counterparts in the House of Representatives. This is quite pertinent insofar as the legislature is a participant in the conclusion of treaties, but in the sphere of performance of treaty obligations, the Senate acts as a legislature laying down national laws in the same manner as Congress acts in the field of domestic legislation. Treaties and statutes have the same effect; both are the laws of the land and affect state and popular interests in the same way.

In the British federations the general rule established by the English Revolution of 1688 has delimited the prerogative in making charges on the people or altering the law of the land by means of the treaty. Though the prerogative of the King in England is unlimited as to "capacity," such treaties require legislation before their terms become national law.[20] This, too, is the practice in Canada and Australia.[21] The tendency in these federations, as in Great Britain, is to submit every important treaty to Parliament for approval before it is ratified, and, if this is not done, to insert in the treaty a provision to the effect that the treaty will be ineffective unless the necessary legislation is forthcoming.[22] This parliamentary approval may take alternative forms. After the agreement has been signed, Parliament may approve it, either in the form of a resolution or a statute. Sometimes this statute may, not only authorize ratification of the treaty, but give it the force of law or possibly empower the Governor General to give effect to its provisions. Or again, before ratification, the international agreement may be "tabled," irrespective whether legislation is necessary or not.[23] Any or all of these practices may be employed but, as yet, there is no legal rule to prevent the executive from ratifying without any parliamentary action whatsoever.

Popular and state rights in these federations receive in effect the same protection, consideration and consequences under a treaty as under any municipal enactment. The Canadian House of Commons and the Australian House of Representatives represent the people on a national basis. Each body provides an instrument of general supervision and constructive criticism of the action of the executive, and is ever cognizant of the fluctuations and trends of public opinion. They are national bodies, theoretically at least, representing all interests of the whole, and they are the supreme governmental organs in the states. The Senates in Canada and Australia, originally intended (on the American model) to represent the interests of the states and the provinces, have been relegated to an inferior position because of their methods of appointment, life terms, party affiliation, and subordinate position with respect to money bills.[24]

There are certain analogies between the House of Representatives and Parliament, in matters of treaty performance. Although treaties and the laws of the United States are declared by the Constitution to be the supreme law of the land, not all treaties are *ipso facto* the supreme law. Occasionally the House of Representatives is called upon to perform, by legislation, treaty provisions which are not considered to be "self-executing." As expressed in the leading case of *Foster and Elam v. Neilson:*[25] "Our Constitution declares a treaty to the law of the land. It is, consequently, to be regarded in the courts of justice as equivalent to an act of the legislature, whenever it operates of itself without the aid of any legislative provision. But when the terms of the stipulation import a contract, when either of the parties engages to perform a particular act, the treaty addresses itself to the political, not the judicial department; and the legislature must execute the contract before it can become a rule for the court."[26] Thus there are certain types of treaties which from their very nature cannot be given effect as the law of the land without further action by the legislature. This is a question of construction for courts, and from the cases it is difficult to extract any principle for judicial guidance.[27] It has been maintained that if a treaty deals with a power within the control of Congress the treaty is not self-executing and demands legislative action; but the courts have not sustained this view.[28] Indeed, the courts have pursued a course of self-abnegation in this respect. They have been hesitant to declare treaties not self-executing because, of course, if the necessary legislation is not forthcoming the treaty will be inoperative.[29] This approach is observed in a recent case[30] which involved interpretation of the effect of the Preamble, Article 1, 2 and 55 of the United Nations Charter. The court, without considering whether such powers were within the control of Congress, held that the provisions of the treaty were intended to be "self-executing"—mainly because legislation was not forthcoming. This was apparently the test adopted which, if valid, is another indication of the tendency of the courts to restrict judicial interference in foreign affairs.[31]

A further similarity between the House of Representatives and the Parliaments of the British federations in the performance of treaty obligations is that acts of Congress are constitutionally

on the same plane as treaties.   This means that Congress may
pass an act which is inconsistent with the terms of a prior treaty
and so render the latter legally ineffective.[32]   Similarly it was
at one time thought that legislative action was necessary for enforcing sanctions for breaches of international agreements by
American citizens, since it had been held that, for the purpose
of imposing criminal sanctions for such breaches, no treaty is
"self-executing."[33]   Prevailing opinion is to the contrary, and
apparently the treaty device can be used to prescribe criminal
offenses for violation of the treaty's terms.[34]

With this general purview of the effect of the division of governmental powers on the performance of treaty obligations, we
shall consider whether the treaty provisions, validly made by
the executive, are nationally effective without legislative sanction.

In view of the practice of the Canadian and Australian federations to at least "table" all proposed international agreements,
a degree of parliamentary control is always present.   Also, the
requirement that legislative approval is essential for any treaty
which purports to alter the existing law, to make a charge on the
subjects, or to alter the Constitutions, leaves little scope for individual executive initiative to affect the rights of the people by
the treaty device.   There is still controversy as to the extent of
the prerogative of the Crown in cessions of British territory.
In certain other minor aspects, when the Crown incidentally
affects the rights of subjects while exercising an undoubted power,
legislation may not be necessary.[35]   The whole subject is considerably beclouded.   Clarification will likely come through
practice rather than judicial expression.[36]

In the United States, the effect of executive agreements, either
under Congressional authority or under the inherent authority
of the President, on the law of the land, is much more definite.
Those made under Congressional authority are under a high
degree of control by Congress, and have the sanction of that body
in the same way and to the same extent as any domestic law.
The legal problem is that of delegation,[37] and attendant constitutional difficulties have been raised and discussed elsewhere.[38]
Though such executive agreements are not specifically provided
for in the Constitution, constitutional practice would appear to
make them interchangeable with the more formal treaty.   With
such legislative sanction, there is no reason why they should not
have the force and effect of law.

Agreements made under the constitutional authority of the President raise different considerations. No legislative sanction is behind them; their provisions, apt to become the laws of the land, are the product of the action of one man. This is a strong argument against their interchangeable use when they affect, modify or terminate the existing law. However, legal authority may be found for giving them the same municipal effect as "treaties." In *United States v. Belmont*,[39] the Supreme Court of the United States was called upon to interpret the effect of an assignment by executive agreement of Russian assets in the United States to the government, in return for United States recognition of the Soviet regime. The Court held that, although an executive agreement does not have the dignity of a treaty, it is an international compact and a treaty under the Court of Appeals Act, and it operates as the law of the land, and overrides conflicting state laws.[40] The *Belmont* and *Pink* cases have given rise to much controversy,[41] and little more can be said to clarify the situation. Professor Edwin M. Borchard, an eminent American authority on this subject, has attempted to distinguish and modify the conclusion advanced above. He claims that the relevant portions of the judgments are dicta, that the assignment was only valid as national law because it was part of one transaction with the recognition of the Soviets, obviously a Presidential function, and dismissed the judgments themselves as being "dangerous and poorly decided." It is his considered opinion that executive agreements (and he would include these with Congressional authorization) do not operate as the law of the land except within the undoubted powers of the President.[42] To the foreign observer, the conclusiveness of the *Pink* and *Belmont* decisions and the references to synonimity with treaties,[43] make the opinion of Professor Borchard difficult to understand.

If it is concluded that executive agreements made under the inherent authority of the President have the same operation as the formal treaty, they are anomalous in American law. They present a perfect method of evading the constitutional participation of the Senate, a practice which will invariably irk that body and raise criticism of the existing treaty process. They are, however, the product of necessity. The President who finds himself with a hostile Senate will certainly look to every means to carry out his policies, and practice has made the wide employment of the executive agreement an excellent means of policy imple-

mentation.   The device, of course, could be misused by an unscrupulous or incompetent executive, and the use of such agreements to the extent of superseding the formal treaty is to be
deprecated.   No doubt their employment is due to a great extent
to an incompleteness of the American treaty process.   Treaties
often call for secrecy, speed, and delicate information, which
might reasonably preclude Senatorial participation.   Often, too,
the executive may find himself politically at odds with the Senate,
and wish to avoid contact with that body.   In conclusion, though
the executive agreement has its uses, it must be kept within strict
confines, and its provisions should receive particular judicial
attention before they operate as national law.

In Switzerland, the situation is quite clear.   From the procedure outlined in studying "capacity," the utmost protection of
cantonal and popular rights is evident.[44]   Not only that, but the
legislature itself must account to popular or cantonal mandate
if called upon to do so.[45]   Treaty provisions are subject to the
same stringent regulations that govern the promulgation of
national laws.   The difficulty, of course, is that such participation tends to restrict the state in international intercourse.[46]

Judical Construction of Constitutional Limitations on the Treaty Processes

In the United States, the difficulties which the government ex-
perienced under the Articles of Confederation have already been
mentioned.[47]   They resulted in the determination of the delegates to make the treaty-making power of the central government
broad and inclusive.   The opinions of these advocates of the
wide power are well known and need little comment.[48]   However, the minority wished to restrict the executive power.   They
feared that the executive might "dismember the empire," override the personal and state rights guaranteed in the first ten
Amendments, and nullify acts of Congress.   They vehemently
advocated a maximum of checks on the power.   The majority
met these arguments in various ways.   It was felt that Congress
would be a sufficient check, that the power was a trust which
would not be breached and exercised except for the ends for which
its bestowal was sought.   They further argued that the Senate
itself was another check on an irresponsible executive, and that
the power could not be used to give the government constitutional
authority to encroach on "the express fundamental principles es-

sential to liberty and those privileges which are declared necessary to all free peoples."

Let us consider some of the arguments for the omnipotence of
treaty provisions. Article 6, Section 2 of the Constitution is
clear and unequivocal: "This Constitution and laws of the United
States which shall be made in pursuance thereof, and all treaties
made, or which shall be made, under the authority of the United
States, shall be the supreme law of the land; and the judges of
every state shall be bound thereby, anything in the Constitution or
laws of the state notwithstanding." The provision itself ex-
presses no limitation, though there would appear to be a distinction made between "laws made in pursuance" and treaties
made "under the authority of the United States." This has
never been authoritatively decided. It could possibly be interpreted to mean that treaties are susceptible to no constitutional
limitation and, apparently, at the state conventions prior to the
acceptance of the Constitution, this was the meaning generally
accepted.

Justice Holmes, in *Missouri v. Holland*,[49] declared that "acts
of Congress are the supreme law of the land only when made in
pursuance of the Constitution, while treaties are declared to be
so when made under the authority of the United States. It is
open to question whether the authority of the United States
means more than the formal acts prescribed to make the convention." It is possible that the learned judge was expressing
a wide view of the inherent sovereignty of every nation to contract and perform international engagements, and that the
agents' power in negotiation with foreign powers was meant to
be covered by the phrase "authority of the United States." Inferentially, this power is unfettered by any constitutional restriction. The Justice goes on to say that there are some limitations
on the power, but they must be ascertained in a different way.[50]
The distinction is indefinite but it supports the theory that the
treaty-making power is an attribute of sovereignty and inheres,
independently of any delegated power, in the federal government.

It is often stated that sovereignty in the United States resides
in the people as a whole, and the Constitution directs and channels the powers delegated to the various organs of government.[51] But there is considerable support, besides the inference
from Justice Holmes's opinion, for the view that the treaty-making power is a basic one, that it is preexisting and inherent, de-

rived from international law and not from the Constitution.[52]
Being derived from international law, it is plenary and cannot
be destroyed or fettered by constitutional limitations or prohibitions.   Thus the federal government possesses to the fullest
extent the power to participate in international intercourse within
the ambit permitted by international law.   As the Constitution
places that power in the hands of the President, with the two-
thirds vote of the Senate, treaties so made become, by Article 6,
Section 2, the supreme law of the land.   This theory has been
apparently accepted by the American Supreme Court in *United
States v. Curtiss-Wright Corporation,*[53] when the Court considered that the "powers of external sovereignty did not depend
on the affirmative grants of the Constitution."[54]   However,
this theory is not completely acceptable.   It is probably true to
say that the capacity to enter into international agreements is
an inherent attribute of every sovereign state.[55]   But the capacity to enter into international agreements and the ability to
perform them are two distinct parts of the treaty process, the
latter being dependent entirely on the condition of state's internal
law.   Thus, though the state might have the capacity to enter
into agreements with other states because of its inherent sovereignty, it might not have, by its Constitution, the ability to perform the obligations incurred.[56]   Should this argument be advanced against the plenary authority of the American treaty-
making power, it may be countered by the opinion that, if the
capacity to enter into all types of agreements is assured, the
power includes the ability to effectuate self-executing provisions
under Article 6, Section 2.   Also, legislation for non-self-execut-
ing agreements may be forthcoming under the authority in the
Constitution giving to Congress the power to "make laws which
shall be necessary and proper for carrying into execution the
foregoing powers."   So there is no doubt of the plenary nature
of the federal government's treaty-making power.

There have been a variety of opinions on possible limitations
on the treaty-making power.   The extreme federalist view of
Charles H. Butler is that the power is unlimited,[57] but Professor
Quincy Wright's opinion is probably more generally prevalent
at this time.   He lists three types of constitutional limitations:
"(1) those based on the division of power between national and
state governments; (2) those based upon general prohibitions of
the power of government in defense of individual rights; (3)

those based upon the separation of the departments of the national government."[58]   A number of judicial decisions support this classification,   For example, Justice Field, in the case of *Fort Leavenworth Railway Company v. Lowe*,[59] declared that "the treaty-making power, as expressed in the Constitution, is in terms unlimited except by those restraints which are found in that instrument against the action of the government or of its departments, and those arising from the nature of the government and of that of the States.   It would not be contended that it extends to authorize what the Constitution forbids, or a change in the character of the government or in that of one of the states, or a cession of any portion of its territory of the latter without its consent.[60]   But with exceptions it is not perceived that there is any limit to the questions which can be adjusted touching any matter which is properly the subject of international negotiation with a foreign country."[61]   These possible limitations demand considerable qualification; they are by no means clearly defined.

In the first place, the United States has ceded territory under the treaty-making power[62] and apparently considers itself to have the power to do so without the consent of the state concerned, although such an eventuality is unlikely to occur.[63]   Secondly, and relative to the doctrine of the separation of powers and the inviolability of American governmental institutions, such a limitation is by no means undisputed.   An example of this is the conflict between the treaty-making executive and the House of Representatives.[64]   The alleged right of Congress to participate in the treaty-making process, when a treaty concerns matters within the legislative domain of Congress, was first brought into focus by the Jay Treaty with Great Britain in 1796.   This right still cannot be considered conclusively settled, although the objections made against such encroachment by the executive on the legislative power has "proved unavailing and a large number of treaties have been made and ratified by the Senate where legislation is necessary to carry them into operation."[65]   Also relative to this possible limitation on the treaty-making power is the proposed tampering with the judicial branch of government. For example, the International Prize Court Convention of 1907[66] contemplated review of decisions of national courts.   In the United States this was considered to be open to the constitutional objection of running counter to Articles 3 and 6 of the Constitution.[67]   Although the convention was not ratified, it

was approved by the Senate,[68] and interference with the national
judiciary by this means is still a matter of doubt. Finally, there
is the question of delegation of powers. By holding that the
powers of the President in foreign affairs were derived from international law and not delegated by the states, an inroad on the
doctrine of separation of powers is apparent.[69]

Similar doubts arise about the correctness of the advocated
limitation on the treaty-making power by the rights guaranteed
to individuals in the Constitution. Actual practice has not sustained the broad theory that the rights of individuals are inviolable by this means. Willard B. Cowles, in attempting to answer the question, examined over one thousand cases and could
find only six definite holdings by the judiciary to the effect that
the power does not extend to negate the "due process" and "just
compensation" provisions of the Fifth Amendment.[70] He points
out that the taking of property rights by the treaty was feared
by many states at the Convention in 1787. He concludes, after
considering the historical background, that the intention of the
framers who designed the amendments was not only to preclude
treaties from being domestic law when repugnant to the above
provisions, but that these clauses were also specifically intended
to defeat what Judge John Bassett Moore states to have been
the first object of the treaty-making clause, namely, to enforce
Article 4 of the Treaty of Peace with Great Britain as paramount
law by virtue of Article 6, Section 2, irrespective of the states'
Bill of Rights.

Although Cowles carefully considers many cases, particularly
the Litvinoff assignment group,[71] his work does not include the
United States v. Pink decision,[72] which sheds more doubt on his
conclusion. In this case, it was held that an executive agreement
required recognition and enforcement by American courts in like
respect to a treaty.[73] Relevant to this particular problem, the
law was upheld on the ground that, as by this agreement the
Soviet decrees of confiscation, with respect to assets in the United
States of certain Russian insurance companies, were recognized in
the United States, claims of foreign creditors against such companies were superseded under the agreement by certain claims of
American citizens and of the United States itself. This result
was reached notwithstanding that "aliens as well as citizens were
entitled to the protection of the fifth Amendment." Justice
Stone dissented, but did so for the reason that "even though the

two governments might have stipulated for alteration by this government of its municipal law and the consequent surrender of the rights of individuals," the inference should have been clearly expressed.[74] The constitutional guarantees in question did not provide a defense to the rights of the individuals in this case.[75]

Thus, this type of restriction on the treaty power in the United States appears very vague. In the field of domestic legislation the general technique employed by the courts has been to determine whether questionable enactments are within the powers of the federal government, and then to pose the question of the basis for the legislation. If the party alleging the violation of "due process" cannot meet this burden, the court will concern itself no more.[76] Since 1937 only two domestic acts of Congress have been declared unconstitutional,[77] and there is no reason to believe that any different method will be employed or result reached in construing the provisions of treaties as allegedly in conflict with the rights of individuals.

It is not contended, nor has the court admitted, that there are no limitations on the American treaty-making power; but what they are or how they are to be determined can only be conjectured. True, a treaty has never been declared unconstitutional in the United States. This might indicate, not so much the timidity of the executive to enter into international agreements in excess of its powers, as the broad scope of the power, and the hesitancy which the courts have shown in interfering with the political arm of the government. Hence the American treaty-making power, both in respect to "capacity" and "performance," is fully competent to cope with the expanding use of the treaty in international intercourse; and the judicial control is ever present to prevent any undue excess of the power. Should a treaty have a subject improper for international negotiation, the judiciary could act to declare it void.[78] But the international obligation would still remain, and necessitate settlement by diplomatic means in accord with international law.

The B.N.A. Act and the Australian Constitution Act are not the comprehensive documents of the other two federations. They do little more than define the governmental mechanism, and, in accord with the British principle of the supremacy of Parliament but within the ambit of the written Constitutions, the Parliaments of the British federations are supreme.[79] To the foreign observer the most startling omissions in these Con-

stitution are rights guaranteed to individuals.   In the United
States, the courts, as interpreters of the Constitution, protect
these rights from infringement by either the executive or the legislature.   In Canada and Australia the courts give protection to
the individual only within the precedents afforded by the common
law, based on judicial decision and on the ancient constitutional
documents, such as the Magna Carta and the Bill of Rights,
which remain untouched by legislation.   Parliament can alter or
annul any of these precedents.   Just as in the United States the
protection of fundamental civil liberties is in the hands of the
courts, in the British federations the protection is afforded by
Parliament.

But the Parliaments of these federations are not omnipotent;
they must act in accord with the Constitutions.   These Constitutions are in the form of statutes of the Imperial Parliament, and
prescribe the functions and powers of the central and regional
governments, which the federal parliaments may not contravene.[80]   In Australia, there is a definite judicial interdiction
against treaties which purport to infringe on the Constitution.
Although the decision in *The King v. Burgess; ex parte Henry*[81]
gives the central executive wide powers relating to "capacity,"[82]
and the central legislature correspondingly wide powers of
"performance,"[83] all the judges of the High Court referred
to the constitutional restrictions on the process.[84]   Justices
McTieran and Evatt referred specifically to Sections 6, 28, 41,
80, 100 116 and 117, which relate respectively to the yearly session of Parliament, the duration of Parliament, the rights of the
electors, the right to trial by jury, the right of the states to
reasonable use of the waters of rivers, to freedom of religion,
and to discrimination among residents of different states.   This
is not so comprehensive as the American "Bill of Rights" but it
does provide definite restrictions on the treaty process.   Such
strong and unanimous pronouncements would prevent any attempt on the part of the executive to alter or abrogate the Constitution by the treaty device.[85]

In Canada there is no authoritative pronouncement that the
Constitution cannot be amended by the treaty process.[86]   The
process is legally obscure.   As in Australia, written provisions
are scanty and provide only for such matters as the right to an
independent judiciary (Section 99), Parliamentary elections
every five years (Section 50), the use of the English and French

language in official intercourse (Section 133) and a few other minor items. However, it is a just inference that, should the Canadian treaty process be clarified to correspond more nearly to her international status, the courts would follow the judicial path of her sister state and of the United States, and preserve to themselves the right to declare unconstitutional any infringement of the constitutional document. Should international relations call for agreements apt to undermine or alter the constitutions of these states, such alteration cannot be effected by the treaty proccess; it must take the form of a constitutional amendment. This would be a judicial determination.

In Switzerland, the Constitution theoretically does not impose any obstacle in the way of the plenary power of the central government to enter into and perform treaty obligations.[87] Further, it would not operate as a bar to any reasonable alteration to conform with international demands of the time. However, the Swiss are very jealous of their constitutional liberties and any attempt to curtail them with no good reason would meet considerable opposition.[88] At the present time, the Constitution, by Article 5, guarantees to the cantons their territory, their sovereignty within the limits fixed by Article 3, the liberty and rights of the people, the constitutional rights of the citizens, and the rights and privileges of the authorities. The nature of their fundamental guarantees illustrates how far the Swiss have traveled the road to political, social, cultural and religious freedom. Article 43 refers to their rights of citizenship; Article 44 to their right not to be expelled; Article 45 to their right of freedom of movement and right to domicile; Article 49 pertains to their right of religious liberty; Article 50 deals with the right to trade; and, finally, Article 55 guarantees the liberty of the press. Although it has the legal power to do so, the Federal Assembly would not lightly derogate from the guaranteed liberties by the treaty device. This will be more fully explained in the next chapter.[89]

[1.] *Supra,* pp. 79-80; *infra,* pp. 165 ff.

[2.] See the recent provisions in the South American Constitutions. Peaslee, Amos J., *Constitutions of the Nations,* (1950), *passim.* But note Section 2 of the Bricker Amendment which proposed, in part, that "a treaty shall become effective as internal law in the United States only through legislation . . ."

[3.] *Mortensen v Peters,* (1906) Scottish Law Reports 227. Of course international law may become national law by judicial decision under certain circumstances, see Oppenheim, L., *International Law.* 7th ed. by Lauterpacht, H., (1947), p. 37.

[4.] *Infra,* pp. 92-93.

[5.] Holdworth, William S., *A History of the English Law,* (1924), Vol. 6, pp. 44 ff, gives a good account of this case and main issues raised respecting foreign affairs.

[6.] McNair, Arnold D., *Law of Treaties,* (1938), Ch. 2.

[7.] See the discussion by Holdworth, William S., "The Treaty Making Power of the Crown," (1942) 58 *Law Quarterly Review* 175.

[8.] *Supra,* pp. 25-26.   [9.] *Infra,* pp. 123 ff.

[10.] *Infra,* pp. 107 ff.   [11.] *Supra,* pp. 79-80.

[12.] See examples in Dangerfield, Royden J., *In Defense of the Senate,* (1933), pp. 175 ff. In particular, note President Theodore Roosevelt's executive agreement respecting the administration of San Domingo. The recent Bricker Amendment controversy is also illustrative.

[13.] As in *The Labor Convention Case,* (1937) Appeal Cases (England) 326.

[14.] *Infra,* p. 138. To obviate this result it is the occasional British practice to include a provision in treaties which require legislative approval as illustrated in the Anglo-American Liquor Treaty, 1924: "In the event that either of the High Contracting Parties shall be prevented by judicial decision or legislative action from giving full effect to the provisions of the present treaty, the said treaty shall automatically lapse, and, on such lapse or whenever this treaty shall cease to be in force, each High Contracting Party shall enjoy all the rights which it would have possessed had this treaty not been concluded." See also McNair, Arnold D., *Law of Treaties,* p. 31.

[15.] *Supra,* p. 24.   [16.] *Supra,* pp. 80-81.

[17.] The Federalist, No. LII, (by Alexander Hamilton or James Madison), (edited by Max Beloff, Oxford 1948), p. 316.

[18.] Pepper, George W., *In the Senate,* Philadelphia, 1930.

[19.] Dangerfield, Royden J., *In Defense of the Senate,* (1933), Ch. 6; Fleming, Denna F., *Treaty Veto of the American Senate,* (1930), p. 286.

[20.] This important principle has been comprehensively explored by McNair, Arnold D., *Law of Treaties,* (1938), Ch. 2; and in an article by the same author, "When Do British Treaties Involve Legislation," (1928), 9 *British Year Book International Law* 59. Dr. McNair lists four categories of treaties which constitutional convention demands that the cabinet seek parliamentary approval for necessary implementation: "1. Treaties requiring for their execution and application in the United Kingdom a change or addition to the laws administered in the courts. 2. Treaties requiring for their application in the United Kingdom that the Crown shall receive some new powers not already possessed by it. 3 and 4. Treaties creating a direct or contingent financial obligation on Great Britain. There is a practice, probably amounting to a constitutional convention, whereby treaties involving the cession of British territory are submitted for the approval of Parliament, and its approval takes the form of a statute." The two modern legal expressions on the subject are *Walker v Baird*, (1892) Appeal Cases (England) 491, and *The Parlement Belge,* (1879) 4 Probate Division (England) 129. However, exceptions to the above rules may occasionally be found. See, for example, *The Chile* (1914) Probate Division (England) 212; *Fenton Textile Association, Limi-*

ted v. Krassin and Others, (1922) 38 Times Law Reports (England) 259; *In re Marten's Patents,* (1915) 112 Law Times (England) 313.

[21.] Legal sanction for this principle in Canada may be found in *Re Arrow River Tributaries Slide and Boom Co. Ltd. v Pigeon Timber Co. Ltd.,* (1932) Supreme Court Reports (Canada) 495. At p. 510 (*per* Justices Lamont and Cannon): "The treaty in itself is not equivalent to an Imperial Act and, without the sanction of Parliament, the Crown cannot alter existing law by entering into a contract with a foreign power." Also see *Albany Packing Co. v Registrar of Trade Marks,* (1940) Exchequer Court Reports (Canada) 256, pp. 265-66. In Australia, although Justice Starke, in *Meyer v. Poynton,* (1920) 27 Commonwealth Law Reports (Australia) 436, p. 441, would express no opinion on whether "the Executive Government of the Commonwealth can, without legislative sanction, make a treaty binding as a law upon the Courts and citizens of Australia," the subsequent case of *The King v. Burgess; ex parte Henry,* (1936) 55 Commonwealth Law Reports (Australia) 618, presents the true view. At p. 664, Chief Justice Latham says: "See *Walker v. Baird,* which settles the principle that, at least as a general rule, a treaty cannot affect the private rights under municipal law of British subjects, so that often legislation is required to implement a treaty."

[22.] *Supra,* p. 102, note 14.

[23.] It is a moot point whether the Senate's approval is necessary or not. Probably the better policy is to conform to the general practice for laying down municipal legislation, which, of course, would give the Senate a measure of voice in the process.

[24.] In Canada, see generally MacKay, Robert A., *The Unreformed Senate of Canada,* (1926). In Australia, Greenwood, Gordon, *The Future of Australian Federalism,* (1946).

[25.] (1829) 2 Peters (United States Supreme Court) 253.

[26.] See examples in Hackworth, Green G., *Digest of International Law,* (1940-44), Vol. 5, pp. 177 ff.

[27.] Anderson, Chandler P., "The Extent and Limitations of the Treaty Making Power Under the Constitution," (1907) 1 *American Journal of International Law* 636, pp. 641 ff.

[28.] See, for example, *Bacardi Corporation of America v. Domenech,* (1940) 311 United States 150.

[29.] An indication by the Department of State to the judiciary that it is an impolitic or embarrassing agreement, and a subsequent determination that the treaty is not self-executing would be a possible way for the executive to repudiate such an obligation. Such a method would be a breach of international law, however, as the treaty is internationally valid on constitutional conclusion. *Infra,* Ch. 7.

[30.] *Fujii v. California,* (1950) 217 Pacific 2nd (United States) 481; (California Appeals, 1950). (1950) 44 *American Journal of International Law* 543, p. 590. This argument has since been overruled. The California Supreme Court has held that the Charter is not "self-executing" and requires congressional implementation before it is binding on the courts. (1952) 242 Pacific 2nd (United States) 617; 38 California 2nd 718.

[31.] To obviate any doubt when the treaty may require legislation either because it is not self-executing or there is doubt that Congress may pass the necessary enabling statute for any reason, as for example, the appropriation of money, stipulation to this effect should be, and generally is, made in the treaty itself. *Supra*, p. 102, note 14.

[82.] The international obligation would still remain although provision against this eventuality could be made by the insertion in the treaty of a clause to this effect and so prevent international default.

[83.] *Over the Top*, (1925) 5 Federal 2nd (United States) 838, p. 845.

[84.] Hackworth, Green H., *Digest of International Law*, (1940-44), Vol. 5, pp. 16-17.

[35.] McNair, Arnold D., *Law of Treaties*, pp. 24 ff; Anson, Sir William R., *Law and Custom of the Constitution*, (4th ed., 1955), Vol. 2, Part 2, pp. 137 ff; Holdsworth, William S., "Treaty Making Power of the Crown," (1942) 58 *Law Quarterly Review* 175.

[36.] Holdsworth, William S., *ibid*, p. 183, says: "The test is, I think, this: if the object of the treaty is the doing of an act which the Crown has the power to do, e. g., the recognition of the status of a foreign sovereign or a public ship or a cession of territory, the fact that it will have the effect of altering the rights of the subject will not preclude the Crown from making it." However, it must be remembered that rights of the Crown under the prerogative are subject to scrutiny by the courts, and still in an indefinite state.

[37.] *Supra*, p. 76.

[38.] For Example, McDougal, Myers S., and Lans, Asher, "Treaties and Executive Agreements," (1945) 54 *Yale Law Journal* 181, 534.

[39.] (1937) 301 United States 324.

[40.] To a similar result, *United States v. Pink*, (1942) 315 United States 203.

[41.] For example, McDougal, Myers S., and Lans, Asher, "Treaties and executive Agreements," (1945) 54 *Yale Law Journal* 181, 534, p. 308; also the reply to this article by Professor Edwin M. Borchard, in the same volume, p. 616.

[42.] *Ibid*, p. 628.

[43.] For example, (1937) 301 United States 324, pp. 330-31.

[44.] *Supra*, p. 79.   [45.] *Supra*, pp. 79-80.

[46.] *Supra*, pp. 80,   [47.] *Supra*, pp. 17, 25-26.

[48.] See generally Corwin, Edward S., *National Supremacy*, (1913), Ch. 4; Butler, Charles H., *Treaty Making Power of the United States*, (1902), Vol. 1, Chs. 6, 7; Crandall, Samuel B., *Treaties: Their Making and Enforcement*, (2nd ed., 1916), Chs. 4, 5.

[49.] (1920) 252 United States 416, p. 433.

[50.] *Ibid*, p. 433.

[51.] For example, *Ware v. Hylton*, (1796) 3 Dallas (United States Supreme Court) 198, p. 236.

[52.] See the arguments advanced by Potter, Pitman B., "Inhibitions Upon the Treaty Making Power of the United States." (1934) 28 *American Journal of International Law* 456; Magnusson, Jon, "Our Membership in the United Nations and the Federal Treaty Power Under the Constitution," (1948) 34 *Virginia Law Review* 137, pp. 145 ff; Butler, Charles G., *Treaty Making Power of the United States*, (1902), Ch. 1. For strenuous arguments to the contrary, see Tucker, Henry St. George, *Limitations on the Treaty Making Power*, (1915), Ch. 5.

[53.] (1936) 299 United States 304. See the quotation from the judgment of Justice Sutherland in this case, *supra*, p. 76.

[54.] To the contrary and apparently admitting no qualification, see *Kansas v. Colorado*, (1907) 206 United States 46; *McCullouch v. Maryland*, (1819) 4. Wheaton

(United States Supreme Court) 316; Quarles, James, "The Federal Government: As to Foreign Affairs, Are Its Powers Inherent?" (1944) 32 *Georgia Law Journal.* 375, is a criticism of this holding.

[55.] Hall, William E., International Law, (8th ed., 1924), p. 380; Corwin, Edward S., *The President's Control of Foreign Relations,* (1917), p. 1. But note the cautious structure of Article 3 of the Harvard Draft Convention, (1935) 29 *American Journal International Law* (Supplement), p. 705; "The capacity to enter into treaties is possessed by all states but the capacity of a state to enter into certain treaties may be limited."

[56.] International law requires, however, that all states carry out in good faith the obligations which it incurs. See Harvard Draft Convention, Article 20, and the authorities quoted therein, *ibid.* pp. 977 ff. Also see, *infra,* pp. 137 ff.

[57.] "If, however, any limitations do exist, they cannot be defined or expressed beyond the statement made in the preceding section that the power must be exercised in accordance with the fundamental principles of our government . . . for the purpose of maintaining national life and not destroying it." *Treaty Making Power of the United States,* (1902), Vol. 1, p. 353.

[58.] "The Constitutionality of Treaties," (1919) 13 *American Journal of International Law* 242, p. 251. For more detailed lists of possible limitations see, Black, Forest R., "Treaty Making Power and Limited Government," (1926) 11 *St. Louis Law Review* 6; Stoke, Harold W., "The Constitution and International Labor Conventions," (1932) 30 *Michigan Law Review* 631.

[59.] (1885) 114 United States 525, p. 541.

[60.] For a more recent expression to the same effect, see *Amaya v. Standolind Oil and Gas Co.,* (1946) 158 Federal 2nd (United States) 554.

[61.] See also *DeGeoffroy v. Riggs,* (1890) 133 United States 266, in which it was held that the power "extends to all proper subjects of negotiation between states."

[62.] For example, the cession of part of Maine to Canada under the Webster-Ashburton Treaty of 1842 with Great Britain, and other examples contained in Magnusson, Jon, "Our Membership in the United Nations and the Federal Treaty Power Under the Constitution," (1948) 34 *Virginia Law Review* 137.

[63.] Hackworth, Green H., *Digest of International Law,* (1940-44), Vol. 5, p. 13, citing the opinion of the Solicitor of the Department of State in 1910.

[64.] *Supra.* pp. 74-75.

[65.] Hackworth, Green H., *Digest of International Law,* (1940-44), Vol. 5, pp.11-12. In particular note that the penal provisions in treaties, constitutionally within the power of Congress, have been upheld as a valid exercise of the power, *ibid,* p. 16.

[66.] For text see (1908) 2 *American Journal of International Law* (Supplement), 174.

[67.] For example, see Brown, Henry B., "The Proposed International Prize Court," (1908) 2 *American Journal of International Law* 476

[68.] But subject to a protocol containing the provision "that it is not for the court to reverse or affirm the decision of the national tribunals", (1911) 5 *American Journal of International Law* (Supplement), 99.

[69.] *United States v. Curtiss-Wright Corporation,* (1936) 299 United States 304

[70.] Cowles, Willard B., *Treaties and Constitutional Laws: Property Interferences and Due Process of Law,* (1941).

[71.] Cowles, Willard B., *ibid,* Ch. 14, pp. 275 ff. He considers in detail *Guaranty*

Trust Co. v. United States, (1938) 304 United States 126; *United States v. Belmont,* (1937) 301 United States 324; *Moscow Fire Insurance Company v. Bank of New York and Trust Company,* (1940) 309 United States 624.

[72.] (1942) 315 United States 203.

[73.] *Supra,* pp. 92-93.   [74.] (1942) 315 United States 203, p. 252.

[75.] In *King's Features Syndicate Inc. v. Valley Broadcasting Co.,* (1942) 43 Federal Supplement (United States) 137, it was held that courts have no right to annul or disregard the provisions of a treaty upon any notion of equity, general convenience or substantial justice and private rights which have suffered by reason of the treaty may be salved by the government which entered into the treaty, and which required the condition causing the injury.

[76.] For example, *Pacific States Box and Basket Co. v. White,* (1935) 296 United States 176, (*per* Justice Brandeis).

[77.] *Tot v. United States,* (1943) 319 United States and *United States v. Lovett,* (1946) 328 United States 303. In dealing with state statutes involving interferences with the rights of individuals, at least with respect to the freedoms of speech and assembly, the present tendency of the courts is to determine whether the statute is justified by any clear and present danger to the public security. For example, *Thomas v. Colins,* (1945) 323 United States 516, p. 530.

[78.] Thus, it is submitted, Section 1 of the Bricker Amendment which provided that "a provision of a treaty which conflicts with this constitution shall not be of any force or effect," is only declaratory of existing law. Also see, *supra,* pp. 71 ff.

[79.] *Regina v. Burah.* (1878) 3 Appeal Cases (England) 889.

[80.] This principle was affirmed in the Statute of Westminster, 22-23 *Statutes of George V,* Ch. 4, 1931, which bestowed on the Dominions powers in accord with their rise to a status of equality with the other members of the international community. Section 7 of the Statute prevents the Parliament of either federation from altering its Constitution in any way.

[81.] (1936) 55 Commonwealth Law Reports (Australia) 618.

[82.] *Supra,* pp. 57 ff.   [83.] *Infra,* pp. 120 ff.   [84.] *Supra,* p. 71.

[85.] See also *Ffrost v. Stevenson,* (1937) 58 Commonwealth Law Reports (Australia) 528, pp. 599-600 (*per* Justice Evatt).

[86.] Except, possibly, the reference contained in Chief Justice Duff's judgment in *The Labor Convention Case,* (1936) Supreme Court Reports (Canada) 461, p. 474, *supra,* p. 71.

[87.] *Infra,* pp. 127-128.

[88.] Huber, Hans, *How Switzerland Is Governed,* (1947), Ch. 10.

[89.] *Infra,* pp. 127-128.

CHAPTER 6

TREATY PERFORMANCE AND THE LEGISLATIVE POWERS OF THE COMPONENT STATES

The third and last classification of constitutional limitations affecting the performance of treaty obligations raises the distinctive federal problem of the distribution of legislative powers. The question may be posed how far judicial interpretations of the constitutions have permitted the legislative powers of the component parts to have effect in the treaty-performing processes of the federal states.

THE UNITED STATES

In addition to the main arguments for limiting the treaty process outlined in Chapter 4[1] there is the more particular and questionable limitation of the Tenth Amendment of the American Constitution, reserving to the states all powers not delegated to the federal government. No more need be said of the wording of Article 6, Section 2. Expressly there are no limitations contained in it, and obviously treaties cannot be the supreme law of the land if the provisions of state constitutions, state laws, and municipal ordinances stand in the way. But the advocates of the implied restriction of the Tenth Amendment present their views in three broad ways. First, they argue that the federal government is an institution operative only within the area of its delegated powers. The treaty-making power is coextensive with these delegated powers, and is only a method of utilizing them. They would restrict the power of the central government in international affairs to the enumerated powers contained in the first Article of the Constitution. Second, they strenuously assert that the states possess certain inalienable rights, that may not be infringed. Third, they consider that the treaty-making power must be restricted to such affairs as are truly the incident of international intercourse, and which cannot be settled in any other way. From this power are excepted the rights reserved to the states, and the treaty-making power cannot be used to do what the government itself may not do.

These arguments, basically identical, have been answered in detail by Professor Edward S. Corwin.[2] He is most vehement in their denunciation, and concludes that the treaty-making power is not limited by the police power of the states. He declares that "the United States cannot, on the one hand, stand in the forefront of those who promote friendship, good faith, and reciprocity among the nations of the world, and on the other hand, reserve to itself the right to recede from its stipulated covenants on the ground that, after all, it is not a real nation."[3]

Probably the best arguments in favor of the reserved powers of the states are advanced by Judge Henry St. George Tucker.[4] In a very detailed study of the problem, he examines the Constitution, and declares that the amendments are all subject to it. They are inviolate and cannot be destroyed or infringed upon by the use of any constitutional power. He maintains that these rights contained in the first ten amendments would never have been demanded by the states and the people if they were apt to be taken away by some power in the federal government. The scope of the treaty power is limited not only by the Constitution but also by the direct and specific prohibitions on the Government itself. For example, Article 1, Section 9, provides that the "writ of habeas corpus shall not be suspended unless," etc., and that "no title of nobility shall be granted by the United States."[5] As any attempt to contravene a specific prohibition of the Constitution would be invalid, so would an infringement on a power reserved to the states. Judge Tucker recognizes that the police power of the states is very difficult to define, and that its precise meaning will never be known.[6] He recognizes the expanding commerce power of the federal government, and the consequent contraction of the police power, but considers this to be a "functional" and "structural" growth of the Constitution. Any expansion of the treaty-making power would be "organic" and "fundamental." He says: "If the limitations suggested (i.e. on the treaty-making power) are evils, and they are upheld by the Constitution, then the Constitution should be changed unless, indeed, such changes would result in the organic and fundamental change of our whole government."[7]

The adherents to this view of "state rights" have the support of judicial utterances concerning the inviolability of the police powers, particularly from those maintaining that the state's legislative power is not subject to the treaty-making power.[8] Considering the more outstanding instances, in *Holmes v. Jennison,*[9] it was maintained that "it must be assumed that the framers of the

Constitution intended that it (the treaty-making power) should extend to all those objects which in the intercourse of nations had usually been regarded as the proper subjects of negotiation and treaty, if not inconsistent with the nature of our government and the relation between the states of the United States." The dicta in the *License*[10] and *Passenger*[11] cases are particularly strong. In the former it was declared that a "treaty no more than an ordinary statute can arbitrarily cede away any one right of a state or of any citizen of a state." In the latter case it was similarly held that "there can be no authority of the United States save what is derived mediately or immediately . . . from the Constitution. A treaty, no more than an ordinary statute, can arbitrarily cede away any one right of a state or any citizen of a state."[12]

In the following cases, emphasis has been placed on the courts' method of interpretation, the scope of operation they have given to state laws and the types of state laws which have been unheld and overriden. Finally, an effort has been made to determine the sphere of the states which the federal government may not invade by the treaty process.

Though the courts maintain that a state constitutional provision, statute, or municipal ordinance will fall when in conflict with a treaty, the treaty should be construed so as not to override state laws if this is reasonably possible.[13] State laws will not be interfered with lightly, but there is nothing to prevent a court from giving the treaty a construction that will conflict with a state statute, even though another construction may be possible, provided the former is more in accordance with the intent manifested in the treaty.[14]

The foremost legal expression in this controversy is that of *Ware v. Hylton*,[15] decided by the American Supreme Court in 1796, with all the judges giving separate opinions. The case involved a suit by a British citizen who was attempting to collect a debt from a citizen of Virginia. The defendant pleaded payment into the hands of state officials, in accordance with a state statute which had been passed during the Confederation. The plaintiff's contention was based on the Treaty of Paris, which provided that "creditors of either side should meet with no lawful impediment to the recovery of the full value in sterling money of all bona fide debts theretofore contracted." Justice Chase, in delivering his opinion, said: "There can be no limitation on the power of the people of the United States.   By their authority the Constitution of the United States was established; and they had the power to change or abolish the state constitutions or make them yield to the central government, and to the treaties made by their authority.   A treaty cannot be the supreme law of the land, that is, of all the United States, if any act of the state legislature can stand in the way . . . it is the declared will of the people of the United States that every treaty made under the authority of the United States shall be superior to the constitutions and laws of the individual states; and their will alone is to decide . . . (otherwise) the will of a small part of the United States may control or defeat the will of the whole."

Questions relating to alien holdings of land, ordinarily within the power of the states, came up at an early date as being in conflict with the Treaty of Peace with England in 1796.   By the treaty it was agreed reciprocally that English subjects who then held lands in the United States might grant, sell or devise the lands so held to whomever they pleased in a like manner as if they were natives.   In numerous cases,[16] it was held that this provision completely removed alien disability of English subjects as to title of land at the time of the conclusion of the treaty, and placed them and their heirs in respect to such land on the same footing as citizens; and that a title defeasible on the date of the treaty was completely protected and confirmed, irrespective of state laws to the contrary.   But, to obtain these rights, the treaty must expressly stipulate for such a broad construction.   Thus in *Terrace v. Thompson,*[17] for example, it was held that a state statute prohibiting aliens from holding lands in the state was not in conflict with an article in a treaty between the United States and Japan, which provided that the citizens and subjects of each contracting party "shall have liberty . . . to lease land for residential and commercial purposes, and generally to do anything necessary to or incidental for trade."   When the alien plaintiff sought to lease agricultural land, the court held that "in the most liberal construction of this language that may be indulged in, it cannot be fairly said that truck farming is incidental to trading."   As it was considered that the leasing of agricultural land should be excluded, the state retained control over such land within its borders.

Other cases respecting tenure, transfer, and descent of land illustrate the broad range of the treaty power in this respect, and of the consequent yielding of state laws. In *Chirac v. Chirac,*[18] the court was called upon to decide the validity of a plaintiff's claim to title through a naturalized Frenchman. By a Maryland statute, certain conditions necessary to the valid transfer of land had not been performed; but it was contended that the necessity of complying was removed by a treaty with France, which granted to French nationals dispositive rights equal to those of natives. Chief Justice Marshall observed that "the direct object of this stipulation is to give French subjects the rights of citizens . . . the act of Maryland has no particular reference to the case of Chirac, but it is the general rule of state policy, prescribing the terms on which French subjects may take and hold lands. This rule is changed by treaty." In *DeGeoffroy v. Riggs,*[19] another leading case, the rights of a French citizen under the treaty were in conflict with Maryland state land law, and the treaty was upheld by Justice Field in an opinion in which he uttered his famous expression "that the treaty power of the United States extends to all proper subjects of negotiation between our government and the governments of other nations."[20]

Analogous questions relating to treaties bestowing the right on consuls to appear and administer the property of deceased nationals have been the subject of somewhat cautious interpretation by the courts. In *re Hansen's Estate,*[21] the question in issue was whether a consul had the right to appear for his minor nationals before any service of process on them, claimed by virtue of a "most-favored" provision in a treaty. The New York Surrogate Court held that the treaty was satisfied by allowing the consul, after the minor had been brought into court regularly under the *lex fori* or had subjected himself to it by personal petition, to appear for the minor in the sense of intervening on his behalf. It was held that the "states only delegated so much of their presumably unbounded sovereignty as was thought necessary for the welfare of the union in respect of interstate and international matters . . . the entire *lex fori* is supreme as to the descent of lands, even in the hands of aliens . . . and this supremacy . . . extends to the procedual steps taken to apply and administer those local matters." In respect to these matters, "there is probably no treaty to be found without a stipulation that, whatever be the representative powers conceded to a foreign consul here, they were, nevertheless, to be exercised here 'so far as the law of each country will permit' or 'conformably to the laws' of the respective tribunals to which the application might be made." The New York Court presumably would have such a phrase read into a treaty even though intentionally omitted. Such rulings that the words of a treaty manifested an intent not to affect the laws of the individual states are, of course, often against the spirit of the treaty;[27] and, although they indicate certain concessions to state laws, such restrictive interpretations represent a circuitous reasoning encouraged by poor or indefinite treaty-drafting, rather than any illustration of the reserve power in the states.

The fate of state inheritance tax statutes in conflict with treaty provisions deserves comment, as illustrating ingenious arguments of state authorities to circumvent them. In *re Anderson's Estate*,[23] the Iowa Code, imposing a collateral inheritance tax of 20% when beneficiaries are non-resident aliens, while 5% was imposed on other categories of beneficiaries, was held not to be in conflict with a treaty with Denmark, which stipulated that no higher taxes be levied by either party "upon any personal property, money or effects of the citizens or subjects of the other party, on the removal of the same from the country." The court held that it was not a tax upon property, but merely a regulation of the transmission of the property of deceased persons. On appeal to the Supreme Court of the United States,[24] the decision was upheld, but on the ground that the relevant article in the treaty was intended to apply only to the property of citizens of one country located within the other, and so placed no limitation upon the power of either government to deal with its own citizens and their property within its own dominion. The decedent, being a citizen of the United States, was not covered by the treaty. In *Neilsen v. Johnson*,[25] another leading case with very similar facts, the argument advanced was that the tax was not prohibited by the treaty since it was a tax on succession, not on property. The Supreme Court considered that this was a narrow and restrictive interpretation, not consonant with the intention of the contracting parties. But a more rational argument was accepted in another taxation case. In *Watson v. Hooey*,[26] it was held that the similar provision in the Hay-Paunceforte Treaty was not violated by a state tax provision which provided a higher rate for non-resident aliens, as it was on another base than for non-resident citizens.[27]

Various labor laws of the states have been in conflict with provisions of treaties, and have received interesting interpretations from the courts. In fact, the states appear to have retained a measure of autonomy in this regard. In *Heim v. McCall*,[28] Articles 1 and 2 of a treaty with Italy, providing for equality of rights and privileges for persons of Italian citizenship with the citizens of the United States, were held not to have been infringed by statutes of New York which provided that only citizens be employed in public works, and that citizens of New York be given preference. A relevant part of the judgment of *Atkins v. Kansas* was quoted and approved:[29] "It belongs to the state, as the guardian and trustee for its people, and having control of its affairs, to prescribe the conditions upon which it will permit public work to be done on its behalf, or on behalf of its municipalities." The language of the treaty was further restricted by the holding that "the equality of rights that the treaty assures is equality only in respect of protection and security for persons and property."[30]

The rights of aliens to work within state borders have brought up questions of property rights. In *Patsone v. Commissioner of Pennsylvania*,[31] the right to carry firearms was denied to an Italian subject, notwithstanding the treaty clause permitting Italians the privilege of carrying on trade on the same terms as citizens of the United States. The court held that a state has the right to protect its wild game for its own citizens if it so pleases. State statutes regulating commercial fishing rights have been similarly upheld. Thus, in *Lubitch v. Pollock*,[32] and in *Leong Mow v. Board of Commissioners for Protection of Birds, Game and Fish*,[33] there is support for the proposition that the regulation of this type of state property is within the control of the state, and may not be touched by the treaty process. In the latter case, it was held that the most-favored nation clause of Chinese treaties, providing that citizens of foreign nations shall have the same privileges and rights of citizens and shall not be charged any higher impost or duties, does not include the right to take fish from the tide-waters of the state. This is a property right and not a mere privilege of citizenship, and since the title to all tide-waters of the state is in the state, the state may impose such conditions on the right to take fish therefrom as it sees fit, notwithstanding that the license fee exacted from foreigners is greater than that required from its own citizens. Thus the state could impose a higher fee on aliens if it saw fit.[34] However, though a measure of support may be obtained for the police power of the state over its own property, that power cannot be said to be inviolable.[35] A recent decision has expressly held otherwise. In *Makah Indian Tribe v. McCauley*,[36] the plaintiff Indians were secured their right to fish at their usual and accustomed grounds in the State of Washington. In bringing suit to prevent interference by state officers, acting under a state statute, the court held that the treaty reserved to the Indians the fishing rights, and that the claimants were not subject to any such interference by the state under its police power. Such property rights in the state will not be interfered with lightly; but it is impossible to conclude that they are outside the scope of the treaty process.

Attempts to prevent aliens from obtaining employment on the same basis as citizens, when there is a treaty on the subject, have likewise generally been held invalid. *In re Tiburcio Parrot*,[37] the provisions of Articles 5 and 6 of the Treaty with China recognized in 1868 the right of citizens of the Chinese race to emigrate to the United States for the purposes of curiosity, trade and permanent residence, and provided that Chinese subjects residing in the United States shall have the same privileges and immunities as citizens of the United States. The court held that the state act which made it a crime for a corporation formed under the laws of the state to employ, directly or indirectly, Mongolian labor was in conflict with the treaty. A similar fate befell anti-Mongolian legislation which provided that these aliens should not work or hold mines within the state.[38]

State workmen compensation acts have given rise to problems of interpretation. In *Vietti v MacKie*,[39] an action was instituted for compensation by the dependents of a workman who were naturalized natives of Italy, but residents of Kansas. It was held that a statute, which provided for a lesser compensation for non-citizens resident in the country than for citizens, was void, as being contrary to the letter and obvious intent of the treaty between Italy and the United States.[40] There are other cases to indicate a restrictive interpretation in this regard. In *Lukich v Department of Labor*,[41] it was held that the most-favored nation clause with Serbia, which covered taxes, trade, commerce, and industry, did not render inapplicable a state statute reducing non-resident aliens' workmen compensation by half. Such a statute is not in conflict with the treaty, which is referable to commerce and navigation, and does not bring "into operation general treaties with other nations concerning matters within the purview of the treaty involved." This is a most narrow interpretation and it is difficult to conceive a more obvious disregard of the true intent of the treaty. Further, it has been held that this clause[40] does not operate to give the subjects of the King of Italy, who have never been in the United States and have no property in that country, the right to maintain an action under a state statute which gives the right of compensation for wrongful death only to citizens or inhabitants of that state.[42] Apparently, so long as there is no discrimination against aliens, the state statute stands.

Leniency towards state statutes may be observed in various health statutes which have been upheld in the face of alledgedly conflicting treaty provisions. In *Compagnie Francaise and Company v. State Board of Health*,[43] the Supreme Court of Louisiana held that a quarantine law enacted by the state in the exercise of its police power, for the protection and preservation of public health, and which empowered the Board of Health to prohibit the introduction of persons into any infected portion of the state, was not in contravention of any treaty of the United States. This decision was upheld by the Supreme Court of the United States on the ground that the treaties did not, and were not intended to, deprive the state of those powers necessarily inherent in it and essential to the health and safety of its people. A similar result was reached in *Minneapolis St. Paul and Sault Ste. Marie Railway Company v. Milner*,[44] when the State of Michigan sought to detain and disinfect immigrants with the purpose of preventing the spread of infectious diseases. It was held that there was nothing in conflict with the usual friendship and commerce treaty with Norway and Sweden by the enforcement of its quarantine regulations. Again, in *re Wong Yung Quy*,[45] it was held that a statute of California which made it an offense to disinter or remove from the place of burial the remains of a deceased person without having obtained a permit, for which a fee was to be paid, did not violate a treaty with China providing that Chinese subjects in the United States should enjoy entire liberty of conscience and should be exempt from all disability or persecution on account of their religious faith. Justice Sawyer said: "Besides, it may well be questioned whether the treaty-making power would extend to the protection of practices under the guise of religious sentiment deleterious to the public health or to a subject matter within the acknowledged power of the state."[46]

Various miscellaneous cases complete the picture. In *Olsen v. Smith*,[47] it was held that a state pilotage law subjecting all vessels, domestic and foreign, to pilotage regulations, but which exempts, pursuant to law, coastwise steam vessels of the United States, was not in conflict with the provisions of the treaty between the United States and Great Britain to the effect that British vessels shall not be subject to any higher duty or other charges than vessels of the United States. Reasonable regulations are permitted notwithstanding that the letter of the treaty may be violated. In *Universal Adjustment Corporation v. Midland*,[48] it was held that the purpose of a treaty is not to secure to an alien corporation rights to sue in the courts of the other country regardless of reasonable rules and regulations. The treaty will not be interpreted as conferring on a corporation the right to sue in all courts in the United States without the payment of the usual fees and without observing all general laws and rules of the court binding upon citizens and aliens. Such rules are not discriminatory and do not fall within the spirit of the treaty. In *Todok v. Union State Bank of Harvard*,[49] a state law providing for the establishment of homesteads, with special exemption from execution and forced sale, and prohibiting conveyances of homestead property by any instrument not joined in by both husband and wife, was held not to be in conflict with a treaty giving subjects of both countries the full right to dispose of goods and effects. "It is not supposed that the treaty intended to secure the right of disposition in any manner whatever regardless of reasonable regulations in accordance with the property law of the country of the location bearing upon aliens and citizens alike."[50]

There are two recent cases in which the police power would appear to be still very much in issue in the American treaty-making process. In *Magnini v. Harnett*,[51] the New York court held that the privilege of operating motor vehicles in public thoroughfares of the state is an exercise of the police power of the state, which cannot be abrogated by international treaty. The court found that it did not violate the reciprocal trade and occupation provisions of the treaty with Great Britain, since there was no question of trade and occupation involved. However, the true basis of the decision appears to be in the holding that "this is clearly an exercise of the police power, the proper enforcement of which cannot be abrogated by international treaty, it being purely a question within the province of the states."[52]   The other decision is the *Pearl Assurance Company of London v. Harrington*.[53]   Here the Supreme Court of the United States held that a Massachusetts statute, which required an alien insurance company to have as its manager a United States citizen, does not violate the treaty with Great Britain of 1815, which provided for the freedom of commerce and the utmost protection of the citizens of each country in the territories of the other.   It was held that the treaty did not diminish the normal scope of the police power.

Though a fuller rationalization will be forthcoming after the leading decision of *Missouri v. Holland* is considered,[54] a few observations will be made here.   In attempting to answer the question whether there is any scope for the operation of the Tenth Amendment in the treaty process, it must be remembered that the above-mentioned decisions represent only a fraction of the cases decided, involving this point, and in no case has an excess of the treaty-making power been found.   The power has embraced all types of subject matters involving the admission of aliens, the imposition of taxes, the removal of disability of the rights and privileges of aliens to hold, devise, and transfer lands, the administration of estates, liquor conventions, extradition, acquisition and cession of territory, the jurisdiction of the courts, the issuance of patents to the public, promulgation of penal sanctions, the raising of revenue, the protection of migratory birds, the control of arms and ammunitions, the control of the drug traffic, air conventions, and copyright.   On all these subjects and others, the treaty-making power has been held supreme, and state laws have fallen when in conflict.   But the Tenth Amendment still has a measure of life in the treaty process, which, together with the operation of the test of the treaty being a "proper subject of international negotiation,"[55] would foil any attempt to ill-use the treaty process.   On the other hand, the Tenth Amendment, as a protection for certain inalienable rights, which cannot be infringed by the treaty making power, is a vague concept indeed, perhaps non-existent.   Although still occasionally brought up in judicial dicta, the Amendment forms no barrier in international intercourse for true subjects of negotiation with foreign states.[56]

The decisions speak for themselves. The American treaty-making power is very wide, but the courts still maintain a measure of control over the process. State laws generally will not be a bar if the subject is one proper for international regulation; but the Tenth Amendment is still a deterrent to a too expansive interpretation of treaty clauses.

AUSTRALIA

The Commonwealth Constitution contains no exact counterpart to Section 132 of the B.N.A. Act. The federal Parliament has the legislative power over subject matters contained in Sections 51 and 52, which the framers intended to be of broad import. Among the powers in Section 51 is *placitum xxix,* which empowers the Parliament to legislate on "external affairs". The history and early interpretation of the clause, at the time of federation, has already been referred to,[57] and, unlike in Canada, the treaty-performing power of the central government is adequately illustrated by reference to this clause only.

The interpretation of this clause has proceeded slowly, and decisions in point are few. At an early date the High Court of Australia interpreted *placitum xxix* to include legislation on fugitive offenders.[58] The Court at that time considered that the clause had the same force as Section 132 of the Canadian Constitution, since in this case it was declared that "the power includes the power to legislate as to the observance of treaties between Great Britain and foreign nations."[59] In *Robtelmas v. Brenan,*[60] it was held that the right to legislate with respect to external affairs included the legislative jurisdiction regarding the exclusion and deportation of subjects of other states. Two years later a somewhat broader dictum was forthcoming in *Attorney-General of New South Wales v. Collector of Customs for New South Wales.*[61] In determining the validity of the exercise of legislative powers concerning the imposition of customs duties that affected the Crown in the state, the Court remarked: " . . . The other powers expressly conferred on the Commonwealth may be considered, the power of controlling in every respect Australia's relations with the outside world. The control of trade and commerce with other countries, the imposition of custom duties, immigration, quarantine, and external affairs are all different aspects of Australia's relations with the outside world."[62] The Commonwealth was already paving the way for a broad interpretation of the clause to meet the demands of modern international life.

In *Roche v. Kronheimer*,[63] it was held that the Treaty of Peace Act of 1919 was within the legislative power of the Commonwealth Parliament.   Section 2 of this Act, which purported to reenact the provisions of Part X of the Treaty of Versailles,[64] was upheld so far as it provided machinery for enforcing those provisions.   Justice Higgins said: "The Constitution gives the Parliament power to make laws with respect a) to external affairs, b) the naval and military defence of the Commonwealth, c) trade and commerce with other countries.   It is difficult to say what limits (if any) can be placed on the power to legislate as to external affairs.   There are none expressed.   No doubt, complications may arise should the Commonwealth Parliament exercise the power in such a way as to produce conflict between relations of the Commonwealth with foreign governments and the relations of the British Government with foreign governments. It may be that the British Parliament preferred to take such a risk rather than curtail the selfgoverning powers of the Commonwealth, trusting, with a well-founded confidence, in the desire of the Australian people to act in cooperation with the British in regard to foreign governments."[65]   The limits of the clause appeared to be directed more by the relationship of Australia as a member of the British Commonwealth rather than by the fear that the power may be utilized to invade a residuary power of the states.[66]

In discussing the nature and extent of the authority of the Commonwealth Parliament over the mandated territory of New Guinea, the Court[67] held that, "it is interesting to observe that in Australia, Section 51, *placitum xxix* of the Constitution—the external affairs power—has been regarded as having the scope and purpose at least as that of Section 132 of the B. N. A. Act."   The decision also quoted a dispatch from the Imperial Secretary of State for the Colonies:[68]   "In the absence of any authoritative interpretation of the provisions of section 51, *placitum xxix*, of the Constitution, it is not for His Majesty's Government to say whether they confer on the Commonwealth Parliament the powers expressly conferred on the Canadian Parliament by the B.N.A. Act.   In matters in which your ministers do not consider it necessary or desirable to consult the state governments as being of federal concern, the Canadian rule must be applied to

Australia." Thus the interpretation of Section 51, *placitum xxix,* was to have the authority of Section 132, and this was affirmed as late as 1933, the date of the decision quoted above. At that time, Section 132 was restricted to the implementation of conventions and treaties made under the title of the British Empire, that is, after the decision in *The Radio Communications Case.*[69] As it was held in this case that the Canadian Parliament did not derive the power to implement the treaty by this Section but under the residuary powers of the federal government, the Commonwealth Parliament proceeded very slowly in implementing international agreements. This is well illustrated by its handling of labor conventions.

In a report to the International Labor Office in 1924, the Commonwealth Prime Minister explained that it was for the states of the Commonwealth to decide whether and to what extent certain draft conventions should be ratified and applied. A series of conferences between the Commonwealth and state authorities did little to clarify the situation.[70] In 1929, the Commonwealth maintained that all states must give their approval before the Parliament would proceed with the ratifications of these conventions. No substantial progress was made in various attempts to reach agreement. Finally, in 1936, the Commonwealth presented to the states two lists of conventions. The first list included conventions fully or substantially covered by existing legislation, and it was hoped that the states would agree to governmental ratification of these conventions. The second list included conventions which were more or less covered by state legislation, and necessitated only minor changes by the states. Thus, before 1936, the Commonwealth recognized that a large number of international subjects dealt with matters mainly within the jurisdiction of the states.

In 1920 the Commonwealth Parliament passed the Air Navigation Act[71] to implement the Convention signed by the representatives of the allied and associated powers relating to the control of aerial navigation.[72] The Act was attacked as being *ultra vires* the central government, and came to judicial attention in *The King v. Burgess; ex parte Henry,*[73] the issue being whether the Commonwealth Parliament has power to legislate with respect to flying operations carried on within the limits of a single state. All the old arguments, already mentioned,[74] for a restrictive interpretation were advanced but not accepted. Chief

Justice Latham referred to the *Aeronautics Case*[75] in Canada, and held that the Australian power to legislate on external affairs is at least as wide as the corresponding Section 132 in the Canadian Constitution, and hence there was authority for upholding the Act in question.[76] But he did not stop there. He referred to the American situation, particularly the case of *Missouri v. Holland*,[77] and concluded that, as both Canada and the United States have the power to legislate on subjects that, without a treaty, would be beyond the scope of the central legislature, Australia has the same power in Section 51, *placitum xxix*. Justice Starke concisely put the situation: "The power conferred by the Constitution upon the Commonwealth to make laws with respect to external affairs must be exercised with regard to the various constitutional limitations expressed or implied in the Constitution, which restrain generally the exercise of Federal powers. The Commonwealth cannot do what the Constitution forbids. But otherwise the power is comprehensive in terms and must be commensurate with the obligations that the Commonwealth may properly assume in its relations with other Powers or States. It is impossible, I think, to define more accurately the precise limits of the power."[78]

Justices Evatt and McTiernan are more definite in their judgment. Referring to the opinion of Sir William H. Moore,[79] on the extent of the "external affairs" power, they dispose of it by holding that it was made at a time when the Commonwealth's power under Sections 51 and 52 of the Constitution was undefined and indefinite. The Constitution must first be interpreted before it is possible to determine the extent of the exclusive power of the states. Inferentially, in foreign relations the power of the state is non-existent.[80] They also refer to an American decision,[81] and note the expanding orbit of proper subjects for international negotiation. Finally, they sum up their conclusions by saying that "the legislative power of the Commonwealth over *external affairs* certainly includes the power to execute within the Commonwealth treaties and conventions entered into with foreign powers. The legislative power in Section 51 is granted *subject to this Constitution* so that such treaties and conventions could not be used to enable Parliament to set at nought constitutional guarantees elsewhere contained, such, for instance, as sections 6, 28, 41, 80, 92, 99, 100, 116, or 117 ... it is certain that the power includes, but also extends further than, the power assigned to the Parliament of Canada by section 132 of the British North America Act."[82]

This decision was pronounced before the Canadian *Labor Conventions Case,*[83] in which it was held that the Canadian Parliament could not override the express grant of legislative authority to the provinces by the treaty process. The effect of this decision in Australia was doubtful, but the doubt was soon to be resolved. In *Ffrost v. Stevenson,*[84] decided in the next year, it was argued that the legislative power over external affairs was not to receive the wide interpretation of that contained in the *King v. Burgess* case, and that the clause was applicable to, and in no wise superior to, the other *placita* in Section 51. In other words, the argument, based on the decision in *The Labor Conventions Case,* was that it could be used only to implement treaties and conventions when the Commonwealth Parliament had the necessary authority to do so. Justice Evatt thought otherwise, and re-affirmed the principle in the previous decision. He distinguished the Canadian Constitution and concluded that "section 51, pl. xxix cannot be limited to treaties entered into by Australia as part of the Empire and necessarily extends to all treaties and conventions entered into by Australia by virtue of her new status as an international entity."[85] Any hopes or fears that *The Labor Conventions Case* might alter the situation were put to rest. In this case, Justice Evatt also answered the common argument in both the United States and Canada, namely that by the treaty process there was nothing to prevent the executive from altering the Constitution. His reply was that the government can do nothing that the Constitution forbids, and, as provisions for amendment of the Constitution are contained in another section, the Constitution is thus protected. This would support the argument of limitation in the United States that, if the subject-matter of the treaty was of such magnitude as to involve a change in the Constitution, it would be an excess of the power and thus void.[86] It would not be a proper subject of international negotiation.

CANADA

Canada has no clause similar to that of Article 6, Section 2 in the American Constitution, providing that treaties shall be the supreme law of the land and override conflicting state laws. The complete array of Canadian powers with respect to the treaty process are, to date, found in Sections 91 and 92 and, exceptionally, in Section 132.

It is evident from the B.N.A. Act itself that the framers intended a pro-federal enactment.[87] The central authority was given a residual power concerning all matters not coming within the sixteen classes of subject-matters contained in Section 92. The obvious intention was that the central government was to have all legislative power, with only the express provincial classes subtracted.   Possibly, if the framers had stopped there, some of the confusion would have been avoided.   But, "for greater certainty" of federal paramountcy, they went on to enumerate twenty-nine classes of subject-matters, intended to illustrate the powers that were within the exclusive central control.   The course of Canadian constitutional interpretation has made it obvious that the concept that the twenty-nine classes are meant to be but illustrations of the federal legislative powers, has been disregarded.   The jurisdiction of the provinces extends to the sixteen classes of subject-matters characterized in the residuary clause of Section 92 as matters of "local or private nature in the provinces," a phrase which correctly describes everything in Section 92.   In terms of antithesis to this phrase, the manifest intention of the framers was to give everything of a non-local, non-private, non-provincial nature, that is, of an interprovincial nature or national character, to the central government.

The Judicial Committee of the Privy Council, apparently concerned to protect the provincial authority, began at an early date to restrict competing federal clauses, so that now it can be justly said that the provincial powers have far outranged the powers of the federal government in many matters.   To consider this proposition briefly, reference will be made to the federal "trade and commerce" clause and its competing provincial counterpart, "property and civil rights in the provinces".   In the *Parson's Case* in 1881,[88] the Privy Council referred to the necessity of restricting the former clause, to preserve from serious curtailment the degree of autonomy that the provinces were intended to possess.   This important case upheld a provincial statute dealing with contracts of insurance as being properly within the provincial power.   Fifteen years later, in *Bank of Toronto v. Lambe,*[89] the same court held that the trade and commerce clause could not be invoked to prevent provincial taxation of Canadian banks.   Again, in *Re Board of Commerce Act*[90] in 1922, the Privy Council denied the right of the Canadian Government to prevent profiteering and the fixation of fair prices. The Court held that the clause did not enable the government to deal with particular trades in which Canadians were otherwise free to engage.[91] All these subject matters denied to federal jurisdiction, of course came within the "property and civil rights" clause of the provinces.

Another important example of this restrictive interpretation, is the course of interpretation of the residuary clause of the British North America Act.[92] This clause, originally intended to assist in giving a broad legislative mandate to the central authority, was first interpreted in *Russell v. The Queen*.[93] The case held that Canadian liquor legislation was valid under the clause, as being a matter of general concern, where uniformity of legislation for the whole was desirable. However this decision was followed by the *Local Prohibition Case*,[94] ruling that the clause was supplementary to the twenty-nine enumerated powers, and prohibited the central government from infringing on provincial legislation unless the power was found in one of the express clauses in Section 91. The power now includes only matters not enumeratively entrusted to the provinces,[95] and necessary legislation under circumstances of grave national emergency.[96]

With these principles of Canadian constitutional law in mind, only four decisions relative to the Canadian treaty-performing power need be considered.[97] In 1911, Great Britain and Japan concluded a treaty providing that the subjects of each nation should have full liberty of residing in each other's territories, and in relation to their industries should be on the same footing as the subjects of the most favored nation. Canada implemented the provisions of this treaty by passing the Japanese Treaty Act in 1913.[98] The province of British Columbia then enacted legislation providing that all leases, contracts, and concessions made by the government should provide that no Japanese or Chinese be employed in connection therewith. In determining the validity of this enactment, the Privy Council held that, as respects the Chinese, the legislation was a valid exercise of the provincial right to manage its own property.[99] However, it was legislation invalid respecting the Japanese, and was overridden by the Canadian statute under the authority of the central government, conferred by Section 132. This government thus had the power to perform obligations of Canada when the treaty was made by the King for Canada, and the exclusive capacity of entering into agreements was within the control of the Imperial government.

In 1919 Canada had entered into the Convention Relating to the Regulation of Aerial Navigation, which resulted from the Peace Conference at Paris.[100]   This Convention was subsequently ratified by His Majesty on behalf of the British Empire, at the time when the Canadian representative signed for Canada under the title of, and as a member of, the British Empire.   In accordance with the treaty obligations, the Canadian Parliament enacted the Air Board Act of 1919[101] relating to the control and regulation of aeronautics, including the granting of certificates to persons to act as pilots, the inspection and licensing of aircraft, and the inspection and licensing of airdromes and air stations. On appeal to the Privy Council,[102] their Lordships considered that the legislation could be supported under Section 132, as giving the Canadian Parliament "all the powers necessary and proper for performing the obligations towards foreign countries arising under treaties between the empire and such foreign countries."   The Convention was literally, in form and in fact, between the British Empire as such, and the foreign countries parties to it, hence, under circumstances in which Section 132 gives the Canadian Parliament supreme and overriding authority.

The Aeronautics Case was followed by *The Radio Communications Case*,[103] the third to be considered.   Canada had concluded an agreement with seventy-nine other countries, known as the International Radio Telegraph Convention, in 1927.   It was subsequently ratified on behalf of His Majesty's Government in Canada by an instrument signed by the Secretary of State for External Affairs.   Parliament then dealt with the subject matter by enacting the Radio Telegraph Act.[104]   In affirming the decision of the Supreme Court of Canada,[105] the Privy council said that "this idea of Canada as a Dominion being bound by a Convention equivalent to a treaty was unthought of in 1867.   It is not expected that such matters should be dealt with in the explicit words of section 91.   The only class of treaty was that expressed in section 132.   Not mentioned explicitly such legislation falls within the general words of the opening section of section 91 which assigns to the Dominion the right to 'make laws for the peace, order and good government of Canada.' "[106]

So the validity of this legislation in *The Radio Communciations Case* was dependent on the operation of the residuary clause, not Section 132.

On the strength of this decision, legal opinion was generally in accord that the central Parliament did have all the state's performing power,[107] and that the provinces were effectively excluded from the process.   However, in 1937, the Privy Council made it clear, in *The Labor Conventions Case*,[108] that such was not the legal position.   In this case, the courts were called upon to decide the validity of legislation which Parliament intended to enact, to fulfill the obligations of three labor conventions, namely, the Weekly Rest Convention, the Minimum Wage-Finding Machinery Convention, of 1928, and the Hours of Work Convention of 1921.[109]   The Privy Council held that any Parliamentary implementing legislation would be invalid.[110]   In their Lordship's opinion, such legislation would not fall either under Section 132 or the residuary clause, the latter being generally thought to be the basis for the decision in *The Radio Communications Case*.   They explained that the Radiotelegraph Act was valid under the residuary clause, only because it dealt with a class of subject-matter not included in the enumeration of either Sections 91 or 92.   Such a matter did not of necessity encroach on provincial legislation, when not mentioned specifically in either of these Sections.   Legislation to effect these labor conventions was an infringement on the exclusive jurisdiction of the provinces to deal with "property and civil rights within the provinces," and also an interference in "matters of a local and private nature."   Section 132 would not assist the Central Parliament since it concerned only legislative powers to perform obligations imposed upon Canada as part of the Empire, by the Imperial executive responsible to and controlled by the Imperial Parliament.[111]   The argument of the federal authorities that, inasmuch as Canadian obligations to enact labor legislation arose ultimately under the Treaty of Versailles, which is without question a treaty between the British Empire and foreign countries, and falls within the category of "empire" treaties, was overruled.   It was held that there was no obligation to legislate on any of the matters "until the Canadian executive, left with an unfettered discretion of their own volition, acceded to the conventions, a *novus actus* not determined by the treaty."[112]

Finally, it was held that not only did the subject matters in question fall within the provincial legislative competence, but the residuary clause could not be utilized to give federal jurisdiction over a matter of general concern affecting the body "national politic", if otherwise it was within the provincial legislative domain. Their Lordships repudiated the existence of such a doctrine.[113]

The present position of Canada is stated by the Privy Council: "In totality of legislative powers the Dominion and provinces together, (Canada) is fully equipped. But the legislative powers remain distributed, and if in the exercise of her new functions derived from her new international status, she incurs obligations, they must, so far as legislation is concerned, when they deal with provincial classes of subjects, be dealt with by the totality of her power."[114]

SWITZERLAND

The Swiss problem of treaty performance is more political than legal. By Article 8 of the Constitution, the Federal Assembly has plenary control over foreign relations. This includes both the capacity to enter into international agreements, and the power to perform their obligations.[115] However, the central authority proceeds very slowly when implementation means transgressing the legislative jurisdiction of the cantons.[116] But even though the necessary implementing legislation is within cantonal control, the federal government has three ways to obtain jurisdiction. It may, by constitutional practice, legislate on the subject within cantonal control, under its power to perform treaty obligations; it may put the treaty to the test of a popular referendum and so acquire legislative jurisdiction, by what would in effect be a constitutional amendment; or the Federal Assembly may institute a constitutional amendment under the authority of Article 121. Theoretically the Swiss central government appears to be in the most advantageous position of all the federations with respect to the problem of treaty performance.

The Federal Assembly has little need for intrusion on the cantonal legislative sphere. The central government is rapidly acquiring the omnipotent powers of a government of a unitary state. Only a few of the more important powers need to be reviewed, to illustrate this trend in Switzerland. The revision of the Constitution in 1874 gave to the central government control over the army, over fishing and hunting, over railways (their construction, maintenance and administration), and over higher education.   Such items as taxes, customs and imports, regulations respecting the exercise of industrial enterprise, posts and tele-graphs, routes and bridges (and their maintenance), money, weights and measures were added to federal jurisdiction.   Since 1880, these subjects have been expanded and cantonal control has decreased markedly.   In 1887, the federal government was given control over patent legislation; in 1897, over dams and for-ests, and pure food laws.   In 1908, the controls over hydraulic power were committed to the Federal Assembly.   In 1921, Articles 37 *bis* and 37 *terti* gave to that body legislative juris-diction over motor vehicles and aerial navigation respectively. In 1925, old age pensions became its responsibility, and in 1929, the control of wheat and its far-reaching consequences on the economy of the State.   In 1938, the control over explosives be-came a federal problem, and, finally, in 1947, a series of economic measures gave the Federal Assembly almost complete control in this sphere.   Notwithstanding these broad powers now within the federal orbit, the cantonal legislatures are still of consider-able consequence in the state.   They have primary jurisdiction over peace and order, the construction of local works, and ele-mentary education.   Also it is by being a citizen of a canton that national citizenship is acquired, and the laws of the cantonal legislatures determine many of the citizens' rights.

CONCLUSION

In attempting a comparative rationale of the decisions that have been discussed, it is important to refer to the leading case in the United States of *Missouri v Holland,* decided in 1920.[117] This case upheld an act of 1918, which prohibited the killing of certain migratory birds, except as permitted by regulations to be made by the Secretary of Agriculture.   This legislation was ex-ecutory of the Migratory Bird Treaty with Great Britain in 1916.[118]   Before the Supreme Court, the argument for the state of Missouri was based on the fact that the states had abso-lute power over the wild game within their borders, and upon the existence of limitations on the treaty process, which included the "purely internal affairs which concern the lives, liberties and prop-erties of the people and the internal order, improvement and prosperity of the state."   This, of course, is the limitation of the Tenth Amendment. The opinion of the Court, handed down by Justice Holmes, disposed of the first contention by maintaining that at least the state control of migratory birds is only a qualified control, and exists only when the state is regulating within its borders. With the second contention, Justice Holmes took direct issue. He said that the question raised is the general one of whether the treaty and statute are void, as an interference with the rights reserved to the states. "To answer this question it is not enough to refer to the Tenth Amendment, reserving the powers not delegated to the United States, because by Article 2, Section 2, the power to make treaties is delegated expressly, and by Article 6 treaties made under the authority of the United States, along with the Constitution and the Laws of the United States made in pursuance thereof, are declared the supreme law of the land. If the treaty is valid there can be no dispute about the validity of the statute under Article 1, Section 8, as a necessary and proper means to execute the powers of the government."[119]

The cases holding the previous legislation invalid are no use here, he pointed out, for "acts of Congress are the supreme law of the land only when made in pursuance of the Constitution, while treaties are declared to be so when made under the authority of the United States." It may be possible to infer from this statement that there are no constitutional limitations on the treaty-making power;[120] but almost in the next sentence he admitted that some limitations do exist, though "such limitations must be ascertained in a different way".[121] "It is obvious that there may be many matters of the sharpest exigency for the national well being that an act of Congress could not deal with but that a treaty followed by such an act could, and it is not lightly to be assumed that, in matters requiring national action, 'a power which must belong to and somewhere reside in every civilized government' is not to be found . . . with regard to that we may add that when we are dealing with words that are also a constituent act, like the Constitution of the United States, we must realize that they have called into life a being the development of which could not have been foreseen completely by the most gifted of its begetters. It was enough for them to realize or to hope that they have created an organism; it has taken a century and has cost their successors much sweat and blood to prove that they have created a nation. The case before us must be considered in the light of our whole experience and not

merely in that of what was said a hundred years ago."[122] In this
factors in the treaty processes of federal states: first, that the
declaration Justice Holmes recognized two salient and important
power must reside somewhere in every civilized government; and,
secondly, that it is a constitution that is to be interpreted. For
the first, the finding is simply a restatement of the truism that a
state cannot maintain satisfactory diplomatic relations, if the
treaty process is subject to divided control in its "capacity" or
"performance" aspects. As for the second, the opinion merely
reiterated the common rule of American constitutional construction. To quote Chief Justice Marshall: "We must never forget
that it is a Constitution we are expounding . . . a Constitution intended to endure for ages and consequently to be adapted to the
various crises of human affairs."[123]

In the light of *Missouri v. Holland*, the positions of the other
federations will be considered. Although the Australian High
Court has abandoned its former position of liberal construction[124]
in the *Engineer's Case* of 1920,[125] this has not prevented it from
taking a realistic stand on the treaty process, as evidenced in
The King v. Burgess; ex parte Henry and *Ffrost v. Stevenson*.[126]
But is the performing power unlimited in this federation? The
vagueness of any limitation in the express words of the Constitution and in the judicial interpretations has already been noted
in the United States.[127] Little assistance may be found in the
Australian decisions or practice, aside from the dicta of judges
to the effect that the provisions of the Constitution itself cannot
be set to nought by this means.[128] The vague phrase that the
power extends to all "proper subjects of international negotiation"
indicates little more than that the judiciary has not renounced all
control over the process. Its limits cannot be defined. The
more particular limitation which Justice Holmes describes as a
possible "radiation of the Tenth Amendment" is equally vague,
and, as already mentioned, probably means little more than a
"brake" on too extensive an interpretation of treaty provisions
that might conflict with state laws.

We may conclude that constitutional limitations on the
treaty process should be ascertained only by the Constitution itself, in the light of current internationalism. In foreign affairs,
the state must act as a whole, not only in entering into treaties,
but also in performing them.

In contradiction to the above, there is the Canadian dilemma. In *The Labor Conventions Case*,[129] the Privy Council emphatically declared that "it would be remarkable that while the Dominion could not initiate legislation, however desirable, which affected civil rights in the Provinces, yet its government, not responsible to the provinces nor controlled by Provincial Parliaments, need only agree with a foreign country to enact such legislation, and its Parliament would be forthwith clothed with authority to affect Provincial rights to the full extent of such agreement. Such a result would appear to undermine the constitutional safeguards of Provincial constitutional autonomy." With such an expression of fear for loss of provincial autonomy in this regard, where can the consideration be found that the "power must reside somewhere," and whence the complete disregard for examining the Constitution "in the light of our whole existence"?

Although Section 132 has an overriding effect over provincial legislation, it has been relegated to a position that no longer exists, that is, in relation to treaties made by Canada as a member of the British Empire. The result is that Canada cannot enter into international agreements which require legislative action outside the orbit of Section 91, without the prior approval of the provinces. Otherwise there is a very real possibility of defaulting her international obligations. In view of the identical histories of these federations, it is difficult to reason that the legislative power with respect to "external affairs" in the Australian Constitution was intended to be broader than the corresponding Section 132. It is also difficult to agree that Section 132 was worded too narrowly.[130] Its phraseology was not a "work of art," but quite broad enough to include implementation of all treaties that Canada might conclude "as a result of her new status." The present unsatisfactory position of Canada's treaty-performing power is due to inaccurate and inconsistent interpretation of the clause.

[1.] *Supra,* pp. 94 ff.   [2.] *National Supremacy,* (1913), Ch. 6.   [3.] *Ibid,* p. 308.

[4.] *Limitations on the Treaty Making Power,* (1915).

[5.] See the similar opinion of Mikell, William E., "Extent of the Treaty Making Power of the President and Senate of the United States," (1909) *University of Pennsylvania Law Review* 435, 528.

[6.] He defines it: "The police power of a state may be said to be that unlimited, inalienable, inherent power in every State to protect the health, the safety, and the morals of the people, and to preserve and protect its autonomy at all times." *Limitations on the Treaty Making Power,* (1915), p. 287.

[7.] *Ibid,* p. 431.

[8.] See the numerous examples collected in Corwin, Edward S., *National Supremacy,* (1913), Ch. 6, and in Tucker, Henry St. George, *ibid,* Ch. 10.

[9.] (1840) 14 Peters (United States Supreme Court) 540.

[10.] (1847) 5 Howard (United States Supreme Court) 504.

[11.] (1849) 7 Howard (United States Supreme Court) 283.

[12.] See also *People v. Naglee.* (1850) 1 California 232. For a more modern expression, see *Antosz (Jantosz) v. State Compensation Commissioner,* (1947) 43 South Eastern 2nd (United States) 397; 130 West Virginia 260. Burke, D. Barlow "Federal Treaties and State Sovereignty," (1942) 46 *Dickinson Law Review* 246, maintains that these dicta have still considerable force today, and have never been overruled.

[13.] *In re Knutzen's Estate,* (1945) 161 Pacific 2nd (United States) 598; California Appeals, 1945.

[14.] *Makah Indian Tribe v. McCauley,* (1941) 39 Federal Supplement (United States) 75; *Watson v. Hooey,* (1943) 59 Federal Supplement (United States) 197.

[15.] (1796) 3 Dallas (United States Supreme Court) 198.

[16.] See those cited in Crandall, Samuel B., *Treaties: Their Making and Enforcement,* (2nd. ed., 1916), pp. 247-51.

[17.] (1921) 274 Federal (United States) 841.

[18.] (1817) 2 Wheaton (United States Supreme Court) 259.

[19.] (1890) 133 United States 258.

[20.] Another leading case, often quoted in this regard, is *Hauenstein v. Lynham,* (1879) 100 United States 48.

[21.] (1935) 281 New York Supplement 617.

[22.] Similarly, see *State v. Staeheli,* (1920) 192 Pacific (United States) 991; 112 Washington 344; *Chryssikos v. Demarco,* (1919) 107 Atlantic (United States) 358; 134 Maryland, 533.

[23.] (1914) 147 North Western (United States) 1098; 166 Iowa 617.

[24.] *Petersen et al v. State of Iowa,* (1917) 245 United States 170. See also *Duus v. Brown,* (1917) 245 United States 176.

[25.] (1929) 279 United States 47.

[26.] (1943) 59 Federal Supplement (United States) 197.

[27.] Similarly in *Succession of Sala,* (1897) 24 Southern (United States) 674, 50 Louisiana Annotated 1009, a provision of a treaty was not violated, since it covered only personal goods, and thus a tax on immovable goods was valid, notwithstanding that the same provision permitted the alien to sell real property and withdraw the proceeds "without molestation and exempt from all rights of detraction".

[28.] (1915) 239 United States 175.

[29.] (1903) 191 United States, 207, p. 223; *ibid,* pp. 191-92.

[30.] To the same effect: *Crane v. People of the State of New York,* (1915) 239 United States 195; *Lee v. City of Lynn,* (1916) 111 North Eastern (United States) 700; 223 Massachusetts 109; *Cornelius v. Seattle,* (1923) 213 Pacific (United States) 17; 123 Washington 550. However, in the previous case of *Baker v. City of Portland,* (1879) 5 Sawyer (United States Federal Court) 566, it was held that a state had no power in any way to limit the operation of a treaty of the United States, and the provision prohibiting the employment of Chinese on street improvements or public works was invalid because it was in conflict with the treaty permitting the Chinese resident to enjoy the rights of the most favored nation.

[31.] (1914) 232 United States, 138 [32.] (1925) 6 Federal 2nd (United States) 237.

[33.] (1911) 185 Federal (United States) 223.

[34.] However, in *Silver v. State*, (1917) 93 South Eastern (United States) 145; 147 Georgia 162, it was held that there must be no discrimination. Similarly, *In re Ah Chong*, (1880) 2 Federal (United States) 733, decided that all out-of-state people can be prevented from taking fish from state waters, but there must be no discrimination against aliens, for otherwise there is conflict with the treaty. *Poon v Miller*, (1921) 234 South Western (United States) 573; Texas Civil Appeals, is an example of a state law, denying the right of the alien to fish, in conflict with a treaty, and so invalid.

[35.] Note the power of the government to cede territory, *supra*, p. 97.

[36.] (1941) 39 Federal Supplement (United States) 75.

[37.] (1880) 1 Federal (United States) 481.

[38.] See also *Chapman v. Toy Long*, (1876) 4 Sawyer (United States Federal Court) 18; *Asskura v. City of Seattle*, (1924) 265 United States 332. But in the case of *Ohio v. Deckenbach*, (1927) 274 United States 392, it was held that some latitude must be permitted to the local authorities to appraise local conditions, and so upheld an act which prevented the issuance of licenses to aliens to operate a pool-and billiard-hall.

[39.] (1921) 197 Pacific (United States) 881; 109 Kansas 179.

[40.] The treaty provision reads as follows: "The citizens of each of the High Contracting Parties shall receive in the states and territories of the other the most constant security and protection for their persons and property and for their rights, including that form of protection granted by any state of national law which establishes a civil responsibility for injuries or for death caused by negligence and gives to the relatives or heirs of the deceased a right of action, which right shall not be restricted on account of the nationality of the said relative or heirs; and shall enjoy in this respect the same rights and privileges as are or shall be granted to nationals, provided that they submit themselves to the conditions imposed upon the latter."

[41.] (1934) 29 Pacific 2nd (United States) 388; 176 Washington, 221.

[42.] *Fulco v. Schuylkill Stone Company*, (1909)) 169 Federal (United States) 98. In *Madonna v. Wheeling Steel Corporation*, (1928) 28 Federal 2nd (United States) 710, the provisions in a Workmen's Compensation Act requiring the injured party's father or mother to be a resident of the United States were held invalid, since they discriminate against aliens.

[43.] (1902) 51 Louisiana Annotated 645; affirmed by the United States Supreme Court, 186 United States 380.

[44.] (1893) 57 Federal (United States) 276.

[45.] (1880) 6 Sawyer (United States Federal Court) 442.

[46.] In the case of the *State v. Barlow*, (1944) 153 Pacific 2nd (United States) 647; 107 Utah 292, an enactment making it unlawful for any person to cohabit with more than one person of the opposite sex did not conflict with the Treaty of Guadaloupe Hildago guaranteeing religious freedom to Mexican citizens during the limited time in which they could remain Mexican citizens or become citizens of the United States. The protection of religous freedom was not intended to protect polygamy.

[47.] (1904) 195 United States 332.

[48.] (1933) North Eastern (United States) 152; 281 Massachusetts 303.

[49.] (1930) 281 United States 449. [50.] *Ibid*, p. 454. [51.] (1938) 8 New York Supplement 2nd 447.

[52.] *Ibid*, p. 448. [53.] (1941) 313 United States 549.

[54.] (1920) 252 United States 416; *infra*, pp. 128 ff. [55.] *Supra*, pp. 71 ff.

[56.] *Infra*, p. 178. Also the expanding judicial constructions of the federal legislative powers have assisted in this position, particularly the commerce clause.

[57.] *Supra*, pp. 33 ff.

[58.] *McKelvy v. Meagher*, (1906) 4 Commonwealth Law Reports (Australia) 265. However, it was not considered necessary to expand it to include extradition.

[59.] *Ibid*, p. 286; *supra*, pp. 28 ff. [60.] (1906) 4 Commonwealth Law Reports (Australia) 395.

[61.] (1908) 5 Commonwealth Law Reports (Australia) 818. [62.] *Ibid*, p. 842.

[63.] (1921) 29 Commonwealth Law Reports (Australia) 329.

[64.] Part X referred to the deprivation of property belonging to German subjects, for the satisfaction of war claims.

[65.] (1921) 29 Commonwealth Law Reports (Australia) 329, p. 339. This statement was upheld by Justice Evatt in *Victorian Stevedoring General Contracting Company Limited and Meakes v. Dignan*, (1931) 46 Commonwealth Law Reports (Australia) 73, p. 122.

[66.] After the decision in this case, it was the opinion of Mr. Latham, then Attorney General for the Commonwealth and later Chief Justice of the High Court, that the power could be used to invade the rights reserved to the state. Staricoff, Joseph, "Australia and the Constitution of the I. L. O," (1935) 32 *International Labor Review* 577.

[67.] *Jolley v. Mainka*, (1933) 49 Commonwealth Law Reports (Australia) 242, p. 284.

[68.] *Ibid*, p. 287. [69.] *Supra*, p. 32; *infra*, p. 125.

[70.] Stewart, Robert B., *Treaty Relations of the British Commonwealth of Nations*, (1939), pp. 306 ff.

[71.] *Commonwealth Acts*, Vol. XVIII, (1920), p. 159. [72.] *Supra*, p. 55.

[73.] (1936) 55 Commonwealth Law Reports (Australia) 618.

[74.] *Supra*, pp. 34-35. [75.] *Supra*, p. 30; *infra*, p. 125.

[76.] However, the High Court found that the regulations made under this Act were invalid because not made with the purpose of implementing the convention.

[77.] (1936) 55 Commonwealth Law Reports (Australia) 618, p. 638.

[78.] *Ibid*, p. 658. [79.] *Supra*, p. 34.

[80.] (1936) 55 Commonwealth Law Reports (Australia) 618, p. 679.

[81.] *Ibid*, p. 680. [82.] *Ibid*, p. 687.

[83.] (1936) Appeal Cases (England) 342; *infra*, pp. 126-127.

[84.] (1937) 58 Commonwealth Law Reports (Australia) 528.

[85.] *Ibid*, p. 599. [86.] *Supra*, p. 73; *infra*, pp. 169-170. [87.] *Supra*, pp. 18-19.

[88.] *Citizen's Insurance Company v. Parsons*, (1881) 7 Appeal Cases (England) 96.

[89.] (1887) 12 Appeal Cases (England) 575. [90.] (1922) 1 Appeal Cases (England) 191.

[91.] Similarly, see *Natural Products Marketing Case, (Attorney-General for British Columbia v. Attorney-General fro Canada)*, (1937) Appeal Cases (England) 377.

[92.] The residuary clause is not one clause, like the Tenth Amendment of the American Constitution. It consists of the general purport of the opening and concluding words of Section 91.

[93.] (1882) 7 Appeal Cases (England) 829.

[94.] *(Attorney-General for Ontario v. Attorney-General for Canada)*, (1896) Appeal Cases (England) 348.

[95.] *The Radio Communication Case*, (1932) Appeal Cases (England) 304.

[96.] *Cooperative Committee on Japanese Canadians v. Attorney-General for Canada*, (1947) Appeal Cases (England) 87. Also see *infra*, note 113.

[97.] Only the major arguments will be discussed to afford a comparative analysis with the other federal states. For more detailed discussions, see Jenks, C. Wilfred, "The Present status of the Bennett Ratifications of International Labour Conventions," (1937) 15 *Canadian Bar Review*, 464; Jennings, W. Ivor, "Dominion Legislation and Treaties," (1937) 15 *Canadian Bar Review*. 455; MacKenzie, Norman A. M., "The Treaty Making Power in Canada," (1925) 19 *American Journal of International Law* 489; MacDonald, Vincent C., "Canada's Power to perform Treaty Obligations," (1933) 11 *Canadian Bar Review* 581.

[98.] (Canada), 3 and 4 *Statutes of George* V, Ch. 27.

[99.] *Brooks-Bidlake and Whittall v. Attorney-General for British Columbia*, (1923) Appeal Cases (England) 450.

[100.] *Supra*, p 30.

[101.] (Canada), 12 and 13 *Statutes of George V*, Ch. 11. Title changed to the Aeronautics Act, *Revised Statutes of Canada*, 1927, Ch. 3.

[102.] (1932) Appeal Cases (England) 54; from the Supreme Court of Canada, (1930) Supreme Court Reports (Canada) 663. Their Lordships also expressed the view that the subject of aerial navigation was now a matter of national importance or of general concern, that is, coming within the residuary clause. This view was held to be the true basis of the Privy Council decision in *Johannesson v. Rural Municipality of West St. Paul*, (1952) 1 Supreme Court Reports (Canada) 292.

[103.] (1932) Appeal Cases (England) 304; *supra*, p. 32.

[104.] (Canada) 3 and 4 *Statutes of George V.*, Ch. 43. *Revised Statutes of Canada*, 1927, Ch. 195.

[105.] (1931) Supreme Court Reports (Canada) 541. [106.] (1932) Appeal Cases (England) 304, p. 312.

[107.] For example, see the Canadian *Debates of the House of Commons*, February, 1935, pp. 90 ff.

[108.] (1937) Appeal Cases (England) 326.

[109.] These conventions were ratified by Canada in April, 1935.

[110.] After the Supreme Court of Canada had evenly divided on the question; (1936) Supreme Court Reports (Canada) 461.

[111.] (1937) Appeal Cases (England) 326, pp. 349-50.   [112.] *Ibid*, p. 350.

[113.] But see *Attorney-General for Ontario v. Canada Temperance Federation*, (1946) Appeal Cases (England) 193; and *Johannesson v. Rural Municipality of West St. Paul*, (1952) Supreme Court Reports (Canada) 292, for recognition of the doctrine by the Privy Council, and now by the Supreme Court of Canada in some form.

[114.] (1937) Appeal Cases (England) 326, p. 354.

[115.] Burckhardt, Walther, *Le Droit Fédéral Suisse,* Vol. 5, pp. 1, 414.

[116.] Secretan, Jacques, "Swiss Constitutional Problems and the I. L. O.," (1947) 56 *International Labour Review* 1.

[117.] (1920) 252 United States, 416.   This case was omitted from discussion when the legislative powers of the component parts of the United States were considered, *supra,* pp. 107-118, because the arguments advanced are better used as a vehicle for comparison and summation of this problem.   It is to be noted that the last part of Section 2 of the Bricker Amendment, the so-called "which clause," was directed specifically at the effect of this decision.   The Section reads: "A treaty shall become effective as internal law in the United States only through legislation *which would be valid in the absence of treaty.*" (Italics supplied).

[118.] Prior to this, an enactment to implement this treaty had been held invalid in *United States v. Shauver,* (1914) 214 Federal (United States) 154, as a violation of powers reserved to the states by the Tenth Amendment.

[119.] (1920) 252 United States 416, p. 432.   [120.] *Supra,* p. 95.

[121.] (1920) 252 United States 416, p. 433.

[122.] *Ibid,* p. 434.

[123.] *McCulloch v. Maryland,* (1819) 4 Wheaton (United States Supreme Court) 316, p. 407.   See also Justice Holmes, *Missouri, Kansas and Texas Railway v. May,* (1904) 194 United States 267, p. 270.

[124.] For example, *Attorney-General for New South Wales v. Brewery Employees Union of New South Wales,* (1908) 6 Commonwealth Law Reports (Australia) 469, p. 612 *per* Justice Higgins quoting Chief Justice Marshall, *ibid.*

[125.] (1920) 28 Commonwealth Law Reports (Australia) 129.

[126.] *Supra,* pp. 120 ff.   [127.] *Supra,* pp. 95-96.

[128.] *Supra,* pp. 71, 121-122.

[129.] (1937) Appeal Cases (England) 326, p. 352.

[180.] *Ffrost v. Stevenson,* (1937) 58 Commonwealth Law Reports (Australia) 528, p. 598, (*per* Justice Evatt).

CHAPTER 7

CONSTITUTIONAL LIMITATIONS AND INTERNATIONAL LAW

International legal rules originate and develop for a reason. Rules relative to the treaty process are designed to further international collaboration and to protect the states from irresponsible and incompetent executives. International cognizance of "organic capacities and incapacities" of the states does neither. It serves only to obscure and makes for further uncertainty in this branch of international law. How far, then, should constitutional limitations receive cognizance in international law?[1]

According to many authorities international law demands that certain types of constitutional limitations must be complied with for the sake of validity, and that if the provisions of such limitations are disregarded, the resultant agreement will be both nationally and internationally void. We propose to disprove this proposition, on legal and practical grounds. However, the thesis of this chapter is directed against any international legal interference in general, rather than to disproving the particular solutions advocated. First, it will be shown unequivocally that constitutional limitations affecting the performance of treaty obligations are within the sole concern of individual states, and thus outside international legal control. Second, consideration will be given to the arguments in favor of international legal cognizance of constitutional limitations. Third, some thoughts on the reality and effect of distinguishing different types of constitutional limitations will be presented. Finally, the law and practice of the states, and some practical considerations will be discussed.

"PERFORMANCE" LIMITATIONS AND INTERNATIONAL LAW

It is a well established principle of international law that each state is responsible for its internal governmental machinery. Subject to the restriction that it must act with due regard for the rights of other states, it is sovereign within its territory. To quote William E. Hall: "A state has a right to live its life in its own way so long as it keeps rigidly to itself."[2] It may burden itself with any type of government or system of regulation that it chooses, and this is of no concern in international law. Thus, such a limitation as that in the American Constitution, which places the control of finances in the hands of Congress, or the federal principle that reserves certain legislative powers in the component states are of internal concern only.[3]   Similarly, it is of internal concern what rights or privileges the government of a state grants to its citizens,[4] and the means and methods to uphold and enforce them.   The above categories correspond to the classification of "performance" limitations already discussed.[5] A few legal holdings will suffice to clarify the matter.

With respect to those limitations caused by the division of governmental powers in the state, a leading source is the Franco-American Convention controversy of 1831.[6]   Ratified in 1832, the Convention provided for the payment by France to the United States of an indemnity for damage done by France during the revolutionary war.   France did not meet the first instalment, and offered the defense that it could not obtain the necessary legislative approval, the control of finances being in the Chamber of Deputies.   The United States did not accept this, and correctly maintained that the Convention, being ratified, "was obligatory on every department of the contracting government."   After a prolonged and violent dispute, France finally paid.[7]

The same international question arises because of the distribution of legislative powers between the central government and the component parts in federations.   Thus, in the *Labor Conventions Case*,[8] legislation to perform the obligations of con- conventions duly ratified by Canada was held *ultra vires* the federal government, since it infringed on the legislative powers of the provinces.   In determining the question of legislative authority, the validity of the ratification was also considered.   Justice Cannon of the Canadian Supreme Court was of the opinion that nations contracting with Canada should have notice of its federal character, and of the fact that its government cannot rightfully invade the sphere of legislation reserved to the provinces, to carry out treaty provisions.[9]   The Privy Council did not accept this reasoning, and held that, "once they (i.e., treaties) are created, while they bind the state as against other contracting parties, Parliament may refuse to perform them and so leave the State in default."[10]   As Professor Robert B. Stewart aptly puts it: "Failure to secure the approval of the competent authorities is recognized generally by international law and specifically by the Constitution of the International Labor Organization as a valid excuse for the non-ratification of agreements. Once ratification has been made, there is an entirely new situation. Failure of a legislative organ to pass measures necessary to give effect to the ratified treaty cannot be offered as an excuse for avoiding the responsibilities incurred."[11]

In connection with the failure of certain federal states to provide adequate protection to aliens within their territory, the defense usually offered is that the central government cannot constitutionally interfere with the state or provincial control over the particular matter of grievance. In the *Montijo Arbitration* between the United States and Columbia,[12] the United States preferred a claim for damages to property in violation of treaty rights. Columbia, of course, advanced the defense that claims of such a nature were outside the constitutional control of the federal government, and within the exclusive jurisdiction of the states. The Arbitrator held that the federal government was responsible for the acts of the component state concerned. In the course of his decision he took the position that "a treaty is superior to the Constitution . . . and if a nation deliberately adopts that form of administering its public it does so with the full consequences it entails."[13]

The principle under discussion has received credence in the Permanent Court of International Justice in the *Case of the Polish Nationals in Danzig.*[14] The question submitted to the Court was whether the treatment of the Polish nationals should be decided solely with reference to certain provisions in the Treaty of Versailles and in the Convention of Paris, or also by reference to the Constitution of the Free City of Danzig. The Court held against Poland, and the Constitution of Danzig remained vis-a-vis Poland as the constitution of a foreign state. The Court said that "a state cannot rely, as against another state, on the provisions of the latter's constitution, but only on international law and obligations duly accepted, and, conversely, a state cannot adduce against another state its own constitution with a view to evading obligations incumbent upon it under international law or treaties in force."

There is no clear judicial authority, either in national or international law, that the third type of "performance" limitation, that is, judicial construction of state constitutional provisions other than the legislative powers, is a matter of internal concern. This classification of constitutional limitation, however, is only one of convenience; it entails the same process and is of the same nature as the one last discussed.[15] The difference is one of degree only.   The Jay Treaty of 1796 between the United States and England affords an adequate example.   To carry out its provisions, the United States was compelled to ask Congress for money.   Considerable and violent discussion arose over the ability of the President to enter into treaties involving appropriations without the prior consent of Congress.   Moreover, the treaty also contained extradition provisions, within an undoubted power of Congress.   One of the major arguments advanced was that the conclusion of this treaty was an interference by the executive with the powers of the judicial and legislative organs of government, an interference with the process of government itself as defined by the Constitution.[16]   There was no judicial construction involved, but the United States recognized that it was internationally obligated to carry out the provisions of the treaty, and did so.   It thereby tacitly admitted that it could not defend the validity of the treaty by any constitutional provision after the treaty was lawfully concluded.

These decisions and practices are sufficient to maintain the legal proposition that constitutional limitations affecting the performing power of a state to carry out its obligations afford no defense against the international validity of the treaty.   It is a necessary conclusion that in all such cases the question of notice of a state's constitutional machinery is immaterial.   The governmental process, such as the distribution of legislative powers within the state, a state's adherence to the principle of separation of powers, or the rights which a state may guarantee to its citizens, are of an internal nature and of no concern to co-contracting states.   In the words of Professor Westel W. Willoughby, "one state is not concerned with and therefore not required to be cognizant of the constitutional law of another state with which it has dealings . . . treaties remain internationally binding even when Congress has refused the necessary legislation to put them into effect or when it has abrogated them by subsequent legislation or when the Supreme Court has declared them unconstitutional."[17]

Many international legal authorities, although generally recognizing the above proposition, maintain that the non-observance of some constitutional limitations by a state may result in the international legal invalidity of a treaty.   They are often not clear, however, about the type of limitation to which they wish the doctrine applied. In view of the overwhelming authority for the conclusion set forth above, it is probable that these authorities are referring to constitutional limitations affecting the capacity of a state to enter into international agreements. But in many cases this is inference. A detailed analysis of the type of constitutional limitation to which they are referring is not too important for the purpose of this discussion, the prime aim of which is to disprove the efficacy of any internal legal interference in the treaty process, rather than to disprove the individual arguments advanced.

"Capacity" Limitations and International Law

In support of the contrary principle that the non-observance of constitutional limitations voids the treaty internationally as well as municipally, it is contended by at least two authoritative writers[18] that it is the state's internal law rather international law which determines the validity of treaties. Professor Edwin D. Dickinson states that "this dictum, that the law of nations has no concern with the constitution of a state, requires revaluation . . . the conclusion is beyond doubt that account must be taken of internal limitations." Though not without merit, this view cannot stand in the face of the proposition that international law considers at least some types of limitations to be unequivocally the sole concern of the state itself.

Another contention which has received the support of at least three writers is that a rule of customary international law has developed to the effect that constitutional limitations have to be observed before the treaty is internationally binding.[19] Professor Francis O. Wilcox refers to Article 1 of the Havana Convention, which provides that treaties will be concluded "by the competent authorities of the states or their representatives according to their respective internal law."[20] Professor J. Mervyn Jones points out that certain "Full Powers" contain this provision, and also finds evidence of it in thirty treaties between the various Latin American states between 1860-1913. He concludes that this is sufficient to establish such a rule of international law, at least in respect to the Latin American states. But this qualification on the valid conclusion of treaties is directed more to the act of ratification, and to the fact that states do not intend to be bound by the simple signature of the representative, rather than to the general proposition contended for, which is that the

states are not bound by treaties made in contravention of some
provision of internal law.   Further, what is the meaning of "internal law"?   If it is meant that treaties are to be made in accordance with all constitutional laws of the state, and are otherwise invalid, the proposition is manifestly not accepted in international law.   Constitutional limitations affecting the performance of treaty obligations are not a defense against the international validity of a treaty.   On the other hand, if the term
"internal law" does not apply to all constitutional limitations, it
is difficult to infer that only those affecting "capacity" are included.   In its present unsatisfactory form, the phrase probably
means little more than that the states must satisfy themselves
that they are negotiating with the agents duly appointed in accordance with the internal law, and that the latter are acting
within their apparent authority.   Professor Wilcox seeks additional support for the contention by observing that Article 6
of the same Convention provides that ratification "must be made
in writing pursuant to the legislation of the state."   But this
provision on its face is also of doubtful import.   It may mean
that the consent of the legislature is necessary before the treaty
binds the state, or it may mean that legislation to fulfill the provisions of the treaty is necessary before it may be properly ratified.   If the former meaning is intended—the words are far
from clear—it is perfectly legitimate for the state to make such a
reservation and the co-contracting state is put on notice to this extent.[21]   If it is the latter meaning which is intended, it is in accord with the practice of many states in qualifying international
obligation by the insertion of relevant clauses.[22]   In any case,
such clauses are still being regularly inserted, and there is no indication that the practice will cease on the ground that an existing
rule of international law now dispenses with the procedure.   If
the clause is not inserted, and the state fails to fulfill its obligation,
the state is in default.[23]   It can hardly be contended, then, that
such rule of customary international law has developed.[24]   This
conclusion is supported inasmuch as other writers, in maintaining
the proposition that internal laws govern the international validity of treaties, do not advance this argument.   They allege
that there is no rule of international law to the contrary that
makes constitutional requirements irrelevant in this determination.[25]

Other arguments of the writers maintaining this position are more generally accepted. Professor L. Oppenheim states that "treaties concluded by Heads of States, or representatives authorized by these Heads, as violate constitutional restrictions are not real treaties, and do not bind the state concerned, because the representatives have exceeded their powers in concluding the treaties."[26] Professor A. Berriedale Keith's edition of Wheaton[27] concludes that, "there is an implied condition in negotiating with foreign powers that treaties concluded by the executive government shall be subject to ratification in the manner prescribed by the fundamental laws of the state. If the ratification is purported to have been given without due authority, it is quite invalid." The author supports this conclusion by invoking the Ulpian axiom "he who contracts with another knows, or ought to know his condition." But does the application of this doctrine of notice to the "condition" of the other state mean that one state has to inform itself of all the peculiarities of the constitutional law of the other with respect to both types of constitutional limitations? Or does the doctrine of notice extend only to those limitations relating to the competence of the treaty-making organ, as prescribing the type of treaty that may be constitutionally concluded, and the procedure or form which must be followed? The latter is unquestionably the view of Professor Keith; but Professor Oppenheim is not so clear, for he states in a footnote:[28] "Normally the contracting parties do not pay much attention to the question whether each of them has complied with its constitutional requirements for the validity of a treaty and regard that as a domestic matter." In view of the soundness of the proposition that "performance" limitations are of internal concern, a rather strained inference is that the author is referring to "capacity" limitations only. He does not distinctly state, however, how far he wishes his advocated proposition to extend.

Article 21 of the Harvard Draft Convention lays down in part:[29] "A state is not bound by a treaty made on its behalf by an organ or authority not competent under its law to conclude the treaty." At first glance, it is doubtful what type of constitutional limitation is intended to be included in the word "competent." However, in a subsequent article,[30] it is explained that Article 21 is to be employed only when questions arise over the actual competence of the Head of State or his representative, that is, over constitutional limitations affecting "capacity." In this, the Harvard Draft Convention is quite clear.

The European writers upholding the contention under examination find their main support in the application of the doctrine of notice to the treaty process. They include the non-observance of all constitutional limitations as a defense against the international validity of a treaty. M. Walther M.A. Schucking[31] appears to place a duty on contracting states, not only to inform themselves as to the competence of the treaty-making authority, but also as to the limits of its competence. M. Karl Strupp,[32] to the same effect, declares "que d' apres la coutume internationale tout Etat est tenu de verifier non seulement qui est l'organe competent d' apres le droit interne pour conclure un traite, mais aussi sous quelles conditione cet organe peut le faire. D'ou il resulte qu'un traite n'est valable que s'il est conclu conformement aux modalites prevues par les lois nationales des parties contractantes."

The noted American authority, Professor Charles C. Hyde, in the first edition of his treatise on international law, definitely asserts that an unconstitutional treaty is void.[33] In his second edition, the statement is considerably modified. He states that since "it is reasonable and necessary for the domestic courts of a country such as the United States to regard an unconstitutional treaty as void . . . and as this arrangement must be presumed to be known to the other contracting party . . . and if the treaty is subsequently declared void by the courts," the treaty is invalid. He admits that, although the constitutional law of a country may give "sharp warning" of a state's treaty-making restrictions, there are limitations which after "diligent search" may not be apparent to the other state. In such cases, "there may be room for the contention" that the treaty is valid not withstanding the constitutional defect. This statement is further qualified in the sense that the state "must hold out assurances" that the terms of the agreement are not violative of the fundamental law of the former. Also the agent must make such assurances by reason "of the character of his connection with the particular department of his government to which is confided the management of foreign affairs." It must further be ascertained that "no written constitution is involved, and no published and authoritative instrument notoriously proclaims an opposing view." Thus, before a state may possibly be bound by a constitutionally defective treaty, in

Professor Hyde's view, the co-contracting state must show that it has diligently taken all steps to acquaint itself with the constitutional structure of the other state, that it relied on assurances by the representative acting in his official capacity, and that it was reasonably unaware of any other method by which it could have obtained the requisite knowledge.[34]

The authority to be finally referred to, Dr. Arnold D. McNair, divides constitutional limitations into two classes: A) municipal limitations upon the creation of the international obligation, and B) municipal requirements for the application and enforcement of a treaty.[35]   He is of the opinion that the non-compliance with the latter type affords no defense against the international validity of a treaty, but non-compliance with those of the first class does if the limitations are of a notorious nature.   As an example of a notorious limitation he refers to Article 2, Section 2 of the United States Constitution.   This Article, he states, possesses such international notoriety as to operate to prevent a state from begin bound it there has been no compliance with it.   Treaties concluded in contravention of any other constitutional limitation, however, are internationally valid.   He is also of the opinion that as states with unwritten constitutions have not the means of a written document to put other states on notice to such limitations, they enter into constitutionally defective treaties at their peril unless, in some way, they disclose the relevant limitations in an unequivocal manner.

THE REALITY AND EFFECT OF DISTINGUISHING CONSTITUTIONAL LIMITATIONS IN NATIONAL LAW

Thus certain types of constitutional limitations—i.e., those classified as "performance" limitations—are of internal concern and are irrelevant in the determination of the treaty's international legal validity.   Most writers advocating international legal interference apparently would distinguish between the different types of limitations, permitting international legal cognizance to some, denying it to others.   The distinctions these writers draw are not clear, but they are not important in this discussion.   It is true that "capacity" and "performance" limitations should be kept distinct for many purposes.   But do the distinctions warrant different international legal rules for each of the two categories, according to their operation in national law?

Suppose, in each of the following four examples, an international agreement is made by a state. First, the constitution of the state permits its head to enter the international agreement, but legislation to perform its provisions necessitates the action of another organ of government. The necessary effectuating legislation is not forthcoming and the agreement is consequently inoperative. Second, the head may constitutionally ratify the agreement, but one of its provisions contains a restriction on the right of freedom of speech. The constitution does not expressly prohibit agreements of this type, yet the right to be restricted is guaranteed to the citizens. The judicial organ of the state subsequently declares the treaty unconstitutional and refuses to give it the force of law. It is thus internally void. Third, the constitution provides that before the agreement becomes internally operative it must receive the consent of some other organ. It is constitutionally invalid bcause this condition is not fulfilled. Fourth, and finally, the Head of the State negotiates and ratifies the agreement. It contains a provision for the cession of part of the state's territory. The constitution provides that agreements of "special importance" have to be referred to the legislature for approval. If not of "special importance," they may be constitutionally concluded by the Head alone. The judicial organ of the state declares that this particular treaty is one of "special importance," and the treaty becomes municipally inoperative because it was concluded in contravention of the constitution. The question now is, when are these hypothetical examples, all municipally inoperative and unenforceable, valid in international law? Why should one be and not the other? It is the view of the writer that they all are, and that their differences are only of degree and not of substance.

All four examples fall within the two types of constitutional limitations considered throughout this discussion. The third and fourth are "capacity" limitations, since the constitution prescribes the form that the agreement must take and the procedure that must be followed before the treaty is constitutionally concluded. In the first two, the limitations do not prescribe the procedure or form of the agreements or the type of agreement which the Head of State can validly enter. They relate to the method and means of implementation, and do not directly affect the treaty-making authority of the Head. These two types of limitations are unquestionably within the internal concern of the state, and international law permits no interference. With respect to "capacity" limitations, international legal authority is inconsistent and obscure. The main reason for upholding the view that such limitations are within international legal cognizance apparently rests on the doctrine of notice. But is it feasible, or possible, for a state to have notice of the constitutional law of the other state, even of those limitations of a notorious nature? Let us now examine in more detail the operation of "capacity" limitations with respect to their effect in national law, to answer this question.

The President of the United States may enter into "treaties" only with the advice and consent of two-thirds of the Senators present. The Swiss Constitution stipulates that the Federal Council must submit to the approval of the Federal Assembly, prior to ratification, treaties concluded in the name of the federation. Article 15 of the Mexican Constitution provides that "no treaty shall be authorized for the extradition of political offenders or offenders of the common class, who have been slaves in the country where the offense was committed." In Norway, the second paragraph of Article 26 of the Constitution, provides that no treaties concerning matters of special importance are binding unless approved by the Storting. Finally Article 27 of the French Constitution states in part that treaties of peace and commerce, treaties which pledge the finances of the state, and treaties which touch the state of the person or the right of property of Frenchmen abroad cannot become final until they have been ratified by an act of the legislature. The writers upholding a distinction between the different classes of constitutional limitations maintain that such "capacity" limitations as these are within the notice of the co-contracting state. They assume that they can be determined with some degree of clarity and that if it does not conform with them, the treaty is internationally invalid. They would apply the doctrine of notice to "capacity" limitations but not to those of "performance," otherwise the latter would not be solely within the internal concern of the state. The reason for this is not clear. Possibly they feel that "performance" limitations are more obscure and indefinite. But it is impossible to accept this view.

Exactly what types of international agreements are to be included in the word "treaties" in Article 2, Section 2 of the American Constitution? The difference between executive agree-

ments and treaties in American constitutional law is ill-defined.[36]
Again, under the Swiss Constitution all treaties do not have to be
submitted to the Federal Assembly for approval, its public law
recognizing that certain types of treaties may be constitutionally
concluded by the Federal Council alone.[37]   Similarly, questions
requiring interpretation would inevitably arise in construing the
phrases "political offenders" and "matters of special importance"
in the Mexican and Norwegian Constitutions respectively.   Finally, in the French Constitution, problems of construction are evident in seeking the true meaning of "commerical treaties" and
in ascertaining those which "pledge the finances of the state and
treaties which touch the state of the person or the right of property of Frenchmen abroad."

It is obvious that these "capacity" limitations are open to interpretation to the same extent as those relating to the performance of treaty obligations, even those of a notorious nature.   An
international legal rule based on this distinction is unreal and
shallow.   Both types of limitations are equally important in
determining the treaty's national validity.   Non-compliance with
either type will render the treaty inoperative.   They are equally
obvious and obscure.   They are both within the power of the
state to change as it sees fit, and only the state has the power to
do so.   Finally, when does a limitation affect "capacity," and
when "performance"?   The line is often indescernible.

We may therefore conclude that there is no basis for an international legal distinction between the constitutional limitations
from their effect in national law.   The treaty process is, and
should be, determined by the state's constitution and by judicial
interpretation thereof.   It is this national law which determines
all questions of negotiation, ratification, and accession relating to
international agreements.   International law recognizes these
powers as being within the state's exclusive control, inherent in
the state's sovereignty, and subject to no interference by other
states, or from international law itself.   It is the state that determines what powers its representatives shall have to negotiate,
sign, and conclude treaties.   This is often defined in the Full
Powers that acknowledge the representative to the foreign state
and authorize him to enter into negotiations.   A state may provide in the Full Powers that he shall have power to conclude on
signature any type of treaty, or only treaties of certain type.   It
may, as is the usual practice in the United States, provide in the

Full Powers that the treaty which the agent has the power to negotiate and sign is subject to ratification before it is effectively concluded. Any or all of these conditions may be invoked by the state before concluding a treaty, subject perhaps to the theory that the State owes a duty in international law not unduly to restrict its relations with other states;[38] there is no question of their validity in international law. These are well established rules that have governed the relations of states for many centuries; they are founded upon reason, convenience, and continual dealings. They lead to no other conclusion than that the treaty process is entirely within municipal concern and brooks no international legal distinction between the different types of constitutional restrictions affecting it.

LAW, PRACTICE, AND PRACTICAL CONSIDERATIONS

The earlier writers were in general agreement that the sovereign was bound by all compacts entered on his behalf by the representative acting within his Full Powers.[39] They followed the concept in Roman Law that an agent may bind his principal within the limits of his patent power. They were not acquainted with the intricacies of modern constitutions and the involved affairs of the modern state. They considered only the problem whether the representative could bind the sovereign without the necessity of ratification (a principle of international law now generally dispelled),[40] not the problem whether the representative could bind the state by a treaty that contravened a provision in its constitution or a tenet of its constitutional law. However, these authorities are of value in recognizing the respect and honor due to the person of the representative, and his representations upon matters of state which he, within the limits of his authority, is competent to make.

Turning to modern authorities, Judge Dionisio Anzilloti[41] concludes that the conditions governing the validity and effectiveness of treaties are exclusively controlled by the principles of international law, and that the internal or constitutional restrictions have nothing to do with it.[42] Professor Pitman B. Potter contends that the state possesses the treaty-making power by virtue of international law, and can not and may not curtail itself unduly in its international intercourse through internal restrictions.[43] The Austrian writer, M. Ludwig Bittner, comes to the same conclusion but in a different way. After an extensive ex-

amination of the phraseology of the Full Powers of representatives, the language, terms and texts of treaties, and the forms
of the instruments of ratification employed by the various states,
he considers that, because of the requirement of legislative consent is omitted more often than it is included, the nations show
by this silence that they do not believe the validity of treaties to
be thus affected.[44]   However, it is doubtful whether it may be
inferred that the nations have assented to the general proposition
that constitutional requirements are of no concern in determining
the international validity of a treaty.   The best summation of
the situation is that stated by Professor Westel W. Willoughby:
"It is not merely the juristic basis or origin of a state that other
states have no concern; they are also, as a technical proposition,
indifferent to its form of government, that is, to the distribution
of powers amongst the several organs of government as provided
for by its system of constitutional law.   Each state, when it
claims recognition as a member of the international society of
states, asserts that it not only has the intention but that it possesses the ability, to fulfil all the duties which International Law lays
upon it.   Under no circumstances, then, is it permitted to plead
a constitutional non possumus as an excuse for a failure to live
up to the full measure of its international responsibilities."   He
continues, after stating that it is correct to say that it is presumed
to be known which organ is qualified to enter into treaties: ". . .
One state is entitled to rely upon the assertion of the executive
head of a State or of his plenipotentiary agent, that he is qualified
to negotiate a treaty which will be immediately binding without ad
referendum proceedings.   The assertion thus made might be
without constitutional warrant, but the State none the less be internationally bound, for it would not be held that the other contracting State would be qualified or obligated to determine the
question, which might be a very technical one, of the proper interpretation and application of the provisions of the other State's
constitutional laws."[45]

The British attitude toward the binding effect of treaties made
in contravention of a "capacity" limitation is amply illustrated
by various incidents reported by Dr. Arnold D. McNair.[46]
One question involved an agreement between Spain and Great
Britain for the erection of a suitable consulate residence in Span-
ish Morocco.   This agreement was based on a treaty concluded
in 1783 with the Maghzen of Morocco and, in disputing the

validity of the treaty, Spain contended that this agreement was not embodied in a Sherfien Decree, as prescribed by Moroccan internal law. This defense was not accepted by the British Government and the parties agreed to arbitration. The Arbitrator upheld the British position and in the course of his decision, stated "that no decisive importance could be attached to the fact that the British proposal was not accepted in the form of a Sherifien Decree. It was not the duty of the Rapporteur to enquire into this point of Moroccan law." The other cases reported by Dr. McNair are equally unequivocal.

A number of situations involving the United States show that the modern American attitude is in agreement but this is a departure from the arbitral decision in the Costa Rica-Nicaragua boundary dispute.[47] Although the United States was not a party to the dispute, the Arbitrator was President Grover Cleveland of the United States, and his decision must be taken to reflect the view of this state at the time. In December, 1886, Costa Rica and Nicaragua signed a treaty in which they agreed that the question pending between the contracting governments in regard to the Treaty of Limits of 1858 should be submitted to arbitration. Nicaragua contended, inter alia, that the treaty was not binding on the state because it had not received the necessary sanction as prescribed by the Constitution. It held that it was a "direct and flagrant violation" of the fundamental law, seeing that, in order to have internal validity, the Constitution prescribed that the treaty must receive the same formal ratification as an amendment to the Constitution, which was not done. The Arbitrator held against Nicaragua on the ground that it was not shown that the Constitution, allegedly violated, was in force at the time of the conclusion of the treaty. However, he stated that "the general doctrine in determining the validity of a treaty [is that] the fundamental laws of such state must furnish the guide for determinition." Possibly, if it had been considered necessary to determine whether the treaty violated some fundamental law, the dictum would not have appeared in such unqualified form.

But the above expression does not indicate the present attitude of the American government.[48] This cannot be better stated than in the words of the former legal adviser and now the American member of the International Court of Justice, Judge Green H. Hackworth. In the hearings before the sub-committee on the Great Lakes-St. Lawrence Basin project,[49] he was asked whether the doctrine of *ultra vires,* in connection with the President's action, would be recognized in international law. His reply was: "Generally speaking . . . in international law the Head of the government is entitled to speak for the state, and if the President enters into an obligation with a foreign government, that foreign government is entitled to rely upon it. It is not under the obligation to enquire into our constitutional processes. It takes the word of the Head of State.[50] If the obligation is violated, it is a violation of an international obligation, pure and simple, whether the President exceeded his authority or not. He is supposed to act within his authority but if he gets outside it, the other government is entitled to rely upon it."[51]

A number of decisions dealing with the binding effect of oral declarations of the Head of State or of his representative have come before the Permanent Court of International Justice, and assist the contention of the present writer. They are in accord that notice of the other state's constitutional law is irrelevant if made within the apparent authority of the agent. The most celebrated is the famous Eastern Greenland decision.[52]

The Danish Foreign Minister had asked the Norwegian Foreign Minister whether Norway would cause any difficulty in the proposed extension of Danish sovereignty over Greenland. The Norwegian Foreign Minister, M. Ihlen, had replied orally that the Norwegian Government would not, and this oral declaration was recorded in the form of a minute by M. Ihlen. When the dispute came before the Court, the Norwegian Government contended that the oral representation was not binding on the State, since by the Norwegian Constitution, Article 26, decisions on matters of "special importance" are not constitutionally valid until approved by the Storting. M. Ihlen's declaration, being a matter of "special importance," was not made in accordance with Norway's constitutional requirements. The Danish Government apparently accepted this proposition that agreements made outside the constitutional competence of the minister are not valid, but rested its case on the fact that M. Ihlen was not acting outside his competence, or, in other words, that the declaration was not one of "special importance." This contention is difficult to accept, in view of the fact that the declaration affected the rights of the two states over such a strategic body of land as Greenland. The Court did not directly pass on this question,

but held that the statement fell "within the province" of the
Norwegian Foreign Minister, and that his government was bound
by it.[53]   The Court did not consider the question whether the
status of Greenland involved a matter of "special importance."
Yet it is a logical inference that the Court considered M. Ihlen's
apparent authority to be "within his province," and was not concerned with the actual authority as limited by the Constitution of
Norway.   Statements and acts by accredited representatives,
occuring in the ordinary course of diplomatic affairs, may be entirely relied on by other states.   Another interpretation of the
decision is possible, however.   Constitutional limitations affecting the capacity of a state to enter into international agreements
which are not clear on their face, and require interpretation, are
not the concern of the other state.   Thus matters of "special
importance" were open to doubt, and the Court abstained from
interpreting them.   It was an internal issue only, and did not
affect the international validity of the declaration.   There is
none the less much authority that the first, broad view of the
decision is correct.[54]

Other decisions of the Permanent Court have sustained this
first view.   In the *Lighthouses Case between France and
Greece*,[55] a decree law issued by the Sultan in 1913 authorized the
Ottoman Minister of Finance to renew a concession to a French
firm for the maintenance of a system of lights on certain coasts.
These coastal areas were later ceded to Greece, and the Greek
government refused to recognize the validity of the concession.
One of the arguments advanced by the Greek government was
that the concession was not constitutionally concluded since, by
Turkish law, the validity of the decree was subject to the approval
of the Turkish Parliament.   The court held, however, that the
concession granted under the apparent authority of the decree
law, regular according to the ordinary course of governmental
dealings, was binding and effective on the state.[56]

From this survey of decisions and practices of governments it
is evident that little legal support can be obtained for differentia-
ting between the two types of constitutional limitations.   Non-
compliance with either type of limitation does not affect the international validity of the treaty.   International law deems it a
matter of internal concern only, and this repudiates the doctrine
of notice as applied in this branch of jurisprudence, a repudiation
sustained by several Permanent Court decisions.   The correct-

ness of this conclusion is inescapable. To maintain otherwise
would cause endless litigation, confusion and uncertainty. Further, the application of any criterion, such as "due diligence,"[57]
in inquiring into the constitutional processes, would be similarly
obscure and uncertain.   Constitutional requirements, no matter
how clear and obvious on their face, are invariably open to interpretation by the municipal judiciary, and are open to being declared unconstitutional by that body.   If a state were permitted
to use such a defense, in answer to the international validity of
an agreement, the law of treaties is on very uncertain ground.
It might take years before the constitutionality of a treaty is
finally decided, and confusion would result from the lack of final-
ity.   Further, non-compliance with constitutional limitations
could conceivably become a device for political manipulation,
malfeasance, and bad faith in international affairs.   Constitutional limitations are of no concern to other states; the representations of the Heads or of their duly accredited agents should
be entirely reliable; and the doctrine of notice should be abandoned in this part of the law of nations.[58]

The theory of Dr. Arnold D. McNair that non-compliance
with constitutional limitations of a "notorious" nature may be
a defense against the international validity of a treaty has some
merit.[59]   But the biggest obstacle to its acceptance is that, no
matter how manifest the language of the constitutional requirement, it may be open to judicial interpretation.   What would be
the criterion whether a limitation was notorious or not?   Such
a determination would lead to endless controversy and litigation.
For example, if a state included a provision in its constitution to
the effect that a treaty must conform to the principles of the constitution and the fundamental laws of the state,[60] would this be
considered notorious?   If so, as the state would invariably contend, it would provide an effective defense.   The resultant confusion and uncertainty is evident.   Indeed, the interpretation
of a notorious limitation might in time be deemed notice of all the
provisions of a written constitution and of all judicial interpretation thereof.[61]

There are practical arguments against requiring notice of the
constitutional law of another state.   If there is a burden on
states to have notice, there is, in all fairness, a concomitant right
to make inquiries as to what the true state of the law is.   Thus,
assuming that reasonable inquiry is necessary before a state can

safely enter into binding contractual agreements with other states, how will it undertake the process of obtaining such information? The observations of Mr. Gerald G. Fitzmaurice are of particular value here.[62]   First, he is dubious whether a state can have official notice unless the information is requested officially and an official reply is received.   Foreign offices might have considerable difficulty in obtaining legal experts and opinions that will measure up to the requirements that an international tribunal may impose, before the evidence would be accepted.   Secondly, Mr. Fitzmaurice shows that the only official way of obtaining this knowledge is through the department concerned with the foreign affairs of the state, which in most if not in all cases, is the executive.   As the executive is also the treaty-making organ, it is the very organ of government that is delinquent, and little assistance may be expected from this source.   Finally, he concludes that "states must, in their intercourse with one another, be able to rely absolutely on the validity of the actions of, and the information given by one another's executive, those being the only channels through which such actions can be performed or such action given."   Again, if the requisite legislative assent is given in secret session, how would it be possible for the other state to obtain such notice unless it is permitted to rely on the assurance of the executive?

There is also the consideration that inquiries into the constitutional law of the other state may be refused on the ground that it is of internal concern only.   An illustration is to be found in an incident between the United States and Great Britain in 1864.[63]   Mr. Adams, the United States Minister in London, had given notice, in accordance with a treaty then in force, that the United States wished to terminate that treaty.   This notice was adopted and ratified by a joint resolution of Congress.   Subsequently, Mr. Seward, then American Secretary of State, informed the British Minister in Washington that a statement made by him was to have the force of withdrawing the previous notice given by Mr. Adams.   In reply, apparently to the inquiry of the British Governemnt as to whether Mr. Seward had the constitutional authority to make such a declaration, the American Government maintained that "as between the United States and Great Britain, this act of withdrawal was no less authoritative than the notification itself . . . into the authority of the Secretary of State to give or withdraw the notice of the British Government was incompetent to inquire, it could only accept and respect the withdrawal as a fact . . . the question of competency being a matter of domestic administration affecting the internal relations of the executive and the legislative powers in no wise concerned Great Britain . . . the raising by her of a question as to the authority of the executive in the matter would have constituted an unprecedented and inadmissible step in the international relations of governments."[64]

Regarding Full Powers issued to diplomatic agents, earlier writers recognized that these qualified the agent to represent his sovereign unreservedly within the limits of the authority granted by the Powers. Although the complexities of modern international intercourse have given rise to different considerations as to their legal effect, Full Powers are still very highly regarded in diplomatic protocol. They imply that the agent is worthy of the dignity of representing his country on formal matters of state, and that he is to be accorded the honor and respect due to the state he represents. Recognition of the agent is recognition of the state.[65] Therefore, no express representation that the treaty is being concluded according to the state's internal law should be necessary, since this representation is implied in the Full Powers. Once they have been verified, the duty of inquiry of the other state is at an end.

Conclusion

There are numerous international legal rules regarding the conclusion of treaties, which afford sufficient protection without requiring cognizance of fundamental laws by contracting states. For example, international law imposes no duty on a state to ratify a treaty that has been signed by an agent. Ratification permits "sober, second thought" on the part of the contracting state before the treaty is validly concluded. It also permits ample time and warning for a state to repudiate any unconstitutional action on the part of the Head of State or the representative. If a state does not or cannot take advantage of this international legal rule, there is a serious defect in the governmental structure of that state. This of itself is sufficient answer to those who maintain that an unconstitutional treaty does not express the will of the state. If this "will" is not expressed, it is the state that has forfeited the right to express it, by failing to provide appropriate protective governmental machinery. Further, there is no international legal rule to prevent a state from making *ad refer-endum* reservations or other conditions, prior to the adoption of the treaty. However, they must be definite and leave no doubt of what exactly is reserved. If a reasonable reservation is made, the other state is put on notice to this extent, and should be permitted the right to make inquiries to ascertain if the requirement or condition has been complied with, as well as the right to rely on the representation of the executive in reply. The other state is still protected from the acts of incompetent or unscrupulous agents, since the principle applies only to acts done within the limits of the patent or apparent authority with which the state has clothed them. If the agents act outside this authority or, with no authority, the state is not responsible.[66]

Moreover, the state may in various ways bring the constitutional limitations to the notice of the other party. Here again the only requirement is that the limitation must be definite and brought to the notice of the other party in good faith.[67]

Finally, good faith on the parties must be mutual. A treaty may be terminated, for example, if it is shown that the other party has taken advantage of the other's constitutional limitations to obtain some selfish end. Such cases depend on the facts.

That a state may be obligated internationally by an unconstitutional treaty or municipally inoperative treaty is, no doubt, an unfortunate anomaly. However, if a treaty obligation exists, which, by some peculiarity of internal governmental organization, a state cannot fulfil, that state cannot invoke its internal law to elude responsibility. It must either abstain from incurring such an obligation or, better, alter its constitutional law appropriately. National capabilities and powers can no longer be used as a justification for the evasion of international duties. At the present time, international agreements are the sole means of reaching international understanding and formulating international rules of conduct. The formulation of a strict body of treaty law is indispensable to the development of international law, upon which the peace and security of the world, in no small measure, depends. International agreements suffer from legal uncertainty and obscurity if the conditions governing their validity are dependent upon the constitutional law of states. Security, clearness, and the duty of the state to exercise due care and diligence in its treaty relations will acquire new meaning when they become en-

tirely dependent on the principles of international, and not on
national law.

[1]. *Supra,* p. 5.   [2]. *International Law,* (8th ed., 1924), p. 51.

[3]. Harvard Draft Convention, Article 23, (1935) 29 *American Journal of International Law* (Supplement), pp. 1029 ff., enumerates the authorities upholding the general rule.

[4]. Subject to the rules of customary or conventional international law.

[5]. *Supra,* pp. 9 ff.

[6]. Accounts of this important precedent may be found in Arnold, Ralph, *Treaty Making Procedure,* (1933), (Arnold D. McNair's introduction, "Constitutional Limitations Upon the Treaty Making Power") p. 7, and in Crandall, Samuel B., *Treaties: Their Making and Enforcement,* (2nd ed., 1916), p. 174.

[7]. Similarly, the *Franco-Swiss Arbitration of 1912,* (1912) 6 *American Journal of International Law* 995. The classic statement in Henry Wheaton's *International Law,* (edited by Richard H. Dana, 1866) p. 715, is often quoted in this regard: "If a treaty requires the payment of money or any other special act, which cannot be done without legislation, the treaty is still binding on the nation; and it is the duty of the nation to pass the necessary laws. If the duty is not performed the result is just as much as if the breach had been an affirmative act by any other department of the government. Each nation is responsible for the right working of its internal system, by which it distributes its sovereign functions; and, as foreign nations dealing with it cannot be permitted to interfere with or control these, so they are not to be affected by them, to their injury."

[8]. (1936) Supreme Court Reports (Canada), 461; (1937) Appeal Cases (England) 326.

[9]. *Ibid,* p. 522. This view is held by Stoke, Harold W., *Foreign Relations of the Federal State,* (1931), p. 227. He says; "It is generally agreed that other nations must acquaint themselves with the legal limitations of the treaty making authorities with which they negotiate, and cannot, in good faith, expect to bind a federation, by a treaty, to more than it can constitutionally fulfil." However, Mr. Stoke and Justice Cannon appear to be alone in this view.

[10]. (1937) Appeal Cases (England) 342, p. 348.

[11]. *Treaty Relations of the British Commonwealth of Nations,* (1939), p. 298. Also see the opinion of Jenks, C. Wilfred, "Present Status of the Bennett Ratifications of the International Labour Conventions," (1937) *Canadian Bar Review* 464.

[12]. Moore, John Bassett, *International Arbitrations,* (1896), Vol. 2, pp. 1439-41.

[13]. The United States has occasionally found itself in the same position in this regard, and in all cases has paid indemnities, thus recognizing, by implication at least, the principle of the *Montijo Case.* Moore, John Bassett, *Digest of International Law,* (1906), Vol. 6, pp. 837 ff. Also see Evatt, Herbert V., *"International Responsibility of States in the Case of Riots or Mob Violence,"* (1935) 9 *Australian Law Journal* (Supplement), 9.

[14]. Publications of the Permanent Court of International Justice, series A/B, no. 44, p. 24, (1932).

[15]. *Supra.* p. 86.

Constitutional Limitations and International Law   159

[16.] The constitutionality of treaties providing for appeal from American courts of last resort to international judicial organs has been seriously doubted on this ground. The question is still open. *Supra*, p. 97.

[17.] *Constitutional Law of the United States*, (2nd ed., 1929), Vol. 1, p. 571.

[18.] Dickinson, D., *Equality of States in International Law*, (1920), particularly at pp. 218-20; Chailley, Pierre, *La Nature Juridique des Traités Internationaux*, (1932), pp. 175, 215; Harvard Draft Convention, (1935) 29 *American Journal of International Law* (Supplement), p. 1000.

[19.] Wilcox, Francis O., *Ratification of International Labour Conventions*, pp. 44 ff; Chailley, *ibid;* Jones, J. Mervyn, "Constitutional Limitations On the Treaty Making Power," (1941) 35 *American Journal of International Law* 462.

[20.] Convention on Treaties adopted at Havana, February 20, 1928, Hudson, Manley O., *International Legislation*, (1931), Vol. 4, p. 2378.

[21.] *Infra*, p. 156-157.

[22.] *Supra*. p. 102, note 14, gives an example.

[23.] In failing to fulfil the terms of the labor conventions which were the subject of the *Labor Conventions Case*, (1937) Appeal Cases (England) 324, Canada was in default in international law. In the arguments of counsel and in the judgment of the court, there is no mention of such a rule to protect Canada from delinquency. Also see Jenks, C. Wilfred, "The Present Status of the Bennett Ratifications of International Labour Conventions," (1937) 15 *Canadian Bar Review* 464.

[24.] Professor Jones admits that the practice of the Latin American states is not common in European countries. "Constitutional Limitations On the Treaty Making Power," (1941) 35 *American Journal of International Law* 462, p. 464, note 5.

[25.] Strupp, Karl, *Eléments du Droit International Public*, (1927), p. 182. Chailley, Pierre, *La Nature Juridique des traités Internationaux;* Harvard Draft Convention, (1935) 29 *American Journal of International Law* (Supplement) pp. 999-1000.

[26.] *International Law*, (7th ed. by Lauterpacht, H., 1947), Vol. 1, p. 799.

[27.] *International Law*, (1929), Vol. 1, p. 498.   [28.] *Ibid*, p. 799, note 4.

[29.] (1935) 29 *American Journal of International Law* (Supplement) p. 992. It is interesting to note that the original draft of Article 21 affirmed the opposite conclusion.

[30.] Article 23, *ibid*, pp. 1029 ff.

[31.] *Annuaire de L'Institut International de Droit Public*, (1930), p. 225; Harvard Draft Convention, *ibid*, pp. 999-1000.

[32.] *Eléments du Droit International Public*, (1927), p. 182; Harvard Draft Convention, *ibid*, p. 999.

[33.] (1st ed., 1922), Vol. 2, p. 8; (2nd ed., 1947), Vol. 2, pp. 1384-85.

[34.] Considerable dicta in American juricial decisions can be cited to support this view. For example, see *Downes v. Bidwell*, (1901) 182 United States 244, p. 370; *Cherokee Tobacco Case*, (1870) 11 Wallace (United States Supreme Court) 616, p. 620; *DeGeofroy v. Riggs*, (1890) 133 United States 258, p. 267.

[35.] "Constitutional Limitations Upon the Treaty Making Power," introductory note by Arnold D. McNair in Arnold, Ralph, *Treaty Making Procedure* (1933), pp. 4 ff.

[36.] *Supra*. pp. 43 ff. 92-93.   [37.] *Supra*. pp. 45-46.

[38.] "International Law of the Future," Principle 5. (1944) 38 *American Journal of International Law* (Supplement), pp. 41, 80.

[39]. For example, Wheaton, Henry, *International Law*, (ed. by Keith, A. Berrie-dale, 1929), Vol. 1, pp. 490 ff. gives a brief summary of these opinions.

[40]. Harvard Draft Convention, Article 7, (1935) 29 *American Journal of International Law* (Supplement) 653, p. 756.

[41]. *Cours de Droit International,* (1929), Vol. 1, pp. 364 ff; Harvard Draft Convention, (1935) 29 *American Journal of International Law* (Supplement), pp. 996.

[42]. Also refer to his dissenting opinion in the *Eastern Greenland Case, infra,* pp. 152, 161, note 54.

[43]. "Inhibitions Upon the Treaty Making Power of the United States," (1934) 28 *American Journal of International Law* 456. However, Professor Potter believes that international law permits some limitations, but he does not indicate exactly what they are.

[44]. *"Die Lehre von den Volkerrechtlichen Vertragsurkunden,"* (1924), pp. 86 ff; Harvard Draft Convention, *ibid,* p. 997.

[45]. *Fundamental Concepts of Public Law,* (1924), pp. 312-14. Also his *Constitutional Law of the United States,* (2nd ed., 1929), Vol. 1, pp. 528, 571. In accord are the views of Fairman, Charles, "Competence to Bind the State to an International Engagement," (1936) 30 *American Journal of International Law* 439; (declarations of the Head of State or his diplomatic agents are binding on the state in international law). Basdevant, Jules, "La Conclusion et La Rédaction des Traités," (1926) 15 *Recueil des Cours,* p. 581; ("L'Autre État n'a pas à la controler, à vérifier son exactitude constitutionelle"). Eagleton, Clyde, *International Government,* (1947), p. 150; ("But it should always be remembered that a treaty properly made by the designated constitutional authorities of a state binds that state in international law and that state will be held for violation of it").

[46]. *Law of Treaties,* (1938), Ch. 3. and "Constitutional Limitations Upon the Treaty Making Power," introductory note to Arnold, Ralph, *Treaty Making Procedure,* (1933), p. 1.

[47]. (1888) *Foreign Relations of the United States,* part 1, p. 459.

[48]. The two incidents reported in Hackworth, Green H., *Digest of International Law,* (1940-44), Vol. 5, pp. 155 ff. are quite conclusive.

[49]. Great Lakes-St. Lawrence Basin, "Hearings before a Subcommittee on Commerce," United States Senate, 1945, p. 235.

[50]. That is, presumably, within his apparent authority, If he exceeded his apparent authority, it is submitted, the state would not be bound. *Infra,* p. 157.

[51]. A number of other situations have been reported, but little principle can be deduced. For the most part, and because of political reasons, they are indecisive. For example, the case of the Austro-Rumanian Convention of 1920, reported by McNair, Arnold D., "Constitutional Limitations Upon the Treaty Making Power," introductory note to Arnold, Ralph, *Treaty Making Procedure,* (1933), p. 12; the boundary dispute between Persia and Iraq, in the League of Nations Council, League of Nations, *Official Journal,* February, 1935, pp. 116 ff; the attitude of the Chinese government reported in Jones, J. Mervyn, *Full Power and Ratification,* (1946), p. 142; Hudson, Manley O., "The Argentine Republic and the League of Nations," (1934) 28 *American Journal of International Law* 125.

[52]. Publications of the Permanent Court of International Justice, series A/A, no. 53, p. 69, (1933).

[53]. "The court considers it beyond all dispute that a reply of this nature given by the Minister of Foreign Affairs on behalf of his government in response to a re-

quest by the diplomatic representative of a Foreign Power in regard to a question falling within his province is binding on the country to which the minister belongs." *Ibid.* p. 71.

[54.] Judge Anzillotti in his dissenting opinion concurred with the majority on this point. He said that, "as regards the question whether the Norwegian constitutional law authorized the Minister of Foreign Affairs to make the declaration, that is a point which, in my opinion, does not concern the Danish Government." *Ibid,* p. 91. See also Professor Manley O. Hudson's interpretation of the decision with reference to the status of Argentina in the League of Nations. (1934) 28 *American Journal of International Law* 125. Similarly Garner, James W., "International Binding Force of Unilateral Oral Declarations," (1933) 27 *American Journal of International Law* 493, is of the same opinion.

[55.] *Annual Digests and Reports of International Law Cases,* 1933-34, no. 36, p. 84.

[56.] Other cases in which oral declarations were held binding on the state by the Permanent Court are the *Serbian Loans Case,* Publications of the Permanent Court of International Justice, series A, no. 21/21, pp. 46-47, (1929) ; *Free Zones of Upper Savoy and Gex Case,* Publications of the Permanent Court of International Justice, series A/B, no. 46, p. 170, (1932) ; *Mavromattis Case,* Publications of the Permanent Court of International Justice, Series A, no. 5, p. 37, (1925) ; *German Interests in Polish Upper Silesia Case, ibid,* no. 7, p. 13.

[57.] *Supra,* p. 144.

[58.] Fairman, Charles, "Competence to Bind the State to an International Engagement," (1936) 30*American Journal of International Law* 439, says that the axiom 'he who contracts with another knows or ought to know, his condition' is applicable in international law only insofar as one state is definitely presumed to know any limits on the international status of another with which it treats, for example, the status of the Free City of Danzig. The axiom has been applied, however, in the dealings with *non sui juris* states. But *non sui juris* states are of anamolous type. In the first place, they have not the international capacity to contract and, secondly, considerations of convenience and policy have led the states to ascribe their assent to the application of the doctrine of notice here.

[59.] *Supra,* p. 145.

[60.] For example, Article 19 of the Argentine Constitution, Peaslee, Amos J., *Constitutions of Nations,* (1950), Vol. 1, p. 65.

[61.] See Professor Charles C. Hyde's conclusion, *supra,* p. 144.

[62.] "Do Treaties Need Ratification," (1934) 15 *British Year Book of International Law* 113, pp. 133 ff.

[63.] Moore, John Bassett, *Digest of International Law,* (1906), Vol. 5, pp. 169-70.

[64.] See also Corwin, Edward S., *The President's Control of Foreign Relations,* (1917), p. 47. Eagleton, Clyde, *International Government,* p. 150, writes: "It would appear that a state has only the duty of assuring itself that it is dealing with the authorities empowered by the constitution of the state with the authority to make treaties; it has not the right to determine whether these authorities have exceeded their constitutional powers."

[65.] Hatschek, Julius, *Outline of International Law,* (1930), pp. 19-20, says: "The rule that a state's honour must never be put in doubt by an invitation to its international organs to show proof that they in fact have for any particular business in hand the proper authorization constitutionally necessary under the municipal law of their state. If, for example, a state asserts that it has obtained from its parliament the constitutional authorization for the conclusion of a treaty, the other state, with which it is entering into such treaty, may not go on to make inquiry as to the foundation for that assertion.   That which gives its importance to what is known in international law as the ratification of treaties is precisely the fact that it simply closes the door to any such investigation."

[66.] There might be occasions when the state may consider itself bound in good faith to support the agreement.   For example, *The Gloire,* (1804) 5 C. Robinson (England) 193, (*per* Lord Stowell).

[67.] Dr. Thomas Baty, in accord with Dr. Arnold D. McNair, is of the opinion that the non-observance of constitutional limitations of a notorious nature may be used as a defense against the international validity of a treaty, or when the limitation has been disclosed to the other party.   *Canons of International Law,* (1930), pp. 418 ff.   Basdevant, Jules, "La Conclusion et La Rédaction des Traités," (1926) 15 *Receuil des Cours* 581, considers that "manifest violations" may be used to deny the validity of a treaty, being contrary to doctrine of mutual respect to compel the performance of such a treaty.   It is to be noted that in such cases the circumstances may amount to a breach of good faith to render it inequitable to enforce the treaty.

CHAPTER 8

CONSTITUTIONAL LIMITATIONS
AND FUNDAMENTAL LAWS

Once treaties are validly concluded in accordance with international legal rules, they are not affected by states' fundamental laws. They constitute a valid international obligation regardless of their possible infringement of a constitutional limitation. International law provides its own safeguards against abuse of the treaty process. Ratification, reservations, amendments, are, within their legal limits, recognized as having valid uses. But once a treaty is ratified it is legally binding and the constitutional provisions respecting "capacity" and "performance" of the individual states entirely a matter of national concern.

This is the international legal position. Now what is the national position? Constitutional limitations now existing on the treaty processes of federal states have been examined in some detail. The next step is to observe their consonance with the best interests of the states themselves and of modern internationalism.

National "Capacity" and Modern Internationalism

There are two separate points here: the first is the question of constitutional limitations on the central governments, which restrict the actions of the federal states as units; the second concerns control over, and participation in, the treaty-making power by other organs of government than the executive.

Concerning the first question little need be said about the treaty-making capacity of the United States and Switzerland. Both these federations have restricted the voice of the component parts by their written Constitutions, and their parts' competency in foreign affairs is negligible. The federal governments represent these states in all branches of international activity and are the sole organs capable of speaking for the whole.

But, as we have already indicated, this is not the unqualified position of the British federations of Canada and Australia. Although both these states now enjoy a status equal to Great Britain itself in the international community, the legal capacity of the central executive to enter into international engagements is

163

obscure. Thus, though the states themselves may have such "capacity" by the combined effort of all their governmental organs, there is confusion, legally at any rate, as to which organ is the competent one to deal with foreign nations.   This "capacity" on the part of the executive may be limited in two ways: first, by the fact that no prerogative exists which unequivocally bestows on the central executive (or the state executives) the right to enter into valid international engagements; second, by the doctrine that executive power follows legislative power, and that, inasmuch as the component parts have the legislative power to perform treaty obligations, the executive power is not in the central executive.   Though the practice is clear, and the central authority does enter into international engagements exclusively, the legal situation needs clarification.

Australia is in a much more advantageous position than Canada.   Although the High Court has not categorically stated that the central executive has now the power to enter into any type of treaty, its method of interpretation, and the broad dicta sustaining the power in *The King v. Burgess*: *ex parte Henry,*[1] demonstrate that the judiciary recognizes the importance of an extensive power in the central executive, and will uphold it to meet future exigencies as they arise.   Legally, it is a fair inference that the power of the component states in foreign affairs is now non-existent.   There is no need of any constitutional alteration in Australia.

The Canadian situation demands more consideration with respect to the treaty-making power or "capacity" of its executive. Constitutional amendment is the obvious remedy, to place the power in control of the central executive once and for all. But this may be objectionable for several reasons.   First, it would most probably preclude the use by Canada of the existing Imperial procedure for concluding formal treaties.   There are undoubted advantages to being a member of the British Commonwealth of Nations. The severance of constitutional ties has already reached the stage where the only ones remaining are those relating to external affairs, and the fact that the Canadian Constitution is a statute of the Imperial Parliament.   To cut off the former completely might well deprive Canada of many advantages of this membership   Many Canadians feel that partnership within the world-wide organization is conducive to world solidarity.   Second, the provinces still maintain a zealous regard for their rights, and look askance at the increase of federal powers.   Expressly giving the federal government power to enter into any type of international agreement by constitutional amendment would entail much controversy and open many old scars.   It is further maintained that since the provinces are effectively cut off from the treaty process, and since their legal claims of participation are so insignificant,[2] the advantages of legal clarification would not outweigh the disadvantages.   The peculiar position of Canada between the United States and Great Britain, the state of world conditions in general, and Canada's inevitable future expansion all speak for cautiousness in constitutional change.   The alternative to constitutional amendment is, of course, judicial construction.   There is considerable precedent and practice to place the legal authority indisputably in the central executive. If this were confirmed formally, it would clarify the Canadian position in international affairs, and strengthen the position of the central government in the performing process.   This point will receive final consideration in the concluding pages of this chapter.

The second question with which this section will deal is that of the control over the executives by other organs of governments in the conclusion of international agreements.   The great objective here should be to select the organ which may best negotiate, sign, and otherwise validly conclude a treaty, whilst also complying with the requirements of constitutionalism as adopted by modern states.   Essentially this means determining how much freedom may be given to the executive in international affairs, concomitantly securing sufficient protection to individuals and to the sovereignty of the component states.   In dealing with this problem, the limitations affecting "capacity" and "performance" should be sharply differentiated and distinguished.

The executive is the logical organ for the conduct of international intercourse.   By its very function in the modern state, it implies the right to act both internally and externally.   These functions are essentially similar.   It is the organ which embodies the most compact group in the state.   The executive is generally empowered to perform the highest functions in the state.   To foreign states, it is the only organ which represents the people as a whole rather than sectional interests or groups.   Supporting this, is the invariable position it occupies as head of the government.   It has at its command all necessary and available information with respect to foreign affairs.   Diplomats, special foreign agents, and other sources of information are appointed by and are responsible to it.   This permits a wealth of knowledge not usually available to the other organs of the government. The executive includes generally the most responsible, tried and competent men in the state, holding the confidence of the people and, in Canada and Australia, the confidence of Parliament itself. Internationalism requires expertness, flexibility in the application of broad policy to unforeseeable future developments.   It demands the utmost in diplomacy, information, and integrity.   Often, particularly in times of strife, it demands secrecy and dispatch.[3]   These, in brief, are the qualities necessary in the organ charged with the conduct of foreign affairs in a state.   Only the executive fills these requirements and, invariably, in modern constitutions, it has charge of foreign affairs.   But various states give different degrees of power in this group to effect international agreements.   In other words, the "capacities" of the executives, though not those of the state, may vary.

International treaties often involve policy consideration of the widest import in social and economic fields.   Doubtlessly there is much to be said for the argument of greater legislative participation.   But there is also great need to break down the barriers set up by the still strong doctrine of sovereignty and its concomitant concept of domestic issues to be regulated by the state alone. Finally, the international community needs a strong group of executives, not too hampered by municipal restrictions, to deal with the complicated issues facing it today.   Hence, the present writer advocates a strong executive, having constitutionally a complete discretion to conclude valid international agreements of all types.

In Canada and Australia, the executive is not only responsible to Parliament but also controls it.   It is the initiator of policy and if its policy is defeated, the usual course for it is to resign and seek a popular mandate.   But it leads the government of these federations and fulfils the definition of a strong executive. In foreign affairs as in internal affairs, it is in complete control. Executive acts are done by it through the agency of the Governor General.   It can do what it pleases subject to the political control of the mandate of the people.   If further restraints are needed, its officers are personally liable in law for their acts, for every act of the Crown must be done through a minister.   The drastic sanction of impeachment is also there, although now practically obsolete.[4]

In Switzerland, though the Federal Council is the constitutional organ for entering into treaties, its treaty-making procedure has such a high degree of legislative participation that the least amount of "capacity" is vested in the executive of this federation. Notwithstanding the influence of the Federal Council, treaties must go through both Chambers, and be duly passed in the form of an ordinary statute, before they are constitutionally concluded. Even at this stage, they are still subject, in many cases, to the optional referendum. Freedom of the executive in foreign affairs is indeed impossible under such conditions. This high degree of legislative participation is undesirable with respect to the executive's ability to enter into international agreements. Possibly, because of its peculiar political situation and diminutive size, Switzerland has no need for a strong organ in control of foreign relations.

The degree of legislative participation is not so evident in the United States where the constitution requires the participation of only two-thirds of the Senators present. But, to a lesser extent, many of our observations are applicable to that state.

It has been mentioned that some body to advise and assist the executive in the conclusion of international agreements is desirable, indeed necessary.[5] In Canada and Australia, the cabinet fulfils this purpose. Although originally intended to perform this function in the United States, the Senate acts only as a "consenting" body prior to the ratification, and as the legislative body in passing a treaty so as to give it validity as internal law. Thus, in the latter respect, it acts like the Federal Assembly in Switzerland; in the former respect, it can hardly be said to act as a deliberate, informed body to advise the executive. In its present capacity, the Senate fills neither role satisfactorily. It is too big and too permeated with sectional and political interests to act in the same capacity as the British cabinet. On the other hand, as a legislative body, it may be justly argued that the two-thirds vote arrangement is undemocratic, and improperly denies participation of the House of Representatives in the process. Most of the proponents of constitutional amendment relative to the treaty process in the United States advocate some participation of the House in the process and, in particular, advocate a majority vote in each House.[6] They argue that this procedure would obviate any doubt of the necessity to obtain prior legislative approval for obligations which require legislation. Also they contend that, inasmuch as the treaty has the same internal effect as a statute, such a system would be more democratic and would preclude the use of the much criticized executive agreement. The latter contention is probably based on the questionable fact that it would be easier for the executive to obtain a majority vote in both Houses of Congress than it is to obtain the required two-thirds vote in the Senate. Though the Senate has not fulfilled the intentions of the framers of the Constitution, its present position in the process at least obviates many of the dangers originally envisaged by them.

Yet even the Senate lends itself to the same objections already observed in the Swiss procedure. An ideal situation is easily proposed and supported by the position in the British federations. The President should have the "capacity" to conclude treaties constitutionally with the aid of a select committee either from the Senate alone or from both Houses. Over this body, the other organs of government should have no direct control. Like the British executive, the President would have the authority to enter into any type of agreement which expediency demanded, and internationally the obligation would be complete. Such a situation is warranted by political and legal considerations. Certainly the tendency of the courts has been to give the executive unprecedented control in the foreign relations of the state. This is amply illustrated by reference to the legal sanction given to executive agreements.[7] Politically, the emancipated position of the party system, together with the probability that the President will be the leader, and the consequent opportunity to assume legislative as well as executive leadership, gives the President great powers in the field of foreign affairs. Again, such a solution would in most cases obviate the use of executive agreements and the consequent by-passing of Senatorial consent.

As in the British situations, there are restrictions other than the political ones, to prevent an executive from entering into an impolitic treaty. The President of the United States is usually responsible, capable, and tried in the domain of statesmanship. His advisers should be of similar stature. Congress itself could impose further control, by passing legislation which to terminate or in some way defeat the purpose of a treaty.[8] Finally, there is always available the drastic remedy of impeachment by Article 2, Section 4 of the Constitution.

There are numerous advantages to a small body exercising the treaty-making power of a state. A select group of legislators, acting as advisers, makes the procedure more harmonious with the general concept of constitutionalism. It lessens criticism of the dictatorial powers of the executive in foreign affairs. It serves as a coordinator of foreign policy between the various departments of the government. It results in reducing danger of tardiness on the part of the legislature, or even refusal, in passing implementing legislation; in the United States, it would preclude Senatorial criticism of its own present position in the process, and obviate use of the executive agreement in an extra-legal manner.

NATIONAL PERFORMANCE AND MODERN INTERNATIONALISM

The advocated power in the central executive would still be subject to further checks from the states' performing powers. These have been classified in Chapter 5 as limitations imposed by the division of governmental powers, by the judicial constructions of the constitutions, and by the division of legislative powers between the component parts and the central powers. Once an executive has concluded a treaty, it is internationally binding and uninfluenced by these "performance" limitations. But this does not alter their national effect. The question now to be considered, from the national point of view, is whether there is any possible basis for reconciliation with regard to an internationally valid but nationally invalid obligation? The answer is to be found only in the fundamental laws of the states. The reconciliation must proceed from them.

On the question of division of governmental powers and judicial constructions of the constitutions, only a few remarks will be made, to point up the conclusions of the previous chapter.[9] The operation of the different procedures in the United States, in Switzerland, and in the British federations has been noted[10] and some conclusions on the advantages and disadvantages mentioned. It will be recalled that the big disadvantage of the American system is the excessive use of the executive agreement, and the consequent fear of an omnipotent and uncontrolled executive. This is probably the chief complaint both in the entering of treaties and their effect as the law of the land. The British procedure more nearly combines the qualities of an effective modern executive with the principle of constitutionalism than does the monistic tendency of the United States and Switzerland. The executive, being the cabinet and the guiding force of the government, initiates policy in an aura of secrecy, presses its implications with dispatch and without any parliamentary sanction except the subsequent one of explaining its action once it is a *fait accompli*. There is no doubt of the international validity of these agreements, and the constitutional law of the British federations recognizes this. But this does not mean that they are *ipso facto* a national obligation. Again however, the enviable position of the cabinet makes the necessary legislation, if any change in the law of the land is required, a forthcoming certainty. This is not so in the United States. Although no legislation has been refused in that state by the legislature, the existence of the system which renders treaties the law of the land gives offense to the House of Representatives. It makes passage of a treaty through the Senate often difficult, and, worst of all, it necessitates other procedures to carry out international commitments, possibly by extra-legal means. On the other hand, it might be argued that a state with the British system will often be in default if the necessary legislation is not forthcoming. This can be refuted, not only by observing the dominant position of the cabinet, but also by the fact that the absence of such legislation would make the state more cognizant of its international responsibilities. It would cause political and international discussion on all phases on point, and even possibly adjustment of constitutional machinery. Treaties which deal with social and economic rights need the full cooperation of the whole people. They should be permitted to run through the same process of constitutional machinery as the promulgation of national law. It is difficult to conclude otherwise than that the British procedure offers many advantages not found in the other federations.

Finally, which of the methods of participation of the different organs offers the best protection to the rights of the component parts and of the people as a whole? No more will be said of the British and Swiss situation. In the United States this is the problem whether the Senate or both Houses of Congress should participate. The latter solution is said to be more democratic and more in accord with the domestic law. Further, it is apt to remove complaints of the House of Representatives and make this body more amenable to the passing of implementing legislation.   Finally, it can prevent the possibility of a minority group obstructing the foreign policy of the state.   On the other hand, the protection afforded to the people as a whole is not greatly affected by having as a requisite to the validity of a treaty a larger than majority vote in the Senate.   It can also be argued that the states' rights are more adequately considered in the Senate.

As the interpreter of the constitutions, the judiciary should keep an ever continuing vigil to prevent an abuse of the process.[11] Though the present writer maintains that the courts' power to declare a treaty unconstitutional has only a national effect, and should be exercised sparingly and with due regard to international exigencies, its omnipresence should be a considerable check on the process.   International sanctions will prevent a treaty from being declared unconstitutional except in a very clear case.   But if the situation occurs, its effect will be that the treaty is void nationally and valid internationally.   This breach must then be settled by the executive, by diplomatic or other means, often at the expense of the state's prestige.

The final problem is the separation of legislative powers between the component states and the central authority.   There is no need to elaborate on the international legal position of a state if it fails to perform its obligations under a treaty or rule of customary international law.   Once the treaty has been validly concluded, the implementing legislation must follow, or the state is internationally in default.

In the international community today, states with the federal form of government are among the foremost, notably the United States.   Their constitutional systems cannot be ignored without adverse effects on the progress of international organization and legislation.   After the First World War, steps were taken to facilitate their position in the International Labor Organization, whose Constitution introduced a new procedure for making international treaties.   The study of the federal situation would not be complete without some reference to it.

Article 19 of the original Constitution of the International Labor Organization provided that draft conventions must be submitted to the authority or authorities within whose competence the matter lies for the enactment of legislation or other action, and imposed on the member states a duty to intimate its ratification to the Director of the Organization.[12]   The state then was obligated to put its laws in accordance with the convention. The state was also legally bound not to alter that law in any way which would lower the standards below those in the convention. Further, it had to submit to the I. L. O. each year a report on the measures it has taken to carry out the law giving effect to the provisions of the convention. Finally, a state had to answer complaints lodged with the I. L. O., regarding the non-obesrvance of the convention, and if it failed to carry out the decision of the Permanent Court of International Justice, it exposed itself to measures of an economic nature being taken against it. Members of the Organization are also obligated within twelve months or, at the most, eighteen months to place recommendations before the authorities within whose competence the matter lies for the enactment of legislation or other action and inform the Director of the action taken. These multiple obligations still stand for all states. However, federal states are placed in a much more favorable position. Article 19 (9) provides: "In the case of a federal state, the power of which to enter into international conventions on labor matters is subject to limitations, it shall be in the discretion of that government to treat a draft convention to which such limitations apply as recommendations only, and the provisions of this article with respect to recommendations shall apply in such a case."

To judge by the history of the Commission set up to create the International Labor Organization,[13] it is obvious that this concession was made with great reluctance and mainly to secure American support for the I. L. O. It was not directed at federal states *per se*. The Commission realized that without the support of the United States, the Organization had little chance of survival at the Peace Conference. These considerations overrode the fears of unitary states that the inequalities would undermine the Organization[14] inasmuch as they would diminish its powers and reduce its effectiveness.[15] It cannot be construed as a sympathetic acknowledgement of the peculiar form of government of the federal state, and a general recognition of the existing differences. It was a compromise, necessary to save the life of the embryo Organization, and nothing more. The situation at the time of the drafting of Article 19 can be summed up in the final report of the Commission to the Plenary Session: "The exception in the case of the federal states is of greater importance. It places the United States and states which are in a similar position under a less degree of obligation than other states in regard to draft conventions.   But it will be observed that the exception extends only to those federal states which are subject to limitations in respect of their treaty making power on labour matters, and further that it extends only in so far as those limitations apply in the particular case.   It will not apply in the case of a convention to which the limitations do not apply, or after such limitations as may be present have been removed.   Though reluctant to contemplate an arrangement under which all states would not be under equal obligations, the Commission felt that it was impossible not to recognize the constitutional difficulties which undoubtedly existed in the case of certain federal states, and therefore proposed the above solution as the best possible means in the circumstances."[16]   So this situation persisted until the constitutional amendments to the Organization were adopted in 1946.

Although the privilege afforded to the federal states was directly due to the American constitutional situation, the United States did not join the Organization until 1934, and has since ratified only seven of the one hundred and three conventions adopted by the Conferences up to 1954.   Canada has a little better record, with eighteen ratifications to her credit.   Australia and Switzerland have ratified sixteen and twenty conventions respectively.[17]   This is not an impressive showing, and compared with unitary states, federal states have also been dilatory in their ratifications.   With respect to handling draft conventions and recommendations, Professor William G. Rice says that there has been little difference in their treatment by federal states.[18] This is because recommendations, like unratified conventions, can be ignored after being sent to "the authorities within whose competence the matter lies."   There is no need to discriminate between conventions and recommendations.   In all the federal states, little has been done by active federal-state cooperation to implement them, although Australia has called several inconclusive conferences for this purpose.[19]

The position of Switzerland is peculiar.   In 1920 it informed the I. L. O. that it was in a position to give conventions to force of law "even in the cases in which the Confederation had no constitutional right to legislate."[20]   However, in 1925, it decided to treat a certain convention as a recommendation, since it involved questions regulated by cantonal as well as federal law.

In view of its stand of 1920, the Director of the I. L. O. replied that the Swiss contention would not be accepted and that Switzerland was under a legal duty to ratify the convention.[21]

The overall action of the federal states with respect to ratifications has been considered satisfactory. In 1928 the Director said it was a source of satisfaction that federal states, "which might take refuge behind their federal constitution . . . are nevertheless endeavouring by agreements between the separate states and inter-state conferences to take their part in the general work of ratification."[22]

The Montreal amendments grew out of the demand by member states to improve the effectiveness of the system of conventions and recommendations, as provided for in the Constitution. Stimulated by the proposed merger with the United Nations, by the end of hostilities, and by the impetus provided by popular opinion for better international collaboration, the whole question was discussed at length at the Paris General Conference in 1946. It was resolved that "certain obligations of states in respect of conventions and recommendations as well as certain aspects of constitutional practice of the Organization in this regard, must be clarified and amplified in order to assure the working of the Organization with increased efficiency."[23] In respect to the alteration of the obligations of federal states, the amendments provide that, in the case of conventions and recommendations which the federal government considers appropriate under its constitutional system for action by the component parts, it must make arrangements for action by these parts for the enactment of the appropriate legislation or other action as necessary. Also, subject to the concurrence of the regional authorities, the federal government must make arrangements for the periodical consultation, with the view of promoting coordination between the federal and regional governments, to give effect to these conventions and recommendations. Further, the federal government must inform the Director of the measures taken to bring the conventions and recommendations before the appropriate regional authorities, giving particulars as to these authorities and the action taken by them.

The most important innovation of the Montreal amendments is that, in respect to conventions and recommendations that the federal government regards as appropriate for federal action, a federal state must make to the Director the usual reports required of another member with regard to the conventions which it has or has not ratified. Further, federal states are made subject to the same procedure in force against delinquent states.

There are several reasons for restricting the concessions granted to federal states in the original Constitution of the I. L.O. The 1946 Report of the Paris Conference Delegation,[24] stresses the fact that in the early stage of the existence of the Organization its social legislation was of a moderate character, and that it did not invoke adverse criticism of the unitary states to have the federal states in a more advantageous position. But this has now changed. The scope of social, economic and, in many cases, cultural legislation is broader and more comprehensive now. It covers many fields of economic activity in which it is detrimental to the interests of certain states to have other, competitive states not in the same position. Unitary states are beginning to feel that their interests are being adversely affected by the ratification of these high-level conventions and will hesitate to ratify them and to undertake obligations, while federal states are not obligated by comparable commitments. Another reason for this change of attitude is the voting procedure. In the voting which determines whether the convention has the necessary two-thirds majority, the votes of all delegates of the Organization are of equal value, whether the member is a federal or unitary state. This is contrary to the spirit of equality of obligation and voting power. Unitary states in such cases may be forced to consider these aspects of the problem, in addition to the merits of the particular convention, before voting for or against its adoption. Another reason advanced for revoking the concessions to federal states is that the number of ratifications deposited does not truly reflect the constitutional position of these states in these matters.

However, there is still considerable concession to the federal form of government in the International Labor Organization.[25] This leads to the concluding question: how far does the state's constitutional structures warrant this concession, and permit an excuse for the non-execution of certain types of agreements?[26]

In general, the present day conviction is that economic and social life must be regulated by governments. Business, labor, and other forms of economic enterprise are now pursued on a national plane. Free trade within the federations, improved transportation, and general economic expansion have led to the need of economic unity within the federal states. There is still the outstanding question whether the federal form of government can survive under these changed conditions. Not only in the economic sphere but also in the social, new measures require central authority for their effective application. Nationalism is another factor, and so is the trend towards universalization; the centralization of all forces in the state is not only desirable, but often politically feasible and necessary.

The federal states themselves remain hampered by constitutional and political restrictions arising out of the desire of the component parts to maintain their sovereignty because of race, local economic needs, and long-standing antipathy to centralization. If the power is within the constitutional division reserved to the states, the federal government may not touch it. The component states themselves are hampered by inadequate financial resources, by the confines of their boundaries, by competition with other states, and by constitutional restrictions of the same character as those of the federal government. The difficulties of cooperation have been mentioned elsewhere.[27] Grants-in-aid, state agreements, conferences, and supplementary legislation have generally proved dilatory, expensive, and often inefficient because of the duality of administration.

The federal states have all recently taken active steps to combat and remedy these drawbacks of federalism. Switzerland would appear to have met the problem with the greatest success. By the flexibility of her Constitution, the federal authority has gathered to itself practically all the powers necessary for a strong central government, in conformance with the principles of democracy, and, with respect for the essential rights of the cantons. The continuous extension of the activities of the federal authority of that state into the economic, social and international fields is to be recognized as an outstanding example of wise government.

In the United States, too, the trend towards centralization is evident. With the exception of the reversal of that trend in the years immediately preceding the Civil War, the Supreme Court has steadily enlarged the powers of the central government by its constitutional interpretations. Although another reversal was indicated in the high mortality rate of the New Deal legislation in the years 1935 and 1936, the President eventually was given the power to carry out his economic and social measures. In the words of the Democratic platform of 1936, "We know that drought, dust storms, floods, minimum wages, maximum hours, child labour, and working conditions in industries, monopolistic and unfair business practices cannot be adequately handled by 48 separate state administrations and 48 separate state courts."[28] The positive attitude of the Supreme Court today does not indicate any change from this position.

The process is not so evident in Australia and Canada, although there is a general realization that good and successful government demands an enlargement of federal powers. In the latter state, a series of Dominion-Provincial conferences, particularly in economic matters, are under way to some satisfactory solution to the problem. It remains for the future to determine their success. In Australia, the impotence of the present government and the necessity for a strong one in the future has been examined in considerable detail by Mr. Gordon Greenwood.[29] He showed that the recent defeat of the referendum carried out in that state, in an attempt to expand the powers of the central government, has left the country in a pre-war condition to deal with post-war needs.[30] He advocated the complete bestowal of legislative power on the central state, leaving it to the discretion of the central government to delegate its powers as it sees fit.

During the last two world wars, the federations have lived up to their duties as belligerent states and have amply displayed their homogeneity and national spirit when an immediate danger was presented to their way of life. In so doing, their constitutions have illustrated their flexibility to provide all the powers in the central government for the successful prosecution of the war. In the United States, in December 1941, Congress conferred on the President broad wartime powers, exceeding even those granted to Woodrow Wilson in 1917. These were supplemented by a Second War Powers Act in 1942, and from this Act the most complete regulation of economic and social life proved possible. There was nothing lacking in the power of the United States that was available to the government of a unitary state. In Australia, the Commonwealth implemented its defense measures under the War Precautions Act of 1914, which enabled the executive to make regulations on a great number of subjects. The Australian High Court, in the case of *Farey v. Burvett*,[31] established the power of Parliament to pass any measure it considered necessary for the successful pursuit of the war. In 1939, the Commonwealth Parliament passed the National Security Act, and by subsequent amendments permits a central control of the highest possible nature. Even Canada, the most delinquent federal state in this trend to centralization, had little difficulty in obtaining the requisite powers once the state was involved in a war. In 1914, the War Measures Act gave the Dominion Parliament authority to enter the provincial field, over which otherwise it had no control, on a wide scale. This Act was again proclaimed in 1939. Valid under the "residue clause" of the Constitution,[32] it is of the broadest import.

Thus, in time of war all federations exhibit the desirable characteristics of unitary states. The courts have had little difficulty in finding the necessary central power inherent in their constitutions. But the war is over, and in its wake follow new problems which cannot be dealt with by the component parts. Unfortunately not all the federations consider the winning of the peace as necessary as the winning of the war. International agreements are at present the only source of international law making, embracing all types of subject matters. The importance of the need that states be constitutionally in the position to carry them out faithfully and without delay cannot be over-emphasized. The need for central control in the sphere of internationalism is just as pressing as in internal economic and social problems.

To answer the question whether the federal states are now in a constitutional position to carry out their commitments, some conclusions may be ventured. Concerning the United States, it is possible to assert categorically that judicial interpretation of the Constitution, judicial abnegation of interference in the field of foreign affairs, the consequent increase in the powers of the President in this regard, and the very faint recognition of component state power, have placed that state in a unitary position with regard to foreign affairs. This view is further supported by the judiciary's liberal interpretation of the Constitution, and by its lack of interference in Congressional legislation. There is no indication that the trend will take a different turn in the future. The Australian position is similar. In the field of foreign affairs, the judicial interpretation in behalf of the strong central state has been most favorable. There is every indication that the trend will continue. Though precise definitions of the "capacity" and "performance" limitations are still obscure, there is certainly no necessity for advocating any change.

But Canada's constitutional situation with regard to the treaty process is indefinite and insufficient to meet her international position and demands. The trend of Canadian constitutional interpretation has been erratic—from literalism to liberalism and back to literalism. The essential method of the courts has been to treat the Constitution as a statute. In the words of Lord Loreburn:[33] "In the interpretation of a completely self-governing Constitution founded upon a written organic instrument, such as the British North America Act, if the text is explicit, the text is conclusive, alike in what it directs and forbids." Although in 1930[34] and in 1935,[35] their Lordships gave lip service to a broad and liberal interpretation, they reverted to the usual rule in the New Deal decisions.[36] The result of this method of construction has been to render Canada delinquent in international law, and to deny to the state a competent treaty process.

Recently, two circumstances of considerable constitutional importance have given the problem a new aspect, though they do not alter the situation. Because of rising criticism of the Privy Council's interpretations of the Constitution, Canada recently abolished appeals for such interpretations, thus making the Supreme Court of Canada the final court of appeal.[37] It has been suggested that a strong judicial declaration, to the effect that the court will henceforth construe the words of the Constitution according to a different standard, which, freeing the judges from the binding force of previous judicial interpretation, would take the place of formal amendment. But would this mean that future courts would restore the decision in the *Radio Communications Case,*[38] and give the central government authority to implement treaties under the residuary clause of the Constitution? Or, perhaps, would the now defunct Section 132 be restored to its rightful place, and provide the authority for future legislative action by the central government?

It is true that this procedure would probably be more acceptable to many in Canada. But its objections are also many. First, the principle of *stare decisis* is too well entrenched in Canadian legal thought to be entirely obliterated by such a declaration, even by a statute of Parliament. Besides, there are many decisions of the Privy Council in other fields of law, which could be advantageously retained. Second, there are always the possible *ex post facto* objections, which might be constitutionally objectionable. Third, there is nothing to prevent the Supreme

Court of Canada from considering that the method of interpretation of the Privy Council is the correct one, and little assistance would be obtained by such a procedure in clarifying the
situation.[39]   Finally, some clarification should be made of the
legal status of Canada, affecting her constitutional capacity to
enter into international agreements.   Canada has now attained
the position in the international community of a full-fledged
state and yet has not legally the most fundamental power inherent in any independent state.   Although the central executive
now exercises the power, and its exercise could quite easily be
supported by legal precedent and by its growth to international
status and changed constitutional position, yet an express provision providing the state with the power would be needed to
confirm the true present status of Canada.   As Professor Vincent
C. MacDonald (now a Justice of the Supreme Court of
Nova Scotia) says,[40] the constitution should be a clear statement
designed for prompt and effective action.   Constitutional amendment is the only way out of the confused situation.

The other circumstance of constitutional importance, besides
the abolition of appeals to the Privy Council, is that the power
to alter the B.N.A. Act has recently been declared to reside in
Canada, thus settling once and for all this age-old question.[41]
What form should the amendment take?   It should be drafted in
specific terms to give the central government all powers of "capacity" and "performance" to carry out obligations incurred in
the ordinary course of international relations.   The terms of the
section should be broad enough to permit the court some access
to the determination of the specific subjects of negotiation with
foreign states.   Although this power would not and should not
be used except in very flagrant cases,[42] it will nevertheless serve
to alleviate the fears of some that too much power is conferred on
the executive.   The section should unequivocally state that the
central government has all the necessary implementing powers,
subject again to judicial control, and that, should it be deemed
that the legislation in fact amends the Constitution, that legislation is invalid.   In this way, the amending section will not break
new ground but be based on principles observed in the treaty
process of the other federations and its operation will be the
same.

The main arguments against giving such a power to the central
government should thus be overcome.   Even the province of

Quebec, where the strongest voice for provincial autonomy may be heard, should have no objections here. Indeed her fears that her "way of life" is threatened should have little foundation if a treaty has been concurred in by a majority of the states of the world. Treaties are not made with the purpose of interfering with religion, education and other similar practices of the component states. They are usually designed to raise the standard of living of the signatory countries, not lower it; to provide for a system of education, not to destroy a particular kind. The fears of the provinces that their autonomy is being given up to the central government in the treaty process are certainly no more, in reality, than a fear of the autonomy of government itself.

That national democratic constitutionalism is on trial is evidenced by the other types of governments with which the democracies have been waging "hot" and "cold" wars for the past five decades. If it is to survive, it must be prepared to adapt itself to changing situations and needs. Modern times call for the closest international relations in the economic, cultural, and social fields. This, so far, can be achieved only by the treaty. Not only is constitutionalism on trial, but civilization itself. To assert her position as an international entity, her faith in the new order and to maintain her place as a leader among the "middle" states of the world, Canada has no other course but to provide her central authority with the same power as that achieved by the other federations.

[1.] (1936) 55 Commonwealth Law Reports (Australia) 618; *supra*, p. 55.

[2.] *Supra*, pp. 58 ff.

[3.] Note particularly the delay in political treaties in the United States. Dangerfield, *In Defense of the Senate*, (1933), p. 117, and his Chapter 5, is an illuminating study of the time element of treaties in the Senate.

[4.] Taswell-Langmead, Thomas P., *English Constitutional History*, (10th ed. by Plucknett, Theodore F. T.,) pp. 590 ff—particularly the impeachment of Lord Danby.

[5.] *Supra*, pp. 77-78.

[6.] See generally, Fleming, *The Treaty Veto of the American Senate*, (1930), Ch. 12.

[7.] *Supra*, pp. 92 ff.   [8.] *Supra*, pp. 91-92.   [9.] *Supra*, Ch. 5.

[10.] *Supra*, pp. 87 ff.   [11.] *Supra*, Ch. 4.

[12.] Article 19 (1) reads: "When the Conference has divided on the adoption of proposals with regard to an item in the agenda, it will rest with the Conference to determine whether these should take the form; (a) of a Recommendation to be submitted to the members for consideration with a view to effect being given to it by national legislation or otherwise, or (b) of an international convention for ratification by the Members."

[13.] Shotwell, James T., *Origins of the International Labour Organization,* (1934), Vol. 1, pp. 143-63; Vol. 2, pp. 361-75.

[14.] Shotwell, James T., *ibid,* Vol. 1, p. 153. Also see Dillon, Conley H., *International Labour Conventions,* (1942), p. 42.

[15.] International Labor Organization. *Official Bulletin,* Vol. 1, p. 182.

[16.] Shotwell, James T., *ibid,* Vol. 2, p. 374.

[17.] *International Labour Organization, Official Chart of Ratifications of International Labour Conventions to March 1, 1954.*

[18.] "Revision of an International Constitution: The New Era for the International Labour Organizations," (1947) 4 *Wisconsin Law Review,* 514, p. 536, note 76.

[19.] Stewart, Robert B., *Treaty Relations of the British Commonwealth of Nations.* pp. 306-7; Staricoff, Joseph, "Australia and the Constitution of the International Labour Organization," (1935) 32 *International Labour Review* 577. Generally, cooperation has not met too much success in the federal states. In Canada, although numerous boards and commissions have been set up, their records of accomplishment have not been good. Professor James A. Corry finds co-operation clumsy, expensive, and restricted by constitutional difficulties of administration. *Report of the Royal Commission on Dominion-Provincial Relations;* "Difficulties of Divided Jurisdiction," (1939), Appendix 7. In Australia, much more has been done by means of grants, Premiers' Conferences, inter-state agreements, and complementary legislation, but Greenwood, Gordon, in *The Future of Australian Federalism,* (1946,), p. 301 concludes: "Cooperation as a technique for securing uniform action upon urgent but highly contentious social, economic and governmental problems has been shown by the Australian experience to be lethargic, complicated and for the most part ineffective." For the United States, a brighter picture is painted by Koenig, Louis W., "Federal and State Cooperation Under the Federal Constitution," (1938) 36 *Michigan Law Review* 752. He says that cooperation "promises to become an acceptable alternative to a highly centralized government with the states as merely passive units."

[20.] International Labor Organization, *Official Bulletin,* Vol. 3, pp. 6-7.

[21.] The Montreal amendments of the Constitution, however, rectify this situation, and Switzerland is able to treat a convention as a recommendation under certain circumstances.

[22.] International Labor Organization, *Report of the Director,* (1928), p. 7.

[23.] International Labor Organization, *Report of the Conference Delegation on Constitutional Questions on the Work of its First Session,* 21 Jan-15 Feb., 1946, Ch. 4.

[24.] International Labor Organization, *Report of the Conference Delegation on the work of its Second Session, 13 May—30 May, 1946.*

[25.] The practice is becoming quite general. For example, it is proposed to include an article in the Draft Covenant on Human Rights and Fundamental Freedoms similar to the amended Article 19 of the I.L.O. Although there have been various suggestions, it will probably provide that, with respect to articles of the covenant which the federal government regards as wholly or in part for federal action, the same obligations exist for them as for unitary states. If action is required by their constituent parts, the federal government shall bring such provisions to the notice of the constituent parts with a favorable recommendation. *United Nations Bulletins,* Jan. 15, 1948. However, the practice is not consistent, and there is no indication that it is now a customary international legal rule to give federal states such a concession. See Liang, Yuen-li, *"Colonial Clauses and Federal Clauses in United Nations Multilateral Instruments,"* (1951) 45 *American Journal International Law* 108.

[26.] For example, in 1922, the United States declined to adhere to the Convention for the Suppression of Traffic in Women and Children, on the ground that Congress was not in a position to enact legislation which might impose on the right of the states. League of Nations,*Official Documents,* C.T.F.E. 542, April, 1932, p.3.

[27.] *Supra.* p. 182, note 19.

[28.] Quoted in Finer, Herman, *The Future of Government,* (2nd ed., 1949), p. 131.

[29.] *Future of Australian Federalism* (1946). [30.] *Ibid,* pp. 271 ff.

[31.] (1916) 21 Commonwealth Law Reports (Australia) 433. [32.] *Supra,* p. 124.

[33.] *Attorney-General for Ontario v. Attorney-General for Canada,* (1912) Appeal Cases (England) 571, p. 583.

[34.] *Edwards v. Attorney-General for Canada,* (1930), Appeal Cases (England) 124, p. 136.

[35.] *British Coal Corporation v The King.* (1935) Appeal Cases (England) 500, p. 518.

[36.] These are the Canadian cases handed down by the Privy Council in 1937. *Attorney-General for Ontario v. Attorney-General for Canada,* (1947) Appeal Cases (England) 127, there are indications that the broad view will be taken. Ironically enough this decision construed the B.N.A. Act to give the central government power to abolish appeals to the Privy Council.

[37.] For criticisms of the interpretations of the Privy Council see the Canadian *Debates of the House of Commons,* April 5th, 1937, pp. 2576 ff. For example, Mr. C. H. Cahan said: "The established foundations of Dominion autonomy are insidiously undermined by the decision of the Judicial Committee to the effect that the Dominion Parliament has not complete legislative jurisdiction to carry into effect treaties, which H.M. may enter into with foreign states, with the advice of H.M. Privy Council in Canada.

[38.] (1932) Appeal Cases (England) 304; *supra,* pp. 125-126. In this connection, note *Johannesson v. Municipality of West St. Paul* (1952) 1 Supreme Court Reports (Canada) 292.

[39.] For example, *Attorney-General for Nova Scotia v. Attorney-General for Canada,* (1951) Supreme Court Reports (Canada) 31; and note, in (1951) 29 *Canadian Bar Review* 79, by John R. Ballem, observing the disposition of the Supreme Court of Canada to follow the restrictive interpretative pattern of the Privy Council.

[40.] "Constitution in a Changing World." (1947) 26 *Canadian Bar Review* 21.

[41.] British North America Act, no. 2, 1949; 12, 13 and 14 *Statutes of George VI,* Ch. 8, now gives the right of amendment to the Constitution to the provinces in all matters coming within Section 92 (1). The federal government has the jurisdiction to amend other matters in the Constitution, with five important exceptions. A Dominion-Provincial Conference has been held, but no definite conclusions reached as to the authority to amend the Constitution on questions of federal and provincial concern.

[42.] *Supra,* pp. 73-74, 128 ff.

acts of state, 24, 68ff, 74; and the courts, 70; in Canada and Australia, 71
Act of 1815, 27.
Act of Mediation, 1803, 27.
advisory opinions, 67.
Aerial Navigation Convention, 30, 55, 120, 125.
Aeronautics Case, 30, 121, 125.
"agreement or compact," 40, 41.
Alaska Purchase Treaty, 75
aliens, 139.
ambassadors, 39.
Anderson's Estate, re, 112.
Anson, Sir William R., 48.
Anzilloti, Dionisio, 149.
Argentina, Constitution of, 8, 12.
Articles of Confederation, 17, 25, 26, 94.
Atkins v Kansas, 113.
Attorney-General of New South Wales v. Collector of Customs for New South Wales, 118.
Australia, constitutional origin in, 19.

Bank of Toronto v. Lambe, 123.
Bate's Case, 88.
Belgium, Constitution of, 8.
"Bill of Rights," 23, 98, 100.
Bittner, Ludwig, 149.
Blackstone, Sir William, 88.
Board of Commerce Act, Re, 123.
Bonanza Creek Gold Mining Company v The King, 50.
Borchard, Edwin D., 93.
Borden, Sir Robert, 30.
Brazil, Constitution of, 12.
Bricker Amendment, 10, 45, 101, 106, 136.
British Commonwealth, and Canada, 164, 165.
British Empire treaties, 30, 32ff, 55.
Brown, George, 29.
Butler, Charles H., 96.

cabinet, and executive power, 46; control by the judiciary, 68ff; in the U. S., 21; relationship to Parliament, 22, 75, 87, 166, 170; role in treaty-making, 167ff.
Canada, constitutional origin in, 18ff.
Chirac v. Chirac, 111.
Cleveland, Grover, 151.
Colonial Laws Validity Act, 37.
commissions, see Governor General.
common law and the constitution, 23, 24, 67, 69.
Compagnie Francaise and Co. v. State Board of Health, 115.
component states, and the treaty process, 61ff; cooperation with federal governments, 182; in Australia, 57; in Canada, 58ff; in Switzerland, 41, 42; in U. S., 25, 26, 40, 41.
Congress of Vienna, 20, 81.
constitutional amendment, 100, 101, 122; in Canada, 164, 167, 180.
constitutional interpretation, and the indivisibility of the Crown, 23; and the residue of powers, 22, 23; and the theory of delegated powers, 25; and the treaty process, 130, 178ff; the judiciary and, 66ff.
constitutional law considered, 17.
constitutionalism, 50, 86, 87, 165, 169, 181.
Corwin, Edward S., 107.
Costa-Rica boundary dispute, 151.
Cowles, Willard B., 98.
Crown, and acts of state, 68ff; in foreign relations, 6, 47ff; one and indivisible, 23, 28.

Declaration of Human Rights and Fundamental Freedoms, 10.
declarations, see oral declarations and Imperial Conferences, legal effect of.
DeGeoffroy v. Riggs, 23, 56, 72, 73, 111.
delegated powers, theory of, 25, 98.
delegation of Congressional power, 42, 43, 75, 76, 92.
Denmark, Constitution of, 8.
Dickinson, Edwin D., 5, 141.
dualistic doctrine, 14, 87.

Eastern Greenland decision, 152, 153.
Empire treaties, see British Empire treaties.
Engineer's Case, 36, 130.
executive, and the Crown, 24, 25; control by the judiciary, 66ff, 73, 74; control by the constitutions, 70, 71, 73, 74; in international affairs, 24, 73, 87, 165ff; responsibility to the legislature, 22, 24, 25.
executive agreements, defined, 44; delegation of authority to make, 75, 76, 92; in Switzerland, 45; interchangeable use with the treaty, 44, 92, 93; in the U. S., 40, 44ff, 81; law of the land, 93, 94; value of, 81, 93, 94.
executive powers, distinction of, 21ff. See also prerogative powers.

Farey v. Burvett, 177.
federal states, and international cooperation, 39; and process of centralization, 176ff; and the I.L.O., 171ff; defined, 11, 12; in time of war, 178.
Ffrost v. Stevenson, 122, 130.
Fifth Amendment, 98.
Fitzmaurice, Gerald G., 155.
"fixed" executive, 14, 22.
Fort Leavenworth Railway Company v. Lowe, 97.
Foster and Elam v. Neilson, 91.
France, Constitution of, 8, 147, 148.
Franco-American Convention, 138.
Fujii v. California, 103.
Full Powers, 29, 31, 53, 141, 148, 149, 150, 156.

General Assembly, 2, 3.
Governor General, 18, 19, 22, 24, 166; appointment of, 52, 53; commissions of, 46, 51, 52; instructions to, 46, 49, 51, 52.
Garran, Sir Robert, 33, 34.
Greenwood, Gordon, 177.

Hackworth, Green H., 151, 152.
Hamilton, Alexander, 26, 85.
Halibut Fisheries Treaty, 31.
Hall, William E., 5, 137.
Hansen's Estate, re, 111.
Hay-Paunceforte Treaty, 112.
Heim v. McCall, 113.
Holmes v. Jennison, 108.
Hudson, Manley O., 1, 2.
Human Rights and Fundamental Freedoms, Commission of, 65; Covenant and the Bricker Amendment, 10; Declaration of, 10.
Hyde, Clyde C., 72, 144.

Immunity of Crown Instrumentalities, doctrine of, 50.
impeachment, 21, 167, 169.
Imperial Conferences: 1911, 29; 1917, 30; 1923, 31, 54; 1926, 31, 32, 52, 54; 1930, 52.

Imperial Conferences, legal effect to declarations, 54.
intergovernmental agreements, 31, 32, 48.
internal law, 142.
international community, and federal states, 171; and the states' executives, 39, 166; and the treaty, 1ff; status of Canada and Australia in, 29ff.
international conventions, see international legislation.
international cooperation and the treaty, 1ff, 11, 157, 181.
international labor conventions, 1, 126, 173.
International Labor Organization, 1, 26, 120, 138, 171ff.
international law, and the treaty, 1, 4, 141, 142.
international legal rules, reasons for, 137.
international legisation, 1ff, 3; effect on the treaty process, 79, 80, 166, 170; increase of, 3, 4; nature of, 2; sanctions, 4; sources of, 2, 3.
International Prize Court Convention, 97.
internationalism, 2, 5, 50, 81, 130, 166, 178.
interpretation, see constitutional interpretation.

Japan, Constitution of, 15.
Jay's Treaty, 74, 97, 140.
Johannesson v. Rural Municipality of West St. Paul, 135, 183.
Jones, J. Mervyn, 141.
judiciary, in foreign affairs, 61, 72, 73, 74, 171; in Switzerland, 15, 83; jurisdiction in the treaty process, 66ff, 171; review of executive action, 24, 68, 72, 73.

Keir, David L., 69.
Keith, A. Berriedale, 34, 35, 50, 143.
Kennedy, William P.M., 53.
King v. Burgess; ex parte Henry, 55, 57, 71, 100, 120, 122, 130, 164.

Labor Conventions Case, 54, 58ff, 71, 122, 126, 131, 138.
Lans, Asher, 44.
law-making treaties, see international legislation.
Lawson, Frederick H., 69.
League of Nations, 1ff.
LeFroy, Augustus H.F., 34, 35.
legation, right of, 31.
legislative referendum, 22, 70, 127, 167.
Leong Mow v. Board of Commissioners, 113.
Letters Patent, 49, 51, 52, 53, 70.
License Case, 109.
Lieutenant-Governors, 58; in Canada, 19, 59; in Australia, 64.
Lighthouses Case Between France and Greece, 153.
limitations on the treaty process, external, 16.
Litvinoff assignment, 44, 93, 98.
Local Prohibition Case, 124.
Lubitch v. Pollock, 113.
Lukich v. Department of Labor, 114.

MacDonald, Sir John A., 18, 29.
MacDonald, Vincent C., 33, 180.
Magnini v. Harnett, 116.
Makah Indian Tribe v. McCauley, 114.
Marbury v. Madison, 68.
Marshall, Chief Justice John, 67, 111.
McDougal, Myers S., 44.
McNair, Arnold D., 145, 150, 151, 154.
Mexico, Constitution of, 9, 12, 147, 148.
Migratory Bird Treaty, 128.
Minneapolis St. Paul & Sault Ste. Marie Railway Co. v. Milner, 115.
Missouri v. Holland, 95, 117, 121, 128ff.
Montijo Arbitration, 139.
Moore, John Bassett, 72, 98.

Moore, Sir William, 34, 35, 56, 121.
monistic doctrine, 14, 87.
"moot" cases, 67.

National Security Act, 178.
Neilson v. Johnson, 112.
negotiation of treaties, and "capacity" limitations, 7; by the Crown, 48; in Switzerland, 43; in the U. S., 42, 75ff; proper subjects of international negotiation, 56, 71ff, 97ff, 111, 117, 121, 122, 130.
New Deal legislation, 176, 179.
Northern Ireland, Constitution of, 13.
Norway, Constitution of, 147, 148, 152, 153.
notice, doctrine of, 140, 143ff, 154ff.

O'Connor, William F., 47, 50.
Olsen v. Smith, 116.
optional referendum, see legislative referendum.
Oppenheim, L., 143.
oral declarations, effect in international law, 152, 153.

parliament, supremacy of, 33, 99, 100.
parliamentary executive, 14, 22.
Parson's Case, 123.
Passenger Case, 109.
Patsone v. Commissioner of Penn., 113.
Pearl Assurance Company of London v. Harrington, 117.
plenipotentiary, appointment of, 39.
police powers of the states, U. S., 108.
Polish Nationals in Danzig, Case of, 139.
political questions, 72. See acts of state.
popular referendum, see legislative referendum.
Potter, Pitman B., 149.
prerogative powers, 24, 47ff; and acts of state, 68ff; barring the Imperial prerogative, 64; control by the judiciary, 68, 74; defined, 47; devolution of, 48ff, 70.
prerogative writs and the executive, 68.
President of the U. S., powers of, 39, 40, 42, 43, 168.

Quick, Sir John, 33, 34.

Radio Communication Case, 62, 60, 120, 125, 179.
Radio Telegraph Convention, 33, 60, 125.
ratification of treaties, 156, 163; and "capacity" limitations, 7; in Canada and Australia, 31, 48, 59ff, 90; in Switzerland, 43; in the U. S., 43, 76ff; Instruments of, 53.
referendum, popular, optional, see legislative referendum.
reservations, 142, 157, 163.
residuary clause in Canada, 124, 126, 127, 178.
residue of powers, comparison of, 22, 23.
resolutions, 42, 76, 90.
responsible government, doctrine of, 22, 75, 86.
Rice, William G., 173.
rights of individuals and the treaty, see treaty.
Robtelmas v. Brenan, 118.
Roche v. Kronheimer, 119.
Russell v. The Queen, 124.
Rustomjee v. The King, 69.

Salaman v. Secretary of State for India, 70.
sanctions, 4.
Schucking, Walther M.A., 144.
seals, 52, 53.
Security Council, 3, 4.
"self-executing" treaties, 91, 92.
Senate of the U. S., 77, 78.

separation of governmental functions, 6,
    9, 24, 86, 97, 98.
sovereignty in the U. S., 95, 96.
stare decisis, principle of, 179.
states, individual, see component states.
"state rights," 35, 108ff, 171.
Statute of Westminster, 50, 64, 106.
Stewart, Robert B., 138.
Strupp, Karl, 144.
Sweden, Constitution of, 8.
Switzerland, constitutional origin in, 20.

Tenth Amendment, 18, 107ff, 117, 118, 128ff.
Terrace v. Thompson, 110.
territory, cession of, 92, 97, 102.
Tiburcio Parrot, re, 114.
Todok v. Union State Bank of Harvard, 116.
Trade Agreements Act of 1934, 75.
treaty, and acts of Congress, 92, 168; and
    the English Revolution, 87, 90; and in-
    ternational cooperation, 1ff; and the
    principle of good faith, 4, 86, 105; and
    rights of individuals, 2, 72, 89, 92, 98ff;
    different classes, 1ff; effectiveness of,
    2ff, 157; law of the land, 71, 87, 90, 91,
    93, 95; termination of, 43.
Treaty of Peace, 1796, 98, 110.
Treaty of Versailles, 30, 33, 55, 60, 61,
    119, 126.
Treaty of Washington, 29.
Tucker, Henry St. George, 108.

unitary states, 11, 39, 178; and the I.L.O.,
    171ff.

Union of South Africa, Constitution of,
    12 13.
United Nations, 1ff, 174.
United States, constitutional origin in, 17,
    18.
United States v. Belmont, 93.
United States v. Curtiss-Wright Corp., 42,
    76, 96.
United States v. Pink, 93, 98.
United States v. Reid, 72.
Universal Adjustment Corp. v. Midland,
    116.
U.S.S.R., Constitution of, 13.

Veneuzuela, Constitution of, 12.
Vietti v. Mackie, 114.

War Measures Act, 178.
War Precautions Act of 1914, 177.
Ware v. Hylton, 72, 109.
Washington, George, and the Senate, 77.
Watson v. Hooey, 112.
Webster-Ashburton Treaty, 105.
Wheare, Kenneth C., 11, 12.
Wilcox, Francis O., 4, 141, 142.
Willoughby, Westel W., 140, 150.
Wilson, Woodrow, 177.
Wong Yung Quy, re, 115.
World Health Organization, 1.
Wright, Quincy, 96.

Youngstown Sheet & Tube Co., v. Sawyer,
    62.